D0248199

© Robert Davies 2005
Crown copyright material reproduced under licence from the
Driving Standards Agency

First published in 2005

A catalogue record for this book is available from the British Library

ISBN 1 84425 220 5
Published by Haynes Publishing, Sparkford,
Yeovil, Somerset BA22 7JJ, England

Tel: 01963 442030 Fax: 01963 440001
Int. tel: +44 1963 442030 Fax: +44 1963 440001
E-mail: sales@haynes.co.uk
Web site: www.haynes.co.uk

Haynes North America, Inc.,
861 Lawrence Drive, Newbury Park,
California 91320, USA

Printed and bound in England by J. H. Haynes & Co. Ltd, Sparkford

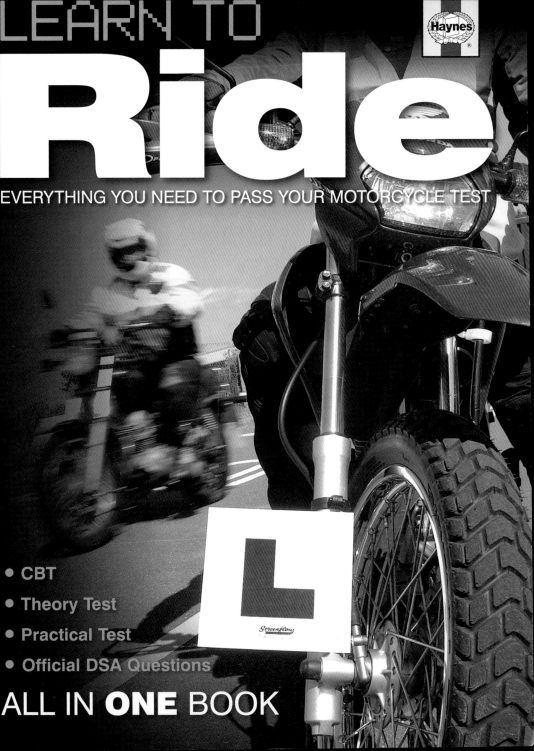

CONTENTS

INTRODUCTION

People come to motorcycling for any number of reasons – some attracted by the economy of a scooter for the urban commute, others by the challenge of mastering the massive performance of a sports bike. You may be learning to ride as a complete novice on the road, or you may already have a car licence. In either case, there's a lot to learn. Riding not only requires a unique set of technical skills, it also demands a rigorous and self-disciplined approach to staying safe. A poorly trained rider is a particularly vulnerable road user, and the testing system has been designed to ensure that riders have to earn the right to go out onto the road by putting in some serious preparation first.

That's where this book comes in. *Learn To Ride* brings together all the information you need to take you through Compulsory Basic Training and on to pass your theory and practical motorcycle tests. We've put all this information in one handy book because it's important to prepare for the theory and practical tests side by side. You won't get the most from your on-road preparation for the practical test without a thorough knowledge of riding theory, and you'll struggle to succeed in the theory test without plenty of practical riding experience under your belt.

One thing all motorcyclists agree on is that riding a bike should be fun – something few drivers can say about their cars. With the help of this book, we hope learning to pass your motorcycle test will be just as enjoyable too.

Safe riding!

01
FIRST STEPS

LEARN TO RACE

There are several routes to getting a motorcycle licence and the one you take will influence your choice of first bike. But whether you're aiming to ride a moped, a light motorcycle, or want to go straight to riding a larger bike through the Direct Access scheme, you first have to undertake Compulsory Basic Training (CBT). And before you even get on your bike you need to make sure it is taxed and insured, and that you are properly kitted out with protective clothing. You also need to check your fitness to ride, to ensure you are physically and mentally prepared to meet the challenge of riding a motorbike safely.

Riding a motorcycle may be many people's idea of freedom, but there's plenty of red tape to tie up before you can get on your bike. Be sure you understand the law as it relates to you before you start to ride.

Think also about the financial investment that motorcycling involves. Don't forget that as well as the cost of your motorbike, you have to budget for specialised clothing and helmet, as well as tax, insurance and the cost of the training you undertake.

rules and regulations

To start riding a motorcycle on a public road you must:

- be at least 17 years old (16 years for mopeds)
- be medically fit, with eyesight to the required standard (corrected with glasses or contact lenses if necessary)
- hold a driving licence that gives provisional entitlement for motorcycles
- undergo a course of Compulsory Basic Training (CBT)
- wear a safety helmet
- ensure that your bike is roadworthy, taxed, insured, and if it is over three years old has a current MOT certificate. (For more information about arranging insurance cover, as well as tax and MOT requirements, see p194.)

licence requirements

You need a driving licence which gives you provisional entitlement for motorcycles. If you hold a full car licence this automatically gives provisional motorcycle entitlement. A full moped licence gives provisional entitlement for motorcycles providing you are aged 17 or over.

If you do not already have one of these licences, you will need to apply for a provisional driving licence. Driving licences are issued by the Driver and Vehicle Licensing Agency (DVLA). Apply using form D1, which you can obtain from the post office. The fee for a provisional licence is currently £38. (In Northern Ireland the licensing authority is Driver and Vehicle Licensing Northern Ireland.)

All new provisional licences are valid until the holder's 70th birthday.

learners and the law

As a learner rider holding a provisional driving licence, these restrictions apply:

- you cannot ride a motorcycle of more than 125cc (unless you are aged 21 or over and are training under the Direct Access scheme)
- you must display L-plates to the front and rear of your motorcycle
- you must not ride on motorways
- you must not carry a pillion passenger
- you may ride a motorcycle and sidecar outfit with a motorcycle of any capacity but the power-to-weight ratio of the outfit must not exceed 0.16kW/kg
- you must not tow a trailer.

As a learner you are not allowed on motorways

L-plates

The size, shape and colour of L-plates is laid down by law, so don't try to economise by making your own. Make sure the plates are positioned on the front and rear of the motorcycle so they are clearly visible. In Wales a D-plate can take the place of an L-plate.

Fix L-plates to the front and back of the motorcycle in as vertical a position as possible

Motorcycle licensing is extraordinarily complicated. In a nutshell, you can aim for a licence that restricts you to riding light motorcycles (under 125cc), or a licence that's valid for any bike. Understandably, most riders take the latter route. Even so, for two years after passing you are restricted to smaller bikes (under 25kW/33bhp) – unless you are aged 21 or over and you take the Direct Access route which lets you ride any size of bike. As this avoids having to wait and trade up from one bike to another, it is again understandably a popular route for those riders who are eligible to take it.

licence categories

Firstly you need to decide whether you want to aim for a licence that will allow you to ride any sort of motorcycle (category A) or one that restricts you to light motorcycles only (category A1).

category A

A category A licence entitles you to ride any size of motorcycle. You have to take the practical test for a category A licence on a learner motorcycle – one that is between 121-125cc and is capable of 100km/h (62mph) – unless you are taking your test under the Direct Access scheme (*see below*).

You are allowed to use motorways and carry a pillion passenger after getting a category A licence, but for the first two years you are restricted to a motorcycle of up to 25kW (33bhp) and with a power-to-weight ratio not exceeding 0.16kW/kg. Motorcycles producing less than 25kW are generally under 400cc, but there is no engine limit specified. This means it is permissible to ride a more powerful motorcycle as long as it has been modified to restrict it to 25kw. After two years, you can have the restrictor kit removed and restore the bike to its original power output.

category A1

A category A1 licence entitles you to ride a light motorcycle, of up to 125cc and with a power output of up to 11kW (14.6bhp). It allows you to ride on motorways and carry a pillion passenger. You can take the practical test for a category A1 licence on a motorcycle of 75-125cc.

Direct Access

Direct Access is an alternative route to obtaining a category A licence which is open only to riders aged 21 and above. It means that, after undergoing CBT (on a motorcycle of any size) and the theory test you take the practical test on a motorcycle with a power output of at least 35kW (46.6bhp). Having

passed, you are then permitted to ride a bike of any size.

You are permitted to practise for the practical test on any bike larger than the learner bike specification, provided that you:

- are accompanied at all times by a qualified instructor on another bike who is in radio contact with you
- wear fluorescent or reflective clothing
- follow all other provisional licence restrictions (ie display L-plates, do not carry pillion passengers and do not use motorways).

Accelerated Access

Accelerated Access is a similar scheme to Direct Access for riders who hold a category A licence and who reach the age of 21 before the end of their two-year restricted period. They can practise on a bike larger than 25kW (33bhp), under the same conditions as Direct Access riders, and take a test on a bike of at least 35kW (46.6bhp). Although the rider reverts to learner status while practising, failing the test will not affect their existing motorcycle licence entitlement.

Under Direct Access, riders over 21 can practise on a larger-engined bike under certain conditions

getting your licence

There are three steps to obtaining a full motorcycle licence. These are summarised in the chart overleaf.

step 1: CBT

All new riders must successfully complete a Compulsory Basic Training course before riding a moped or motorcycle on the road. The only exemptions are:

- riding a moped with the full entitlement automatically given by a full car licence obtained before February 1 2001
- learning to ride a motorcycle after having already obtained full moped entitlement as a result of passing a moped test on or after December 1 1990
- upgrading from one category of motorcycle licence to a higher category, eg full A1 to category A
- riders resident on certain offshore islands (see It's the law panel).

CBT is not a pass-or-fail examination, but you must demonstrate a basic level of skill and understanding of the topics covered in order to satisfy the instructor. On successfully completing CBT, you will be given a certificate of completion (DL196) which is valid for two years. You need to keep this safe as you have to show it when you apply for and take your practical test, and you may be required to produce it by a police officer. If you do not pass the practical test within two years of gaining your certificate of completion, you will have to re-take CBT and obtain a new certificate. A DL196 obtained on a moped is valid for a motorcycle when the rider reaches the age of 17.

See p18 for further details about booking and attending your CBT.

step 2: theory test

You must pass the theory test before you can take (or book) your practical test.

The theory test is split into two elements. First is a touch-screen multiple-choice exam which takes 40 minutes. This is followed by a video-clip based hazard perception test, which takes up to half an hour.

You are not required to take the theory test if you already hold a lower category of motorcycle licence or have passed a moped test since July 1 1996. However, if you hold a licence for a different type of vehicle, such as a car, you do still have to take a theory test. When you pass the theory test you will receive a pass certificate which is valid for two years: you must pass the practical test within this time or you have to retake the theory test.

See p226 for further details about booking and attending your theory test.

step 3: practical test

The practical test consists of a 40-minute ride accompanied by an examiner who follows you by car or motorcycle. You also have to answer questions about basic motorcycle safety checks and carrying a pillion passenger.

You must take your practical test on a motorcycle of the appropriate size:

- **category A1:** a bike with engine capacity of 75cc to 125cc
- **category A:** a bike with engine capacity of 121cc to 125cc and capable of 100km/h (62mph)
- **category A (Direct Access/Accelerated Access):** a bike with a power output of at least 35kW (46.6bhp).

If you pass your practical test on an automatic motorcycle such as a scooter your licence will be valid only for riding automatics.

See p230 for further details about booking and attending your practical test.

mopeds

A moped is a motorcycle which:
- cannot go faster than 50km/h (31mph)
- has an engine no larger than 50cc
- can be moved by pedals (if the moped was first used before August 1 1977).

At age 16 you are able to apply for a driving licence that gives provisional moped entitlement. However, you must successfully complete a CBT course before going on the road, you must display L-plates and you cannot carry a pillion passenger. The CBT certificate is valid for two years and if you wish to continue riding a moped for longer than this you must take and pass the theory test and moped practical test and obtain a category P moped licence. Once you have this, you can discard your L-plates and are permitted to carry a pillion passenger (though not to ride on motorways, from which all mopeds are excluded).

There is an alternative route to riding a moped, and this is to acquire a full car licence. You then have to undergo CBT and obtain a DL196 certificate, upon which you are fully qualified, can ride without L-plates and carry a pillion passenger (a DL196 certificate obtained in this way lets you ride a moped indefinitely, but lasts the usual two years for motorcycles).

Drivers who passed their car test before February 1 2001 are automatically fully qualified to ride a moped, although taking a training course still makes a lot of sense.

A moped is the only form of motorised transport that you are permitted to ride at age 16

motorcycle and sidecar

Learners wishing to ride a motorcycle and sidecar can practise on an outfit with a power to weight ratio not exceeding 0.16kW/kg. On obtaining a category A licence, they are restricted to riding this size of outfit for two years. However, riders aged 21 and above may practise on a larger outfit, within the Direct Access or Accelerated Access provisions.

In any case all riders must take their test on a solo motorbike (except physically disabled riders, who may take their test using a motorcycle and sidecar, but on gaining their licence will be restricted to motorcycle and sidecar outfits only).

Direct Access provisions also apply to riders wishing to use a motorcycle and sidecar

HOW TO GET A MOPED LICENCE

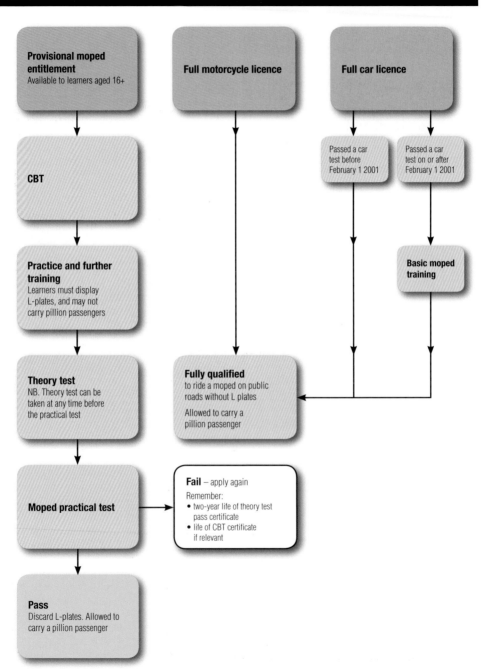

Provisional moped entitlement
Available to learners aged 16+

Full motorcycle licence

Full car licence

Passed a car test before February 1 2001

Passed a car test on or after February 1 2001

CBT

Basic moped training

Practice and further training
Learners must display L-plates, and may not carry pillion passengers

Theory test
NB. Theory test can be taken at any time before the practical test

Fully qualified
to ride a moped on public roads without L plates

Allowed to carry a pillion passenger

Moped practical test

Fail – apply again
Remember:
• two-year life of theory test pass certificate
• life of CBT certificate if relevant

Pass
Discard L-plates. Allowed to carry a pillion passenger

HOW TO GET A MOTORCYCLE LICENCE

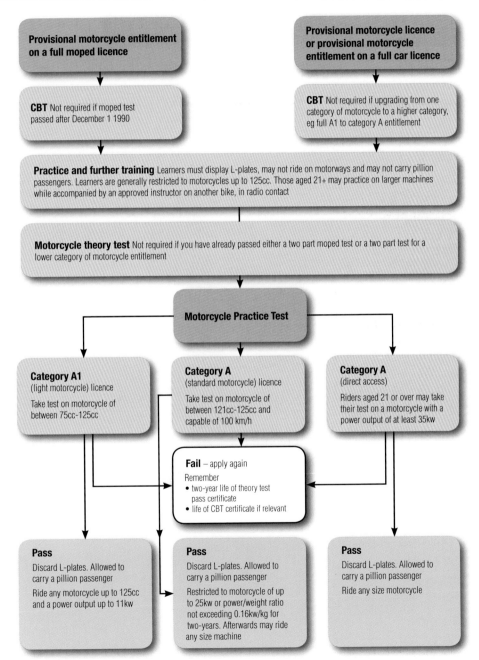

Provisional motorcycle entitlement on a full moped licence

CBT Not required if moped test passed after December 1 1990

Provisional motorcycle licence or provisional motorcycle entitlement on a full car licence

CBT Not required if upgrading from one category of motorcycle to a higher category, eg full A1 to category A entitlement

Practice and further training Learners must display L-plates, may not ride on motorways and may not carry pillion passengers. Learners are generally restricted to motorcycles up to 125cc. Those aged 21+ may practice on larger machines while accompanied by an approved instructor on another bike, in radio contact

Motorcycle theory test Not required if you have already passed either a two part moped test or a two part test for a lower category of motorcycle entitlement

Motorcycle Practice Test

Category A1
(light motorcycle) licence

Take test on motorcycle of between 75cc-125cc

Category A
(standard motorcycle) licence

Take test on motorcycle of between 121cc-125cc and capable of 100 km/h

Category A
(direct access)

Riders aged 21 or over may take their test on a motorcycle with a power output of at least 35kw

Fail – apply again

Remember
- two-year life of theory test pass certificate
- life of CBT certificate if relevant

Pass

Discard L-plates. Allowed to carry a pillion passenger

Ride any motorcycle up to 125cc and a power output up to 11kw

Pass

Discard L-plates. Allowed to carry a pillion passenger

Restricted to motorcycle of up to 25kw or power/weight ratio not exceeding 0.16kw/kg for two-years. Afterwards may ride any size machine

Pass

Discard L-plates. Allowed to carry a pillion passenger

Ride any size motorcycle

17

01

COMPULSORY BASIC
TRAINING

Since it was introduced in 1990, Compulsory Basic Training (CBT) has made a significant reduction to casualty rates among new riders. The course costs around £100 and generally takes a full day, although it can be spread over two days if desired. It provides a thorough grounding in the practical aspects of bike control, and lets you ask questions about any aspect of riding you are unsure about – as well as being an enjoyable opportunity to meet fellow riders.

attending CBT

CBT courses can be given only by Approved Training Bodies (ATBs) whose instructors have been assessed by the DSA and who have sites approved by the DSA for off-road training.

Remember to take your driving licence. If you attend CBT with your own bike, you must also ensure you have all the bike's documentation for the trainer to check, including your insurance certificate, MOT certificate (if the bike is three or more years old), and a current tax disc fixed to the bike.

Most training centres can hire or loan bikes and helmets for use during CBT.

Be sure to wear suitable clothing for the course: this should include a stout pair of boots, a strong pair of gloves, and tough, warm and comfortable jacket and trousers – and if rain looks likely don't forget your waterproofs.

Your trainer will provide a high-visibility overjacket with the name of the ATB on it which you must wear during the course.

what CBT involves

The content of the CBT course is broken down into five elements: the first four take place at the training site, before heading out onto local roads for a session of practical riding under the guidance of the instructor.

Element A: introduction

Your instructor will take you through:
- the aims of the CBT course
- legal requirements, including a check of your documents
- the importance of wearing the correct helmet, visor and clothing
- eyesight test. You must be able to read the current style of numberplate in good daylight at a distance of 20m (66ft). You may wear glasses or contact lenses if necessary but in this case you must wear them for the rest of the course and at all other times while riding. If you fail the eyesight test then you will not be able to proceed with the course.

Your Compulsory Basic Training course will include some classroom instruction as well as practical training

Element B:
practical on-site training

Your instructor will show you round the motorcycle, making sure you understand:

- ⊜ how the controls work
- ⊜ how to carry out basic safety checks, including tyres, suspension, steering, electrics, fuel, oil and chain
- ⊜ using the stand
- ⊜ wheeling the motorcycle
- ⊜ starting and stopping the engine.

Element C:
practical on-site riding

You will practise riding in the controlled conditions of the training site until you can demonstrate that you are competent at:

- ⊜ clutch control
- ⊜ slow riding
- ⊜ changing gear
- ⊜ riding in a figure of eight
- ⊜ braking and emergency stops
- ⊜ rear observation
- ⊜ road junctions
- ⊜ turning left and right
- ⊜ U-turns.

After making sure everyone is familiar with how the motorbike operates, the instructor conducts a range of on-site exercises including road junctions, slow riding and the emergency stop (clockwise from top left)

Element D:
practical on-road training

Your instructor will talk to you about:

- legal requirements for riding a motorcycle
- the *Highway Code*
- the importance of being clearly visible
- the vulnerability of riders as road users
- positioning on the road
- leaving space when following another vehicle
- weather conditions
- road surfaces
- use of speed
- observation and anticipation
- hazard perception
- how attitude affects safety
- the dangers of drink and drug-driving.

Element E:
practical on-road riding

You will go out on to the road for a minimum two-hour session to demonstrate that you can ride safely and deal with a variety of different road situations, including:

- traffic lights
- roundabouts
- junctions
- pedestrian crossings
- hills
- bends
- obstructions in the road
- performing U-turns
- carrying out an emergency stop.

CBT ends with a session of practical riding on the public road under the instructor's supervision

after CBT

Although CBT covers a lot of ground, it should be regarded as only the first step in gaining your full motorcycle licence. Next you need to get in plenty of practice, and should arrange some further training to take you on to test standard.

choosing an instructor

Most ATBs are able to provide further instruction to practical test standard. You may be able to arrange this after completing your CBT. Training usually takes place with a group of learners – up to a maximum of four learners to one instructor.

practice makes perfect

Get in as much practice as you can in the run up to your practical test. Try to experience as many different riding situations as possible: ride in the country as well as in town, on dual carriageways with a 70mph limit, and don't neglect to go out in wet weather – it may be raining on your test day. Get plenty of practice of the essential exercises such as the U-turn and emergency stop (but remember not to obstruct other traffic, and don't repeat them endlessly in the same quiet back streets or you will irritate local residents).

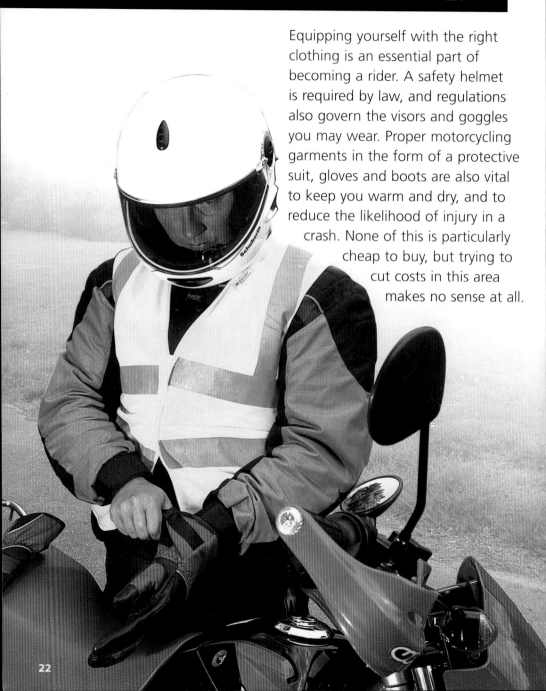

Equipping yourself with the right clothing is an essential part of becoming a rider. A safety helmet is required by law, and regulations also govern the visors and goggles you may wear. Proper motorcycling garments in the form of a protective suit, gloves and boots are also vital to keep you warm and dry, and to reduce the likelihood of injury in a crash. None of this is particularly cheap to buy, but trying to cut costs in this area makes no sense at all.

safety helmets

By law motorcyclists must wear an approved safety helmet (the one exception is for members of the Sikh religion who wear a turban).

A helmet is a vital safety aid. More than 75 per cent of motorcyclist deaths or serious injuries involve head injuries, and a helmet significantly reduces the risk of serious head injury and brain damage in a crash. Helmets also help to cut down wind noise which can be distracting and damaging to the hearing, as well as protecting your face and eyes from flying debris, cold and wind blast.

which helmet?

All helmets sold in the UK must comply with one of the following:

- British Standard BS 6658:1985 and carry the BSI kitemark
- UNECE Regulation 22.05 (look for the UN E-mark, with '05' as the first two digits of the approval number)
- any standard accepted by a member of the European Economic Area (EEA) which offers the same safety standard as the British Standard, and which carries a mark equivalent to the BSI kitemark.

In a crash a helmet can be a life saver, so don't try to economise when buying one. And don't use a secondhand helmet: it may have sustained damage that is not obvious to the naked eye.

There are two types of helmet, open-face and full-face. The full-face has chin protection and a hinged visor, and is the better choice as it protects the face in a crash and gives fuller protection from the weather. Some riders prefer the more open feel of the open-face style, which lacks chin protection and can be worn with a visor or goggles.

The outer shell of a helmet may be made of polycarbonate, glassfibre or kevlar. Polycarbonate is lighter than glassfibre but less long-lasting. It is important not to paint or fix stickers to a polycarbonate helmet,

and it must never be cleaned using solvents. Kevlar has the advantage of combining great strength with light weight, but kevlar helmets tend to be expensive.

Whichever type of helmet you buy, choose one which fits firmly but comfortably. The padding will bed down with wear so if it isn't a tight fit when new the helmet could later become loose, which means there's a risk of it coming off in a crash.

It also makes sense to go for a light-coloured helmet which helps to make you more visible to other road users.

By law a helmet must always be correctly fastened. There are two systems commonly in use – the double D-ring and quick release. Some helmets also have a velcro tab but this is intended solely to secure the strap and stop it flapping in the wind – it must never be used on its own to fasten the helmet.

Take good care of your helmet. Don't leave it on the seat of your bike, where it may fall off and be damaged, or let it roll around on the floor. If your helmet does ever suffer a serious impact, it should be discarded and replaced.

A full face helmet is the best choice because it provides the highest level of protection in a crash

visors and goggles

You should always wear a visor or a pair of goggles to protect your eyes from flying debris, insects, wind and rain. It must comply with British Standard BS 4110 Grade X, XA, YA or ZA, and display the BSI kitemark. Alternatively, it can comply with a European Standard which offers the same safety level as the British Standard, and which carries a mark equivalent to the BSI kitemark (goggles may comply with the EU Directive on personal protective equipment and carry the CE mark).

Never use a tinted visor or goggles in poor visibility or at night.

It is essential to keep your visor or goggles clean at all times. Use warm soapy water to wash off dirt and smears – never use solvents or petrol.

When riding in the cold or wet your visor or goggles may mist up on the inside, impairing your vision. If this happens, find somewhere safe to pull over and clear it with a clean moist cloth. You can buy anti-fog sprays and laminates which help to reduce misting in bad weather.

Avoid using a visor or goggles that has scratches or other damage. This will impair your view, and can cause glare when the sun is low in the sky, as well as dazzle from the lights of oncoming vehicles. Renew your visor or goggles as soon as you notice any damage that might affect your vision.

ear plugs

One medical problem motorcyclists are prone to is hearing impairment caused by excessive wind noise. You are strongly recommended to use ear plugs to reduce the risk of hearing damage. They can also help to reduce fatigue on a long journey.

protective clothing

Wearing the right clothing is vital at all times when riding a motorcycle, not only to keep you warm and dry but also to help protect you if you fall off. Specially designed motorcycling clothing may not be cheap but it is well worth the money for the extra comfort, weather protection and security it provides.

Leather is traditionally a popular choice as it gives a high degree of resistance to abrasion injuries. A one-piece leather suit offers more windproofing and better protection in a crash than a separate jacket and trousers, but most allow little room underneath for putting on extra layers in cold weather. They are also only showerproof so a rain suit will be needed in wet weather.

Alternatively, there is a wide choice of man-made fabrics available, some of which are fully waterproof without the need for a separate rain suit. Try on a good selection, paying particular attention to the fit around the neck, wrists and ankles where cold draughts can penetrate.

Whichever type you prefer, choose clothing which is fully reinforced with body armour, particularly on vulnerable points such as shoulders, elbows, knees and hips. This can play a vital role in cushioning the impact in a crash.

visibility

When choosing clothing, make it a priority to ensure you are as conspicuous as possible to other road users. For a motorcyclist, this is a vital element in staying safe on the road, so don't put fashion before common sense. For optimum visiblity, your outer garments (either your jacket or a specially designed high-visibilty vest designed to slip over your jacket) should be:

- fluorescent to give high visibility in all weathers
- include reflective belts or strips which will make you more easy to see at night.

A one-piece suit is more likely to keep out wind and cold than a jacket and trouser combination

Leather is still a popular choice as it provides a high level of protection from abrasion injuries

Wearing a fluorescent overjacket significantly improves your visiblity to other road users

Plenty of body armour is essential to protect vulnerable points such as knees and elbows

gloves

If you come off your bike, by instinct you'll put out your hands to try to stop your fall. That's why a strong pair of gloves or gauntlets is essential to help prevent serious injury to the hands.

Leather is still the best material for gloves, as it provides a high level of protection but remains supple enough to let you work the controls. Look for extra protection over the knuckles, a long wrist to help keep out the weather and a velcro strap to ensure the glove stays securely in place in a crash.

Leather gloves will quickly become sodden in bad weather, so you'll also need a pair of waterproof overmitts. Check before buying that you can operate the controls easily while wearing your gloves with the overmitts in place.

boots

Always wear a stout pair of over-the-ankle boots when riding. These help to keep your feet warm and also provide protection, both in the event of a fall and against inadvertent knocks and burns from your bike.

When choosing a pair of boots, look for a pair that offers plenty of protection for the shin and ankle. Remember to leave space for an extra pair of socks to keep your feet warm in cold weather. Most boots are made

of leather, which is strong and flexible, but not always fully waterproof in the worst conditions.

Whichever boots you buy, check that they are comfortable and that it is easy to operate the foot controls while wearing them.

weather conditions

Getting cold and wet while riding isn't just unpleasant – it can seriously reduce your concentration and slow your reaction times. Even in mild weather a rider can experience a wind-chill factor that makes it feel more like freezing, and this can quickly lead to the onset of hypothermia if you are inadequately dressed.

When riding in wintry conditions, don't underestimate the amount of extra clothing you will need to keep warm. Wear several layers, starting with thermal underwear and a thin balaclava under your helmet. If you plan to do a lot of riding in all weathers, there are more effective options to consider, such as investing in an electrically heated suit or vest, heated inner gloves or heated handlebar grips.

Waterproof overclothes are worth carrying in case of serious rain. Modern synthetic suits are breathable for comfort, and can be folded into a conveniently small package.

As well as wearing the right clothing, your bike's fairing plays an important part in keeping you protected from the worst of the weather too. If you plan to ride in all weathers, then a touring fairing is a better choice than a sports fairing as it gives much better wind protection to hands, legs and feet. Even fitting handlebar muffs can help to reduce the wind-chill factor.

In hot weather, you may feel overdressed wearing a motorcycle suit. But no matter how warm it is, never be tempted to ride in shorts, a t-shirt, training shoes or sandals – the abrasion injuries from even a slow speed spill onto the tarmac would be severe, extremely painful and could leave you permanently scarred.

KNOW THE CODE

HIGHWAY CODE
RULE 67

On all journeys, the rider and pillion passenger on a motorcycle, scooter or moped MUST wear a protective helmet. Helmets MUST comply with the Regulations and they MUST be fastened securely. It is also advisable to wear eye protectors, which MUST comply with the Regulations. Consider wearing ear protection. Strong boots, gloves and suitable clothing may help to protect you if you fall off.

Always wear a pair of sturdy over-the-ankle boots that offer adequate protection in a crash

Gloves should be strong but also supple enough to let you operate the controls easily

Wearing thermal underwear is an excellent way to help keep out the worst of the winter chill

A waterproof oversuit can be folded up small and carried on the bike in case the weather turrns wet

27

Riding a motorcycle demands a high degree of alertness, concentration, quick reactions and a sober, safety-conscious state of mind. Many forms of illness or disability, alcohol or drug use, or simply tiredness can affect your ability to the point where you are not safe to be on the road. Remember: it doesn't matter how important it seems to get to a job appointment or friend's party – if you're not fit to ride, stay off your bike.

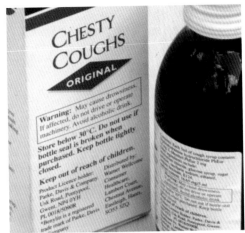

You must by law contact the DVLA if you develop an illness which may affect your riding ability

Even everyday medicines can impair your ability to ride safely, so check the packet for warnings

health and safety

How you feel affects how safely you ride. If you develop a serious illness (see *It's the law* overleaf) then you must inform the DVLA. This won't necessarily mean you'll lose your licence, but the DVLA may ask you to undergo a medical check-up to ensure you are still fit to ride.

Less serious medical problems can also affect your safety on the road. Even a severe cold or flu can lower your concentration and reactions and make you unfit to ride. If you're feeling unwell enough to need medication, then ask yourself if you are really fit enough to get on your motorbike.

medicines

Many medicines can affect your ability to ride. Some of these are available without a prescription across the counter at a chemists.

Certain drugs prescribed to treat depression cause drowsiness and impair concentration. Riding should be avoided while taking these and for some months afterwards. Some tranquillisers and sleeping pills have similar side-effects.

Drugs available at a chemists without a prescription which impair driving include certain hayfever treatments and cold remedies. These can reduce concentration, slow reaction times and promote drowsiness, and they make riding particularly dangerous when taken with any amount of alcohol.

Whenever you take a medicine, carefully check the label for a warning – sometimes not as prominent as it might be – that you should not drive or ride while using it. If prescribed a drug by your doctor, always ask if it will affect your riding ability.

alcohol

Drinking doesn't mix with riding a motorcycle. The anti drink-drive message has been rammed home to all road users by endless publicity campaigns in the last 25 years, but still around one in five drivers and riders killed on the road is under the influence of alcohol.

When a rider has been drinking alcohol it makes them less in control of their machine, slows their reactions and impairs their ability to concentrate and judge speed accurately. It also gives them a false sense of confidence which can lead them to take dangerous risks. Researchers have even suggested that because riding a motorcycle demands a higher level of skill than driving a car, the legal blood-alcohol limit for riders should be lower than for drivers. By far the most sensible course is to drink no alcohol at all if you are planning to use your bike.

The police treat drink-driving very seriously. Drivers and riders involved in an accident are now routinely breathalysed; if

If you ride to the pub, either don't drink any alcohol at all, or arrange to go home by taxi

convicted they face at least a one-year ban. A conviction for riding under the influence of alcohol may invalidate your insurance, and also means you will pay much higher insurance premiums when you do get back on the road.

Remember:

- you must not ride if your breath alcohol level is higher than 35µg per 100ml (equivalent to a blood-alcohol level of 80mg per 100ml)
- alcohol takes time to be broken down by the body and if you have had a heavy night's drinking session the chances are that you will still be over the limit the next morning
- any amount of alcohol impairs your ability to ride safely, even if you're still under the legal limit. So if you plan to drink anything at all, the safest option is to leave your bike at home.

Don't mix motorcycling with drugs or alcohol: it's dangerous, illegal and the penalties are severe

Pay a visit to an optician and get your eyesight checked before you start learning to ride

illegal drugs

Outlawed drugs such as cannabis, ecstasy, cocaine and heroin have the potential to impair your safety and it is an offence to ride under their influence. The police are cracking down on this by introducing roadside tests to identify drivers and riders who are under the influence of drugs, and there are serious penalties for offenders.

eyesight

You must be able to read the current style of numberplate (introduced in September 2001) at a distance of 20 metres (66 feet). If you need to wear contact lenses or spectacles to do this then you must wear them at all times when riding (it makes sense to keep a spare pair with you too, in case you lose or damage your usual pair). Other eye defects such as tunnel vision can also affect your safety on the road so it's a good idea to take a full eye test before starting to ride, and again at the intervals recommended by your optician.

IT'S THE LAW

FIT TO RIDE?

You must by law inform the DVLA if you suffer any of the following:

- ➔ epilepsy
- ➔ giddiness, fainting or blackouts
- ➔ a severe mental handicap
- ➔ diabetes
- ➔ heart pain while riding
- ➔ Parkinson's disease
- ➔ any chronic neurological condition
- ➔ a serious memory problem
- ➔ a stroke
- ➔ brain surgery, a brain tumour or a severe head injury
- ➔ severe psychiatric illness or mental disorder
- ➔ long-term problems with your arms or legs
- ➔ dependence on alcohol or drugs or chemical substances in the past three years
- ➔ any visual disability which affects both eyes (not short/long sightedness or colour blindness)
- ➔ have a pacemaker, defibrillator or anti-ventricular tachycardia device fitted.

31

02
IN CONTROL

LEARN TO RIDE

You've signed your provisional licence, your motorbike is roadworthy, taxed and insured, you've checked your eyesight and health and you can't wait to start the engine and ride off down the road. But try to be patient. A modern motorbike is a complex piece of machinery and before you go anywhere you need to understand exactly how all the controls work, what the various switches do and what the warning lights mean. Whenever you ride a different bike to the one you are used to, always take time to make certain you know how everything operates before moving off.

On the left handlebar you'll usually find the:

- clutch lever
- choke
- direction indicators
- horn
- headlight dip switch
- headlight flasher.

clutch lever

Operating the clutch lever (*below*) disconnects the engine from the rear wheel. This allows the bike to come to a standstill without stalling the engine, and lets you change from one gear to another more easily.

The clutch itself consists of a pair of friction plates which are pulled apart when the clutch lever is operated.

As you let the clutch lever out, the two plates touch and power starts to be transmitted to the rear wheel. This is termed the 'biting point'. The further you release the lever, the more power is transmitted. Once the clutch lever is fully released the clutch plates lock together and all the power from the engine is delivered to the rear wheel.

When you hold the lever so that the clutch is only half engaged, it is called 'slipping the clutch' or 'clutch control'. Clutch control is useful when you want to ride very slowly – for instance when carrying out low-speed manoeuvres.

choke

The choke enriches the fuel mixture entering the engine and is used to start the engine from cold. Put the choke fully on before starting a cold engine. Gradually push the choke back in over the first mile or so of riding (the exact distance depends on the type of bike and the air temperature, but if you turn off the choke too early the engine may stall when you come to a halt at a junction).

Make sure the choke is pushed all the way back in as soon as the engine is warm, or it will cause the engine to run fast and make it difficult to control the motorcycle, particularly when slowing down. Leaving the choke on too long also wastes fuel and if done repeatedly can cause engine damage.

Some models, including many scooters, have an automatic choke fitted. Models with fuel injection do not have a choke but compensate automatically for the richer mixture needed on a cold start.

automatics

Some motorcycles (especially mopeds and scooters) are fitted with an automatic or semi-automatic gearbox.

- **fully automatic:** there is no clutch lever and no gear shift; when ready to move off you shift from neutral into drive. Often a lever operating the rear brakes is fitted instead of a clutch lever.

- **semi-automatic:** there is no clutch lever; you operate the gear shift as you would with a manual and the clutch works automatically.

headlight flasher

Use this for the same purpose as the horn, to warn other road users of your presence if you think they haven't seen you. A headlight flash is useful where the horn may not be audible, for instance at higher speeds.

headlight dip switch

This lowers your headlight beam from main beam to dipped beam to avoid dazzling other road users (*below*).

indicators

Flick the switch to the right to activate the right indicators, to the left for the left indicators. It is important to use your indicators to let other road users know that you intend to change direction. Unlike cars, few motorcycles have self-cancelling indicators so don't forget to cancel them once you have completed your manoeuvre.

horn

Used only to warn other road users that you are there. Make sure you know where the horn is before you have to use it in an emergency (*below*).

RIGHT HANDLEBAR CONTROLS

The right handlebar normally has fitted to it the:

- ➡ throttle
- ➡ front brake lever
- ➡ electric starter
- ➡ engine cut-out
- ➡ light switch.

throttle

Opening the throttle (*below*) by twisting it towards you increases the flow of fuel and air to the engine, giving extra power when you need to increase speed or ride uphill. The throttle automatically springs back to the closed position when released (in the fully closed position it still allows the engine to tick over). Light and gentle use of the throttle improves fuel economy and promotes a smooth riding style.

front brake lever

This lever (*below*) operates the front brake only (except on bikes which have a linked braking system – see p58). Operating this lever also illuminates the rear brake light, giving a warning to following traffic that you are slowing.

electric starter

Fitted on many bikes instead of (or as well as) the manual kick starter. (*See p51 for use.*)

engine cut-out

Used (*below*) to stop the engine in an emergency (the ignition switch should be used when stopping the engine normally).

lights

An increasing number of bikes do not have a separate light switch – the headlight comes on automatically whenever the ignition is switched on. Where a light switch is fitted, it usually has three settings:

⊜ off
⊜ parking lights (in this position the rear position light and numberplate light also illuminate). Parking lights must be displayed when parking at night on a road with a speed limit greater than 30mph (*see p139*)
⊜ headlight (plus rear position light and numberplate light). To maximise your visibility to other road users, use your headlight at all times when riding.

37

FOOT CONTROLS

On most motorcycles the right foot controls the rear brake pedal, and the left foot operates the gear selector. Most modern bikes have an electric starter, but there may also be a kick starter, used for starting the engine manually (*see p51*). Where fitted, this is usually on the right side of the engine in front of the footrest, and it should be securely folded away when not in use.

rear brake pedal

This is usually situated on the right side of the motorcycle, in front of the footrest (although some automatic bikes have a brake lever on the left handlebar that operates the rear brake). The brake pedal operates the rear brake only (except on bikes which have a linked braking system). Operating the pedal also illuminates the rear brake light, giving a warning to following traffic that you are slowing.

gear selector

Usually situated on the left side of the motorcycle, in front of the footrest. Push down on the selector with your left foot to change to a lower gear, or lift it up with your foot beneath it to change to a higher gear. The number of gears varies from bike to bike, though five or six is usual. In addition there is a neutral position, where no gear is engaged. In neutral the engine can tick over without power being transmitted to the rear wheel.

02

INSTRUMENTS

On or around the instrument panel you'll find the:

- ignition switch
- speedometer
- odometer
- trip meter
- rev counter
- warning lights.

ignition switch

This turns on the motorbike's electrical systems in readiness to start the engine. The ignition switch usually has four positions:

- off
- on: this allows the engine to be started
- lock: in this position the steering locks into place if the handlebars are turned without the key in the ignition. It makes the bike more secure against theft
- park (P): this is used when the bike needs to be parked on the road at night with the parking light illuminated.

speedometer

The speedometer shows both miles per hour (mph) and kilometres per hour (km/h). The kilometre scale is marked in smaller figures on the inner ring of the dial and should be ignored unless the bike is ridden overseas. Some bikes have a digital speedometer – although these aren't always any easier to read at a glance. It is a legal requirement to have a working speedometer and it must not show a reading lower than the actual speed.

odometer

Shows the total mileage the motorcycle has covered from new (see top line of numbers within speedometer, *right*).

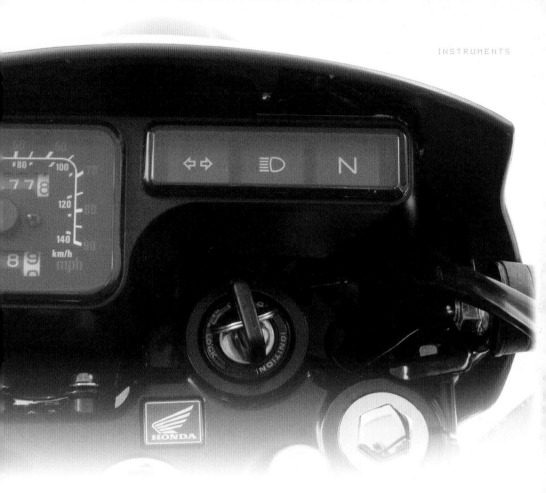

trip meter

Gives a mileage reading which can be reset. This is useful to show how many miles you have ridden since last refuelling (see lower line of numbers within speedometer, *right*).

rev counter

Most bikes are fitted with a rev counter (or tachometer) which shows the engine speed in revolutions per minute (rpm). The maximum engine speed permitted is usually indicated by a red line marked on the dial.

warning lights

Warning lights are fitted to alert you to serious faults and remind you about electrical items that are switched on.

Lights monitoring your motorcycle's systems (such as the ignition and oil pressure) should come on when you turn on the ignition, then extinguish. If they come on while you are riding, stop and investigate why.

Reminder lights (such as headlight main beam) remain illuminated whenever the item is in use.

neutral light

Glows when the gear selector is in neutral. Some bikes also have a digital gear position indicator to help you monitor which gear you are in.

temperature gauge

A temperature warning light and/or gauge is fitted to motorbikes with water-cooled engines. If the light illuminates or the needle of the gauge enters the red zone the engine is overheating and you should stop as soon as possible. When cold the engine does not operate so efficiently. Avoid working the engine hard until the gauge reaches its normal working temperature, or you will waste fuel and cause extra engine wear.

fuel gauge

The fuel gauge gives a rough indication of how much fuel remains in the fuel tank. On some bikes, as this reaches the lower limit a fuel warning light may illuminate, indicating that only a few litres (check the handbook for the exact amount) of fuel are left. Some bikes have a reserve fuel tank. If the main tank runs dry you need to turn the fuel tap to the reserve position to supply the engine with fuel from the reserve tank.

oil pressure

If this light comes on when riding it means the oil pressure is low. Stop as soon as possible and turn off the engine to avoid serious damage. Check the oil level and top up if necessary, but do not continue riding if the light stays on.

ignition

If lit when the engine is running this indicates there is a problem with the battery charging system.

ABS

If fitted, this should light up when you turn on the ignition and extinguish once you get underway. If it stays illuminated or comes on while riding it indicates a problem with the anti-lock braking system (see p58). Stop and consult the handbook to see if the bike is still safe to ride, and get the braking system checked immediately.

left/right indicator

Shows that the indicators are operating.

headlamp main beam

Warns that the headlight is on main beam setting which may dazzle other road users.

03

BASIC SKILLS

LEARN TO RIDE

Riding a motorbike is a more physical task than driving a car. As well as controlling your bike at speed, you have to be able to take it on and off its stand, and wheel it with the engine off. If you already drive a car, you will be familiar with clutch control, but getting used to using your left hand instead of your left foot to find the biting point needs a little practice. Braking too is more complicated than with a car because on most bikes the front and rear brakes are operated by separate controls.

For something that feels so agile when you're riding it, a bike can be a heavy and cumbersome object to manhandle when it's stationary. Bear this in mind when choosing your bike and don't buy one that you don't feel comfortable taking on and off its stand and wheeling about. In any exercise with a stationary bike, you should stand on the left-hand side of the bike, away from approaching traffic.

motorcycle stands

When parked, your motorcycle is supported on its stand. There are two types – the centre stand and side stand – and many bikes are fitted with both.

The side stand is quicker and easier to use, and relies for stability on the bike leaning onto the stand. However, take care that the surface is firm or the stand may sink into the ground, causing the bike to fall over. Care is also needed when leaning the bike against a slope: if the bike is too upright on the stand it will not be stable and may fall over.

The centre stand gives more stability, and can be used to support the bike while you are carrying out maintenance such as adjusting the drive chain. However, take care to use the centre stand on a flat, firm surface only.

Both the centre and side stands can pose a serious hazard if they are not fully retracted while the motorcycle is being ridden, as the stand may dig into the road when cornering, throw the bike off balance and cause an accident. For this reason, it is essential to double check that the stand is fully up before riding off. Some bikes feature an inhibitor switch which prevents them from being ridden when the side stand is down. If your bike is fitted with such a switch and the engine refuses to start, or starts but cuts out when you select a gear, check to make sure that the stand is in its fully retracted position.

using the centre stand

To put the motorbike on its stand:

- position yourself on the left of the bike, holding the left handlebar with your left hand and the frame near the saddle with your right hand (on some bikes there is a special handle to grab)
- push the stand down with your right foot (or left, if preferred)
- hold down the stand with your foot while pulling the bike backwards and upwards.

To take the motorbike off its stand:

- position yourself on the left of the bike, holding the left handlebar with your left hand and the frame near the saddle (or grab handle) with your right hand
- put your left foot (or right, if preferred) in front of the stand
- pull the bike forwards
- as the bike comes off the stand move your right hand on to the front brake lever to control it.

The centre stand gives better support than the side stand, so use it when carrying out maintenance

using the side stand

To put the motorbike on its stand:

- ● position yourself on the left of the bike, holding the left handlebar with your left hand
- ● holding the bike upright, push down the stand with your foot
- ● let the bike lean towards you until its weight is taken by the stand.

To take the motorbike off its stand:

- ● position yourself on the left of the bike, holding both handlebars
- ● push the motorbike upright
- ● pull the bike forwards
- ● push the stand up with your foot
- ● check that the stand has locked securely in its fully retracted position.

wheeling

It is important to be able to move your motorbike by wheeling it with the engine off and the gearbox in neutral. With the bike off its stand, position yourself on the left of the bike and hold both handlebars firmly, keeping your right hand on the brake to control the speed. Let the bike lean towards you, finding the angle which is most comfortable and easiest to balance, and practise wheeling it forwards and in circles left and right.

Take care to use the side stand on a firm, level surface; if it is used on a slope or on soft ground there is a danger of the bike toppling over

Wheeling your motorbike is an important skill; as part of the practical test your examiner will ask you to walk with your motorbike, usually in a U-turn

mounting and dismounting

Mount the motorcycle from the left-hand side, away from the traffic. As you get on, apply the front brake to prevent the bike from moving.

riding position

When sitting on the stationary bike you should be able to place both feet on the ground, and balance securely on one foot while using the other to work the foot controls. You should also be able to reach all the controls without stretching. If necessary, the main controls such as brake, clutch and gear levers can all be adjusted to give a more comfortable fit.

Make sure you apply the front brake lever to keep the motorbike steady as you mount it

You should be able to reach all the controls without stretching; if not, adjust them to fit

03

MOVING OFF

Turning a stationary motorbike into a moving one requires a fair degree of balance and coordination. You need be able to modulate the clutch and throttle to move off in any road situation, whether on the level or a steep gradient, or if you have to pull out at an angle from a tight parking space. But at the same time it's essential you don't overlook the need for observation: when moving off you need to be fully aware of what is happening all around you and act on this information to stay safe.

starting the engine

Different motorcycles have different starting procedures. Some bikes will not start except in neutral, others won't unless the clutch lever is pulled in. On many scooters the brake must be applied before the engine will start. You should consult the handbook for advice on starting your particular bike. However, this is the general procedure:

- ➡ check the gear selector is in neutral. If you try to start the motorcycle when it is in gear it will lurch forwards dangerously. The neutral light on the instrument panel should glow with the ignition turned on. If there is no neutral light fitted, push the motorcycle forward: if it is in neutral the rear wheel should turn freely

With an electric starter, release the button once the engine fires or the starter could be damaged

- ➡ turn on the fuel tap (if fitted)
- ➡ if starting a cold engine, put the choke on
- ➡ check that the engine cut-out switch is in the on position
- ➡ if an electric starter is fitted, press the starter button. Release the button as soon as the engine fires or the starter motor may be damaged. Open the throttle to help it catch until it settles to a steady tickover (tickover speed will be higher than usual when the choke is used)

Don't forget to turn on the fuel tap, if one is fitted, before trying to start the engine

- ➡ if a kick starter is fitted, fold out the kick start lever (you may have to fold up the footrest first). Tread down briskly on the starter lever and allow it to return to its upright position. Repeat this until the engine fires, and open the throttle until it settles to a steady tickover. Fold the kick start lever back into its normal position
- ➡ check that the ignition and oil pressure lights go out once the engine is running steadily
- ➡ remember to move the choke to its off position as the engine warms up.

When starting a cold engine the choke is needed (on this bike it operates directly on the carburettor, but it is more usually situated on the left handlebar)

moving off

To get the motorbike underway:

- ➡ apply the front brake and start the engine
- ➡ squeeze the clutch lever in all the way
- ➡ select first gear
- ➡ take your weight on your left foot, place your right foot on the footrest and apply the rear brake. Take your right hand off the front brake ready to use the throttle
- ➡ start to release the clutch lever until you feel the 'biting point' when the bike starts to move forward
- ➡ open the throttle wider while smoothly continuing to release the clutch. As you move off let off the rear brake and put your left foot onto the footrest.

avoiding stalls

If you release the clutch too quickly or don't apply enough power, the engine may cut out or 'stall'. Clutch control can be a difficult knack to acquire at first so be prepared to practice before you can move off seamlessly every time.

While learning you're most likely to stall when trying to move off uphill. You will need to use more throttle, and be precise about releasing the rear brake – too soon and the motorbike will roll back, too late and it will stall. Practise moving off uphill until you are confident you can carry out this manoeuvre even in tricky circumstances, such as when pulling out from behind a parked vehicle.

low-speed manoeuvres

Careful clutch control is also required when riding at low speeds. You may need to slip the clutch in order to keep the engine running smoothly. The front brake can be fierce at low speeds, so use the rear brake instead. When moving slowly a motorcycle can feel heavy and unwieldy, so practise to improve your balance when slow-riding. Looking well ahead can increase your stability: never look down at the front wheel when riding as this can seriously upset your sense of balance.

Moving off at an angle may be necessary when you have stopped behind a parked vehicle. It requires careful balance and clutch control. Be extra alert for traffic approaching from all directions, be ready to stop for pedestrians and leave plenty of room as you pull past the parked vehicle in case a door opens in front of you

KNOW THE CODE   HIGHWAY CODE RULE 135

Before moving off you should

- ➡ use all mirrors to check the road is clear
- ➡ look round to check the blind spots (the areas you are unable to see in the mirrors)
- ➡ signal if necessary before moving out
- ➡ look round for a final check.

Move off only when it is safe to do so.

Performing a U-turn: you must check all around before starting the turn, and take a final look behind to ensure it is safe before moving off

U-turns

A U-turn is a useful way to turn around. It needs to be performed at low speed so practise until you are confident. You should only carry out a U-turn where it is safe and legal to do so, with no signs or road markings prohibiting this manoeuvre. Take special care to make sure the road is clear in both directions, and always look behind for a final check before starting the turn.

stopping

To bring the motorbike to a halt:
- close the throttle
- apply both front and rear brakes smoothly
- just before coming to a standstill pull in the clutch lever to prevent the engine from stalling
- as the bike stops put your left foot on the ground to support it
- keeping the front brake applied, take your right foot off the brake and put it on the ground so you are now supporting the bike with your right foot

- take your left foot off the ground and shift the gear selector to neutral
- release the clutch lever
- put both feet firmly on the ground.

At very low speeds you may need to pull in the clutch before you brake. However, avoid riding for longer than necessary with the clutch lever pulled in, as this reduces the control you have over the motorbike.

where to stop

When stopping at the side of the road always make sure you select somewhere safe to pull in: never stop where you would obstruct other road users or where road markings prohibit stopping. Don't stop or park:
- near a school entrance
- where you would prevent emergency access
- at or near a bus stop or taxi rank
- on the approach to a level crossing
- opposite or within ten metres of a junction
- near the brow of a hill or hump bridge
- opposite a traffic island
- opposite another parked vehicle if it would cause an obstruction
- where you would force other traffic to enter a tram lane
- where the kerb has been lowered to help wheelchair users
- in front of an entrance to a property
- on a bend.

turning off the engine

To stop the engine running:
- close the throttle
- check that the gear selector is in neutral
- turn the key to switch off the ignition (do not use the engine cut-out switch to turn off the engine – this is for emergency use only)
- turn off the fuel tap (if fitted).

If you've ridden a bicycle fitted with gears you'll understand the effect that choice of gear has on speed and effort. Try to move off in too high a gear and you'll struggle to turn the pedals. Stay in a low gear on a level stretch of road and you'll find yourself pedalling furiously for no extra forward velocity. It's the same on a motorcycle, except that the engine does the work instead of the rider. The low gears provide lots of acceleration but run out of steam before the bike is travelling very quickly. Higher gears provide plenty of road speed, but not as much acceleration. Your job is to match the gears to the speed of the bike, moving up the gearbox as your speed rises, and to select a lower gear when more power is needed, for instance when overtaking or approaching a steep hill.

how to change gear

Changing gear requires careful coordination of foot and hand movements, so don't be surprised if your gear changes feel clumsy at first. To change gear:

- close the throttle and at the same time pull in the clutch lever to disengage the engine from the gearbox
- select the gear required with your left foot: to change up, put your toe under the selector and lift it up; to change down, press down on the selector
- release the clutch lever and simultaneously open the throttle.

To make even smoother changes going down the gearbox, keep the throttle slightly open as you shift the gear selector. This means the engine revs rise to match the new gear selected, and with practice you can make your changes down the gearbox almost seamless.

selecting the right gear

Listen to the engine to indicate when you should change gear. Don't race the engine unnecessarily, which simply wastes fuel, but also don't make it labour by riding in too high a gear for the conditions.

riding an automatic

Mopeds and scooters generally have automatic gearboxes which give an easy ride, especially in town. Simply engage drive, twist the throttle and away you go.

Even if you intend to ride an automatic motorcycle, it still makes a lot of sense to take your test on a manual bike, because passing on a manual qualifies you to ride both manual and automatic bikes, whereas if you pass on an automatic your licence restricts you to riding automatic bikes only.

Select a lower gear when you need more acceleration, for instance when gaining speed on a slip road to merge with fast-moving traffic

KNOW THE CODE

HIGHWAY CODE RULE 102

Coasting This term describes a vehicle travelling in neutral or with the clutch pressed down. Do not coast, whatever the driving conditions. It reduces driver control because:

- engine braking is eliminated
- vehicle speed downhill will increase quickly
- increased use of the footbrake can reduce its effectiveness
- steering response will be affected particularly on bends and corners
- it may be more difficult to select the appropriate gear when needed.

The forces acting on a cornering motorcycle are highly complex but at speed a bike has a natural balance and most novice riders soon get the feel of leaning their bike through bends. At lower speeds a bike has less natural stability and the rider has to compensate by balancing and steering more actively. Low-speed riding is examined during the practical test and it is important to practise this element of bike control until you are thoroughly competent.

holding the bars

To be fully in control of your motorcycle you need to keep both hands firmly gripping the handlebars. Remove a hand from the handlebars only when absolutely necessary (for instance, to give a hand signal). Always replace both hands on the grips before starting any manoeuvre such as turning a corner. Never take both hands off the handlebars while you are riding.

steering technique

How you steer a motorcycle depends on how quickly you are riding.

➡ low-speed steering

At low speeds you need to turn the handlebars in the direction of the turn as you would steer a bicycle. The motorbike will tend to fall inwards, so you need to shift your weight in the other direction to balance it and stay upright. Try to keep your movements as smooth and coordinated as possible and you will find it easy to stay in balance.

➡ high-speed steering

At higher speeds more complex forces come into play. To change direction you need to shift your body weight so that you and your bike lean into the direction of the turn. On sharp bends or at higher speeds you will need a greater angle of lean to maintain your balance, but do not lean so far that you risk your tyres losing grip on the road. As you exit the turn, you need to progressively bring the bike back upright again.

counter-steering

This may not make sense until you experience it for yourself, but at higher speeds, if you try to steer a motorbike as you would at low speeds (that is, by turning the handlebars right to turn right) the bike will do the opposite – lean to the left and make a left turn.

Many riders actively use counter-steering

as an aid to turning into a corner. When approaching a left-hand curve, a gentle forward pressure on the left handlebar encourages the bike to start leaning towards the left. The rider then shifts his or her weight to balance the bike into the curve.

steering lock

When you turn the handlebars as far as they will go in either direction they are at full steering lock. Some bikes have a restricted steering lock which means you may have to allow more space when making slow manouevres such as U-turns.

To steer at low speed you need to move the handlebars in the direction you want to turn

The tighter the steering lock, the easier it is to manoeuvre the bike in and out of confined spaces

03 BRAKING

Braking a motorcycle demands considerably more skill than using the brakes in a car. Firstly, most bikes have separate controls for front and rear brakes and you must learn to balance the two. And secondly, few bikes yet have anti-lock brakes which means extra care must be taken not to provoke a skid in an emergency. In everyday riding you should aim to use the brakes as little as possible by anticipating the need to slow down well in advance. Harsh, late braking is a sign of poor riding and it will not impress the examiner on your practical test.

using the brakes

Although a bike has front and rear brakes the two shouldn't be used evenly. Under braking the weight of the bike and rider is thrown forwards, over the front wheel. This presses the front tyre downwards, making it grip the road harder. It means that the front brake is capable of stopping the bike much more effectively than the rear brake.

You should apply the front brake slightly before the rear brake and, when road and weather conditions are good, use more force on the front brake. In poor weather you need to apply a more equal amount of force on front and rear brakes.

Apply the brakes gently at first, then progressively increase the pressure. Never brake harshly, or you risk making the wheels 'lock up' – stop rotating – and the bike will skid. Special care is needed when the roads are wet or icy as the risk of skidding becomes much higher.

Plan your braking well in advance of a hazard so you have to brake only when the bike is upright and travelling in a straight line. If you brake while leaning into a bend it will upset the balance of the bike and you may lose control. If you have no choice but to brake on a bend, try to use the rear brake only. If you have to use the front brake, do so very gently or the front wheel may skid. If possible, bring your bike back upright so you can apply the brakes normally.

emergency stop

By developing good observation and anticipation skills you should rarely have to stop in an emergency. However, emergency braking is a vital skill to master, and you will be required to carry out an emergency stop during your practical test.

To stop in an emergency, brake firmly but don't snatch violently at the brakes as this may cause the wheels to lock up and skid. Apply the front brake a fraction before the rear and progressively increase the braking pressure. If a wheel does lock, ease off the appropriate brake until it starts to rotate again then reapply the brake less harshly. Pull in the clutch lever just before you come to a halt to prevent the engine stalling. Make sure emergency braking is carried out with the bike upright or you risk causing a skid and losing control. Always keep both hands firmly on the handlebars during an emergency stop.

engine braking

When you release the throttle the engine slows the bike even if you don't touch the brakes. Engine braking is hardly noticeable in top gear, but in the lower ratios it is much more effective. Make use of engine braking by selecting a lower gear to give more control over your bike when descending a steep hill.

linked brakes

Some bikes have a braking system which links the front and rear brakes so that whether you use the front brake lever or the rear brake pedal, braking force is apportioned to both front and rear wheels. The system varies between manufacturers so where fitted it is important to read the handbook. Not all riders are enthusiastic about linked brakes, but they do make it less likely that a skid will occur during emergency braking.

anti-lock brakes

An anti-lock braking system (ABS) works electronically to prevent the wheels from locking up under emergency braking. This means that in an emergency you can apply maximum pressure to the brakes without the risk of the wheels skidding. Anti-lock braking cannot, however, overcome the laws of physics: it will not necessarily make you stop any quicker, and it may not remove the risk of a skid if you brake while you are cornering or riding on a loose or slippery surface.

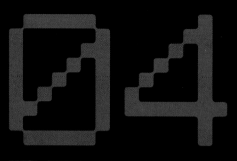

04
READING
THE ROAD

There's a vast amount of information on the road to help you ride safely – providing you see it and respond to it properly. Road markings and signs warn of a whole range of hazards as well as giving you instructions and information. Then there are the signals coming from other road users. Their indicators, brake lights and even how they position themselves on the road tell you a lot about what they are going to do. And at the same time you need to communicate to everyone else what you intend to do by giving clear and accurate signals yourself.

It's as important to be aware of what's happening on the road behind you as it is to see what's going on ahead. Rear observation takes two forms: you need to keep checking your mirrors to monitor traffic movements behind, and you also need to turn your head and look behind to confirm everything is safe before making a manoeuvre.

adjusting mirrors

To get the best view behind, it makes sense to have mirrors fitted on both sides of your motorcycle

Make sure both mirrors are correctly adjusted to give the fullest view of the road behind. You may find that your elbows obscure the view, in which case you should add extensions to the mirror arms. Make sure you keep your mirrors clean at all times. On some bikes vibration may impair the image quality in the mirror – consult your dealer for advice on how to reduce this.

Adjust the mirrors so that you have a clear view of traffic approaching from behind

image distortion

Some mirrors are flat, giving an accurate view of traffic behind. Other mirrors are convex, or slightly curved. This has the advantage of giving a wider field of view but it also means that vehicles can look like they are further away than they really are. Take this into account before acting on information from your mirrors.

Some mirrors have curved glass which makes vehicles seem further away than they really are

looking behind

Even with your mirrors perfectly adjusted there are blindspots – areas behind you which do not appear in the mirrors. This means there are times when it is essential to turn your head to get a full view of what's happening behind you. This rear glance is sometimes aptly called the lifesaver.

Looking behind gives a more accurate view of how fast traffic is approaching than you can get from your mirrors. It can also give an extra warning to following drivers that you are about to make a manoeuvre.

Of course while looking behind you have to take your eyes off the road ahead, which is in itself potentially dangerous. So use your judgement about when to look behind. Don't do it when there is a developing hazard ahead which requires all your concentration, or in the middle of making a hazardous manoeuvre such as overtaking, or when you are close behind another vehicle.

Your mirrors can only tell you so much: before making a manoeuvre you should also look behind

using rear observation

You must always take adequate rear observation before carrying out any manoeuvre that affects your speed or position on the road. This includes:

➲ **moving off**
Check your mirrors, and look over your right shoulder to confirm that nothing is in your blind spot

➲ **changing lanes**
Use your mirrors plus a look behind to check for vehicles that are in your blind spot or moving into the lane you want to enter

➲ **overtaking**
Use your mirrors, and look behind if necessary, to check no one is about to overtake you before you begin your manoeuvre

➲ **turning right**
Check your mirrors as you approach the turn. Look over your right shoulder just before you make the turn to check no one is about to overtake you

➲ **turning left**
Check your mirrors as you approach the turn. Look over your left shoulder before you make the turn to check for a cyclist or other motorcyclist who could be about to pass you on the inside

➲ **exiting a roundabout**
Look over your left shoulder before you turn off to check for another vehicle passing you on the inside

➲ **slowing down or stopping**
A vehicle that is following you too closely may not be able to stop in time when you brake. Check your mirror in good time so you can lose speed more gently if necessary

➲ **increasing speed**
Check your mirrors before accelerating, for instance when leaving a lower speed limit, in case a following vehicle is about to overtake you.

Check over your right shoulder before changing lanes in case there's a vehicle in your blind spot

Look over your left shoulder before turning left in case someone is passing you on your nearside

observation-signal-manoeuvre

The observation-signal-manoeuvre (OSM) routine is fundamental to safe riding. Every time you intend to change your speed or position you must first take **observation** of what's happening in all directions around you. Next give a **signal** if it might help other road users. Only then can you begin to carry out the **manoeuvre**.

The manoeuvre itself involves three consecutive actions: this is called the position-speed-look (PSL) routine.

First you get into the correct **position** on the road to negotiate the hazard.

Next you adjust your **speed** to suit the hazard and select the appropriate gear.

Then you take a last good **look** all around, including taking rear observation, to check that it is safe for you to carry out the manoeuvre.

Only then can you make the manoeuvre if it is safe to do so.

Get into the habit of carrying out the OSM/PSL routine whenever you plan to make a manoeuvre. The sequence is the same for any type of manoeuvre: the diagram on the right illustrates how it works when making a right turn.

1 look all round and take rear observation

2 signal if necessary

3 change position towards the centre of the road

4 slow progressively to the required speed

5 select the appropriate gear

6 look all round including a last check over your right shoulder

7 make the turn if it is safe to do so

SIGNALS

It is essential to let other road users know what you intend to do well in advance. Giving clear and accurate signals cuts down misunderstandings which can lead to dangerous situations on the road. And fellow road users appreciate the courtesy of being given clear signals so they don't have to slow or stop for no reason and wait to see what you are going to do.

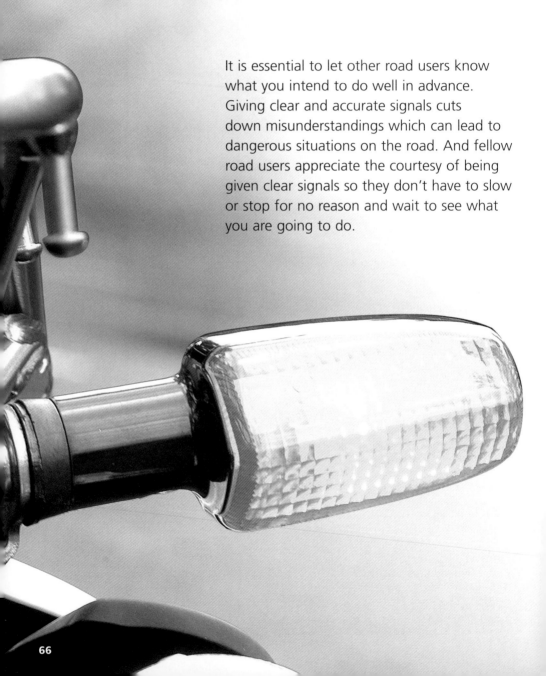

indicators

Use your indicators to signal that you intend to move off or change direction. Always:

- give a signal in good time so other road users have time to react to it before you start changing your speed or position. If a road user shows no sign of reacting to your signal, don't carry out the manoeuvre until you're sure they have seen you
- think before using your indicators. Identify who may benefit from a signal and make that signal as clear as possible. There's no point indicating if there is no one in the vicinity to see your signals
- avoid making ambiguous signals. For instance, if you want to pull into the kerb just beyond a side road on the left, don't indicate until you are past the side road, or other road users may think you're turning left into it
- make sure your indicator is cancelled after carrying out a manoeuvre, or you could mislead other road users.

Give a signal well in advance when you have to change lanes so that other road users have plenty of time to see and react to your signal

Don't signal where it might confuse other road users. For instance, if you want to pull into the kerb immediately after this junction, you should wait until you are past the junction before signalling. If you signal too early, the driver waiting to emerge might pull out in front of you, thinking you intend to turn into the side road

Your brake light gives a useful warning to other road users that you are slowing down or stopping

Use a headlight flash to alert another road user if you think they haven't seen you

brake signal

Each time you use the brakes, the brake warning light on the back of your motorcycle comes on, giving a signal to traffic behind that you are slowing down. You can use the brake controls very gently to illuminate the brake light and warn following drivers that you intend to slow for a hazard which they may not yet have noticed.

There are other situations where the brake lights can give a useful warning. For instance, holding on the brakes while you are stopped waiting to make a right turn, or when you are stationary at roadworks or traffic lights, can help to warn approaching drivers that your bike is stationary.

horn

The horn is one of the most misused signals on the road. Never sound the horn to tick off another road user who you think has behaved badly. This achieves nothing, and it may provoke an aggressive response. Use the horn only to alert another road user who you think may not have noticed that you are there. Give a short toot and consider raising your hand to show there was no aggressive intent on your part.

It is illegal to sound the horn when you are stationary, or in a built-up area between 11.30pm and 7.00am except when another moving vehicle poses a danger to you.

headlight flash

This signal has only one meaning, which is to alert another road user to your presence. A headlight flash is useful in situations where a horn may not be heard, such as at high speed on a motorway, or at night when horn use is not permitted.

Don't flash your headlight for the wrong reason. It must never be done to intimidate or give instructions to another road user – you might know what you mean when you flash your headlight, but the other road user may not, with potentially dangerous consequences.

The same reasoning applies if another vehicle flashes its headlights at you. Don't assume this is an invitation to ride on – the driver may intend it to mean 'stop, I'm coming through'. Always wait until you are certain what the other vehicle is doing before proceeding.

Treat signals from other drivers with caution: they may not necessarily mean what you think they do

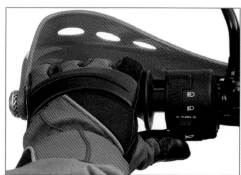

Make sure you know where the horn button is so that you can use it instantly in an emergency

hazard warning lights

A few bikes have a hazard warning light facility. When in use all four indicators operate, giving a warning to other road users. Hazard warning lights should be used for the following purposes only:

- when you have broken down
- when your motorcycle is temporarily obstructing traffic
- while riding on a dual carriageway or motorway, to alert other road users that there is a hazard ahead.

acting on signals

Imagine you are waiting to emerge from a T-junction. The road is clear to the left, and a car is approaching from the right with its left-hand indicator flashing. Does it mean that the driver is about to turn into your junction so it's safe for you to pull out ahead of it? Or does it mean that the driver:

- is hard of hearing and has forgotten to cancel the indicator since their last manoeuvre
- has knocked on the indicator by accident while reaching for the radio
- intends to pull left into a driveway immediately past your junction
- has a faulty indicator switch?

The answer, of course, is any of the above. Never assume another vehicle is about to do something simply because it is indicating. Always wait for some confirmation of the signal, for instance until you see the vehicle slow down or start to turn, before making any manoeuvre in front of it.

Be cautious if you see a driver signalling for no apparent reason. Never overtake a vehicle that is indicating right, even if you think that the driver has left on their indicator by mistake.

arm signals

There are certain situations when an arm signal can be really useful to confirm another signal given by your indicators or brake light, or to make your intentions certain if these lights cannot be seen. For instance:

- → a right turn arm signal can emphasise that you are about to make a right turn into a side road and are not just moving out to pass a parked car
- → a slowing down arm signal makes your intention clear when you want to show you are pulling in to the kerb, not turning left
- → an arm signal is clearly visible when your brake or indicator light is hard to see because of strong sunlight
- → pedestrians waiting at a crossing can't see your brake lights as you approach. Giving a slowing down arm signal tells them you are about to stop.

Never wave pedestrians across the road. You could put them in danger if they walk out without checking for themselves that the road is clear

Giving an arm signal means taking a hand off the handlebars, which reduces your control over your bike. Avoid giving arm signals at high speed, and if giving an arm signal before making a turn, make sure you return both hands securely to the handlebars before starting to make the turn.

Few car drivers give hand signals nowadays but you do need to learn to recognise them.

police directing traffic

When traffic lights fail or when traffic is unusually heavy, a police officer may use arm signals to direct the traffic flow.

You must by law obey arm signals given by any authorised persons – police officers and traffic wardens – as well as signs displayed by school crossing patrols.

arm signals given by riders and drivers

I intend to move to the left or turn left	*I intend to move to the right or turn right*	*I intend to slow down or stop*

arm signals given by authorised persons

Traffic coming from the front must stop	*Traffic approaching from behind must stop*	*Traffic from both front and behind must stop*
Traffic from the side may proceed	*Traffic from the front may proceed*	*Traffic from behind may proceed*

Keep your speed down when approaching a school crossing patrol: you must by law stop and wait when one signals you to do so

Consider making an arm signal where it would be helpful, for example to show waiting pedestrians you are slowing as you approach a zebra crossing

ROAD SIGNS

Road signs give vital information and you must obey them to stay safe and within the law. Many signs show simplified pictures instead of written instructions, which makes it easier to take in what they mean at a glance. You must be able to recognise and understand the meaning of all road signs. More importantly, you must act on the information given by signs. If a sign warns of a hazard ahead – such as an uneven road surface, no footway, slippery road or traffic queues – you should consider adjusting your speed and position on the road so that you are ready to deal safely with the hazard when you encounter it.

shapes and colours

You'll know that some signs are round, some square and some triangular, and that they come in different colours, but you may not realise why. In fact, all these shapes and colours have distinct meanings.

Circular signs give orders. Those with a red border tell you what you must not do. For example:

Triangular signs warn of a hazard on the road ahead.

For example:

Blue rectangular signs give information.

For example:

no left turn   *no overtaking*

children crossing   *low bridge*

no through road   *end of motorway*

Blue circular signs tell you what you must do.
For example:

minimum speed 30 mph   *turn left ahead*

unique shapes

Two particularly important traffic signs have unique shapes: the give way sign is an upside down triangle, and the stop sign is an octagon.

The reason? So that even if these signs are obscured by snow and can't be read, they can still be recognised by their shape alone.

give way sign is an inverted triangle

stop sign is octagonal

TRICKETTS CROSS

Bournemouth
A 347
Poole (A 348)
Ferndown

Stapehill
Knoll Gardens
Stapehill Abbey Gardens

Superstore

Stewart Lodge

Direction signs use different colours depending on what sort of road they are on. Signs on motorways are blue, those on primary routes are green, those on other roads are white with a black border, diversion signs are yellow and signs showing local attractions are brown.

route finding

Route directions are generally clearly signposted, but it's not a good idea to rely on signs alone. Carry a map, and if you lose your way stop somewhere safe to consult it.

It's a good idea to plan your route before starting out. Use a map, or one of the route planning services available on the internet or from motoring organisations. Print off your route or write it down clearly, and plan an alternative route too, in case your first choice is blocked. Allow plenty of time for your journey, especially when travelling a long distance, and plan some rest breaks too. If you can avoid busy times you'll have an easier journey and be less likely to be delayed by heavy traffic – and you won't be adding to traffic congestion yourself.

motorways (blue signs)

left-hand lane leads to a different destination (the arrows pointing downwards mean 'get in lane')

inclined arrow indicates the destinations that can be reached by leaving motorway at next junction

sign placed at a junction leading onto a motorway

on approach to motorway junction ('25' is the junction number)

route confirmed after the junction

diversions (yellow signs)

when you encounter a diversion, follow the signs or the symbols that indicate the alternative route

non-primary and local routes (white signs)

signs on the approach to the junction. Route numbers on a blue background show the way to a motorway; those on green show the way to a primary road

sign at the junction

primary routes (green signs)

on the approach to the junction

at the junction (symbol warns of a hazard on this route)

blue panel indicates that the motorway starts at the next junction; motorways in brackets can also be reached along the route indicated

bilingual sign in Wales

route confirmed after junction

local attractions (brown signs)

tourist attraction *camp site* *picnic site*

other direction signs

ring road (by-passes town)

ring road (non-primary road)

holiday route

75

ROAD MARKINGS

Road markings are a vital source of information.
They are often placed alongside road signs, and
have the advantage of being visible even when
the signs are hidden by traffic. Or they may be
used without other signs to give a continuous
message along the road. Remember the general
rule that the more paint there is on the road,
the greater the danger. When you approach an
area criss-crossed with white lines and warnings,
take note, slow down and prepare to negotiate a
serious hazard ahead.

types of road marking

There are a number of different types of road marking which each have distinct meanings. The main types are (with specific examples):

Lane arrows tell you in advance which lane you need to get into, and are often accompanied by road numbers or place names marked on the road.

traffic lane directions

Lines across the road separate traffic at road junctions, telling you where you must stop or give way to other vehicles.

give way

Written warnings on the road give specific commands or warnings of hazards ahead.

do not block entrance to side road

Lines along the road divide lanes of traffic and give information about hazards on the road ahead.

do not cross centre line

Parking restrictions are shown by yellow lines running alongside the kerb. They indicate that waiting restrictions are in force.

no waiting

Speed reduction lines are raised yellow lines across the road at the approach to a hazard such as a lower speed limit. They make road users aware of their speed so they slow down well in time. Rumble strips are red and give an audible warning too.

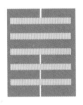

slow down for hazard ahead

KNOW THE CODE — HIGHWAY CODE RULE 111

Reflective road studs may be used with white lines.

- White studs mark the lanes or the middle of the road
- Red studs mark the left edge of the road
- Amber studs mark the central reservation of a dual carriageway or motorway
- Green studs mark the edge of the main carriageway at lay-bys, side roads and slip roads.

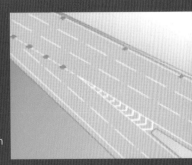

TRAFFIC LIGHTS

Traffic lights automatically control busy junctions.
They ease traffic flow by switching priorities in
sequence, allowing vehicles from one direction to
flow freely while vehicles from another direction
are held back to wait their turn. Approach
junctions controlled by traffic lights with caution
and be prepared for the lights to change.

approaching traffic lights

Use the observation-signal-manoeuvre routine as you approach a junction controlled by traffic lights. Slow down and be prepared to stop. Never speed up to try and get through while the lights are still green.

Remember that green means go only if the road is clear and it is safe to do so. Always check the road is clear before you proceed when the lights go green. Serious collisions occur at junctions controlled by traffic lights when one vehicle moves off through a green light at the same time as another from the other direction has left it too late to stop after the lights have changed.

When a green filter arrow is illuminated you may proceed only in the direction it indicates

traffic light sequence

1 RED means stop. Wait at the stop line.

2 RED AND **AMBER** also means stop. Do not start to move off until the lights change to green.

3 GREEN means go if it is clear and safe to do so. Give way to any pedestrians who are crossing.

4 AMBER means stop. You may only continue if the amber light appears after you have crossed the stop line or if you are so close to it that it might be dangerous to pull up. (Red then follows amber and the sequence repeats itself.)

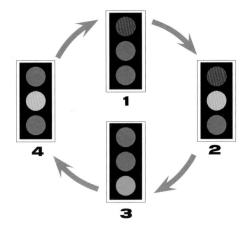

traffic light failure

If a set of traffic lights is not working, you should treat the intersection as an uncontrolled one where no one has priority. Be prepared to stop as traffic from other directions may assume they have right of way. If a police officer is controlling the junction, follow the signals you are given. When signalled to stop by a police officer, wait at the stop line.

Proceed with great care when traffic lights are out of order

KNOW THE CODE

HIGHWAY CODE RULE 154

Advanced stop lines Some junctions have advanced stop lines or bus advance areas to allow cycles and buses to be positioned ahead of other traffic. Motorists MUST wait behind the first white line reached, and not encroach on the marked area. Allow cyclists and buses time and space to move off when the green signal shows.

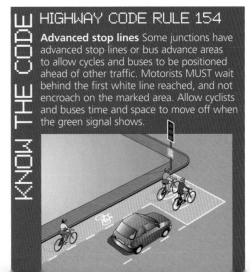

Learning how to control a motorcycle – making it start and stop and go round corners – is the easy bit. On today's busy roads, the real riding skill is interacting with other road users. Good riders blend in with the traffic flow, watch what other road users are doing, communicate their own intentions clearly, make good progress without needing to brake or accelerate harshly, and arrive at their destination relaxed and unruffled. Bad riders fail to observe what other road users are doing, get into misunderstandings, ride too close and too fast, and arrive feeling frustrated and tired. Learning to cope with traffic requires concentration and self-discipline, but it's a skill you must master to pass your motorcycle test.

POSITIONING

As a motorcyclist you have the advantage that the narrow width of your bike allows you to position yourself to best advantage at all times. By always being in the right place on the road you will maximise your vision, make your intentions clearer to other road users and increase your margin of safety when approaching hazardous situations.

road position

Normally you should position your motorbike in the centre of your lane. You should ensure that your position makes you clearly visible to other traffic, especially vehicles emerging from junctions ahead, and that you can be seen in the mirror of any vehicle in front of you.

There are times when it is useful to move a little nearer to the kerb. For instance:
➔ to make space for oncoming traffic through a narrow gap
➔ to increase your vision and safety when approaching a right-hand bend.

But avoid getting too close to the kerb: the road surface is more loose and uneven near the gutter and if you accidentally clip the kerb you may lose control.

Conversely, you should move out towards the centre of the road, if it is safe to do so:
➔ when the pavement is busy with pedestrians
➔ when making a right-hand turn; this confirms your intentions to other road users and gives following vehicles space to overtake you on your left.

IT'S THE LAW

CROSSING WHITE LINES

You are permitted to cross a central solid white line only if it is safe and necessary to do so in order to:

➔ enter or leave a side turning or driveway
➔ pass a stationary vehicle
➔ avoid an accident
➔ pass a working road maintenance vehicle displaying a keep left/right arrow and moving no faster than 10mph
➔ pass a pedal cycle or horse moving no faster than 10mph
➔ comply with the direction of a police constable or traffic warden.

lane markings

A broken white line marks the centre of the road

Longer broken white lines indicate a hazard ahead. Never cross a hazard warning line unless you are sure it is safe

Lane lines divide the lanes on dual carriageways and motorways: keep between them except when changing lane

You may cross the centre lines where there are double white lines and the line nearest to you is broken, if it is safe to do

You must not cross the centre lines where the line nearest to you is solid. You also must not park on a road with double white lines whether broken or solid

Where there are double solid white lines, vehicles from either direction are prohibited from crossing the lines

An edge line marks the left-hand side of the carriageway

Diagonal hatching is used to separate lanes of traffic and to protect vehicles waiting to turn off the road. If the area is bordered by a broken white line you can enter it, but only if it is necessary and safe to do so; if it is bounded by a solid white line then you must not enter it except in an emergency

Positioning yourself towards the nearside will improve your vision round a right-hand bend

Leave enough room for a door to open unexpectedly when passing parked vehicles

lane discipline

Always keep within the road markings indicating your lane unless you are changing lane or direction. Try to anticipate when lanes will have to split, and get ready to move across into the correct lane. Don't change lanes at the last moment if you find you have got into the wrong lane: instead carry on and find another way back onto your route. Never straddle lanes or weave in and out of lanes.

Get into the correct lane in good time when arrows indicate that lanes are changing direction

passing parked vehicles

When passing parked vehicles, leave plenty of space in case one of them starts pulling out, or a door opens unexpectedly. Making more space also helps you to see children coming out from between parked cars to cross the road. If you have to pass closer to parked cars, then reduce your speed and be ready to stop.

When passing a series of parked cars, don't weave in and out between them: maintain a straight course which clearly indicates your intentions to other road users.

HIGHWAY CODE RULE 121

One-way streets Traffic MUST travel in the direction indicated by signs. Buses and/or cycles may have a contraflow lane. Choose the correct lane for your exit as soon as you can. Do not change lanes suddenly. Unless road signs or markings indicate otherwise, you should use:

- ⊖ the left-hand lane when going left
- ⊖ the right-hand lane when going right
- ⊖ the most appropriate lane when going straight ahead. Remember – traffic could be passing on both sides.

KNOW THE CODE

Take care to observe lane markings in one-way streets, and beware of vehicles passing on your left

You must not ride in a bus lane except during the times indicated by the accompanying sign

one-way systems

In a one-way street select the most appropriate lane in good time before you have to turn at the end of the street.

It is legal to overtake on either the left or the right in a one-way street, so take particular care when changing lanes. If you ride down a one-way street by mistake, you must continue to the end of the road – don't try to turn round.

One-way streets may have contra-flow bus or cycle lanes, allowing these vehicles to proceed against the direction of traffic flow.

keep out

Remember that you must not ride in a bus lane, cycle lane or tram lane unless signs state otherwise. (At the time of publication it is under consideration whether motorcyclists should be permitted to use bus lanes, so look out for any changes in the law on this point.)

You must also not ride on the pavement except to cross it when using a driveway into a property, or where signs specifically permit parking on the pavement.

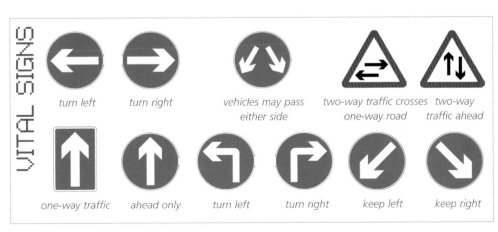

VITAL SIGNS

turn left turn right vehicles may pass either side two-way traffic crosses one-way road two-way traffic ahead

one-way traffic ahead only turn left turn right keep left keep right

On our busy roads we spend much of our time following the vehicle in front, yet far too many riders commit the serious error of following too closely. They get away with this until one day the vehicle ahead brakes unexpectedly and they end up careering into the back of it. Most serious collisions – such as motorway pile-ups – could be avoided if everyone left more space between their vehicles.

how close?

When you are following another vehicle, ask yourself: 'if it slams on its brakes without warning, have I left myself enough space to be able to react and stop without hitting it?'

If the answer is no, pull back until you have created a safe gap. A useful way to ensure you are keeping a safe distance in dry, bright conditions is to use the two-second rule. Watch as the vehicle in front goes by a lamp post or driveway, then count how long it takes for you to pass the same point. If you can slowly count 'one thousand – two thousand' (or repeat the apt phrase 'only a fool breaks the two-second rule') before you reach the marker then you are keeping a safe distance.

wet roads

On wet, greasy or icy roads you will take much longer to stop in an emergency. When it rains, double the two-second rule and leave a four-second gap. If the road is slippery or icy you should leave up to ten times the distance in which to stop.

Wet roads mean you will need further to stop in an emergency, so leave at least a four-second gap

large vehicles

Another time you need to leave extra space is when you're following a large truck or bus. If you are too close to it your view past will be obscured and you won't be able to anticipate what is happening on the road ahead. Keeping well back also means you don't have to breathe in the truck's diesel exhaust fumes, or get your visor smeared by spray thrown up from its rear wheels on a wet road.

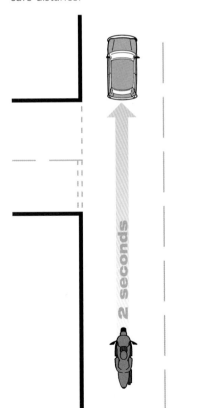

Use a fixed point on the road side to help measure a two-second gap from the vehicle in front

Keep well back when following a bus or you won't be able to see past to overtake it when it stops

tailgating

This is the dangerous habit of following too closely behind the vehicle in front. If someone is tailgating you, it means that if you have to stop in an emergency they may not be able to avoid running into the back of your bike. Reduce this risk by easing off the throttle and increasing your following distance from the vehicle in front. Because you have created more space in front of yourself, you won't have to slow so abruptly in an emergency, which in turn gives the driver behind more time to react.

Often road users tailgate because they are impatient to get past. If this is the case, let them overtake at the first opportunity. Never try to retaliate to a tailgater by putting on your brakes or riding obstructively. The fact that they are behaving dangerously means that you have to take even more care to ride responsibly to help ensure everyone's safety.

queues

When in a slow-moving traffic queue, hold back if keeping up with the queue would mean obstructing the exit of a junction or straddling a pedestrian crossing or level crossing. Wait till the traffic in front has moved forward far enough for you to be able to clear the junction or crossing before proceeding.

filtering

One advantage of the small size and manoeuvrability of a motorcycle is that it's possible to make progress in congested traffic by filtering past queuing vehicles. This is a potentially highly dangerous manoeuvre so do it only with great caution, remembering that other road users may not be expecting you to filter. Always:

- keep your speed low and be ready to brake
- be ready to use your horn to warn anyone who hasn't seen you
- identify the space where you intend to rejoin the queue *before* you move out

- be especially vigilant for pedestrians crossing between vehicles, vehicles emerging from junctions (especially where there is a gap in the queue at a 'keep clear' road marking), vehicles changing lanes or doing a U-turn without warning, and car doors opening
- take extra care if riding across road markings which may become slippery in wet weather
- look out for other motorbikes and bicycles which may also be filtering.

being overtaken

When you're in a line of traffic on the open road, remember that even if you don't intend to overtake, a rider or driver behind may want to overtake you. Leave enough space for them to do so safely.

If someone else is trying to overtake, you should help them get past quickly and safely. Keep a steady course, slow down if necessary and leave plenty of space from the vehicle in front for the overtaking vehicle to move into. But leave the decision to overtake to the other person – don't beckon them to pass, or indicate left, as there may be hazards which you haven't spotted.

Don't ever try to obstruct or prevent someone from overtaking, even if you are riding at the speed limit. Let the other vehicle get by and concentrate on ensuring your own safety. Slow down if someone overtakes where there is not enough forward vision for them to carry out the manoeuvre safely, or to assist a large vehicle which is taking a long time to pull past you.

Never be the cause of a tailback of traffic. If you are riding a slow-moving scooter and a queue forms behind you, pull over as soon as it is safe and let the traffic pass before resuming your journey.

When leaving a safe gap on a dual carriageway or motorway, you may find

Filtering is a hazardous manoeuvre so ride slowly and don't expect others to see you coming

Leave a gap when approaching side turnings in queuing traffic so you don't obstruct access to them

that other vehicles pull in too closely in front of you. Don't think of this as a problem – simply ease off the throttle and pull back until you open up a safe gap again. Even if ten vehicles pull in front of you during the course of a journey you'll still get where you're going only a few seconds later – and more importantly, you'll get there safely.

stopping in traffic

Avoid getting too close to the vehicle in front when it stops at traffic lights or a junction. Leave enough space so that if it stalls or breaks down you have plenty of room to manoeuvre safely past without getting stuck behind it. On a slope leaving this gap also gives room for the car in front to roll back if its driver performs a bad hill start.

KNOW THE CODE

HIGHWAY CODE RULE 129

In slow moving traffic you should:

→ reduce the distance between you and the vehicle ahead to maintain traffic flow

→ never get so close to the vehicle in front that you cannot stop safely

→ leave enough space to be able to manoeuvre if the vehicle in front breaks down or an emergency vehicle needs to get past

→ not change lanes to the left to overtake

→ allow access into and from side roads, as blocking these will add to congestion.

If you meet an oncoming vehicle where an obstruction such as a parked car reduces the width of the road so there is room for only one vehicle to proceed, one of you has to give way. Forward thinking and anticipation make all the difference when dealing with this sort of situation. You need to anticipate, and adjust your speed and position well in advance so that if it is necessary for you to give way you can do so smoothly and safely.

A hump bridge is a potentially dangerous meeting place because the brow of the bridge restricts your forward view. Hump bridges are often narrow so you may encounter oncoming vehicles or pedestrians in the middle of the road. Slow right down and consider sounding your horn to give a warning of your approach

giving way

Where the obstruction is on your side of the road you should be prepared to stop and give way to oncoming traffic. But don't assume you necessarily have priority if the obstruction is on the other side of the road. If an oncoming vehicle carries straight on through, you must be able to stop safely and give way to it. Thinking in terms of 'right of way' in this sort of situation isn't helpful: riders who insist on always taking what they see as their 'right of way' end up in a collision sooner or later.

judging the gap

As you approach a meeting situation use the observation-signal-manoeuvre routine. The oncoming vehicle may pull nearer to the kerb to create enough space for you to continue through the gap. But if you are not absolutely certain there is enough room, hold back until the other vehicle is through. Never pull past an obstruction expecting the oncoming vehicle to move over to make space for you.

hills

It's courteous to give way to vehicles, particularly large lorries and buses, which are coming towards you up a steep hill. If a heavily-laden truck loses momentum to give way on a hill it has to work hard to regain it.

Where parked vehicles cause an obstruction ahead, stop and give way to oncoming traffic

Use passing places to pull in and give way to oncoming vehicles on single track roads

VITAL SIGNS

give way to vehicles from other direction

you have priority over oncoming vehicles

road narrows on both sides

road narrows on right (left if symbol reversed)

KNOW THE CODE

HIGHWAY CODE RULE 133

Single-track roads These are only wide enough for one vehicle. They may have special passing places. If you see a vehicle coming towards you, or the driver behind wants to overtake, pull into a passing place on your left, or wait opposite a passing place on your right. Give way to vehicles coming uphill whenever you can. If necessary, reverse until you reach a passing place to let the other vehicle pass.

OVERTAKING

Many motorbikes are capable of rapid acceleration which makes it possible to exploit overtaking opportunities not open to most other vehicles. But overtaking is also one of the most potentially dangerous riding manoeuvres, and it demands careful judgement and a full assessment of the risks involved. Always remember the golden rule: if you're not absolutely sure it is safe to overtake, don't.

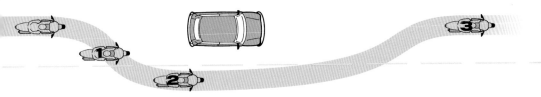

how to overtake

1 Maximise your observation of the road ahead before overtaking. Don't get too close or you will reduce your view past the vehicle you want to overtake. Position yourself towards the centre of the road so you can see past. (When following a large vehicle it can also be useful to move towards the kerb to get a view along its nearside.) Check your mirrors. Consider whether you need to look over your right shoulder and give a signal before pulling out. Make sure you are in a gear that gives enough power to get past quickly, but try to avoid having to change gear in the middle of an overtaking manoeuvre.

2 Move to the other side of the road to make a final check of the road ahead. If it is clear then overtake. You need to accelerate quickly to spend as little time as possible on the other side of the road, but take care not to accelerate too harshly, especially on a slippery road surface, or you may provoke a skid.

3 Don't cut in too early after overtaking. Take appropriate rear observation to ensure that it is safe to pull back in.

when to overtake

The only reason to overtake is when it will help you to make progress. There's no point overtaking when you are approaching a built-up area or if you intend to turn off the road soon.

Keep back and move towards the centre line to maximise your field of view past a slow vehicle

IT'S THE LAW

NO OVERTAKING

It is illegal to overtake:

- ➔ if you would have to cross or straddle double white lines with a solid line nearest to you (apart from the exceptions mentioned on p83)
- ➔ if you would have to enter an area surrounded by a solid white line that is designed to divide traffic streams
- ➔ the nearest vehicle to a pedestrian crossing
- ➔ if you would have to enter a lane reserved for buses, trams or cycles during its hours of operation
- ➔ after a 'no overtaking' sign until you pass the sign cancelling it

A white arrow in the middle of the road is warning you to move back to the left when overtaking. Never overtake where you see this marking

Don't try to squeeze past a cyclist or slower motorcyclist: hold back until it is safe to pass, and leave as much room as when overtaking a car

dangers from other vehicles

If you overtake at 60mph while an oncoming vehicle approaches at the same speed, it means you are closing at a combined speed of 120mph. This leaves little margin for error. Never overtake where you may force another vehicle to swerve or slow down.

While you are deciding whether to overtake, be aware that a driver or rider behind may be thinking about overtaking you. Take appropriate rear observation, and give a signal to indicate your intentions both to following traffic and to the vehicle you are overtaking.

Make sure there is no possibility that the vehicle you intend to overtake is about to make a right turn or swerve across the road to overtake a cyclist or pedestrian you haven't seen. Take care before overtaking at the start of a downhill stretch or when leaving a lower speed restriction in case the vehicle in front speeds up. If you are unsure that the vehicle you want to overtake is aware of your presence consider sounding your horn or flashing your headlamp briefly to warn that you are about to overtake.

If the driver in front waves or indicates left to encourage you to overtake, don't rely on their judgement: overtake only if you can see to your own satisfaction that it is safe.

It is very dangerous to follow straight after another overtaking vehicle as your view ahead will be obscured and oncoming vehicles may not be able to see you. Hold back and make sure the road is clear before overtaking.

overtaking hazards

Overtaking is potentially dangerous because there are so many different hazards to assess before making the manoeuvre. Never overtake:

⮕ where there are road junctions or driveways from which a vehicle may emerge in front of you

⮕ where the road narrows

⮕ where you cannot see the road ahead to be clear, such as on the approach to a bend, a hump bridge, the brow of a hill or a dip in the road

⮕ when approaching a school crossing patrol

⮕ between the kerb and a bus or tram when it is at a stop

⮕ where traffic is queuing at junctions or road works

⮕ at a level crossing.

Caution is required when overtaking on three-lane roads, especially where traffic from either direction is allowed to overtake on the same stretch

Overtaking on the left is legal in some situations, such as on a one-way street, but take extra care as other road users may not be expecting you to do so

three-lane roads

Take special care when overtaking on a road which is divided into three lanes so that traffic from either direction may use the middle lane to overtake. Don't pull out unless you are completely certain there is no risk of an oncoming vehicle trying to overtake at the same time.

overtaking on the left

You must normally overtake on the right. However, there are a few situations where you are permitted to pass slower moving vehicles on the left-hand side:

⊖ where a vehicle is signalling to turn right
⊖ where traffic is moving slowly in queues on a multi-lane road
⊖ in a one-way street
⊖ in a lane turning left at a junction.

KNOW THE CODE

HIGHWAY CODE RULE 140

Large vehicles Overtaking these is more difficult. You should

⊖ drop back to increase your ability to see ahead. Getting too close to large vehicles will obscure your view of the road ahead and there may be another slow moving vehicle in front

⊖ make sure that you have enough room to complete your overtaking manoeuvre before committing yourself. It takes longer to pass a large vehicle. If in doubt do not overtake

⊖ not assume you can follow a vehicle ahead which is overtaking a long vehicle. If a problem develops, they may abort overtaking and pull back in.

VITAL SIGNS

side winds: take special care when overtaking cyclists, other motorbikes or high-sided vehicles

Hidden dip

hidden dip in road: don't overtake as oncoming traffic may be obscured

no overtaking

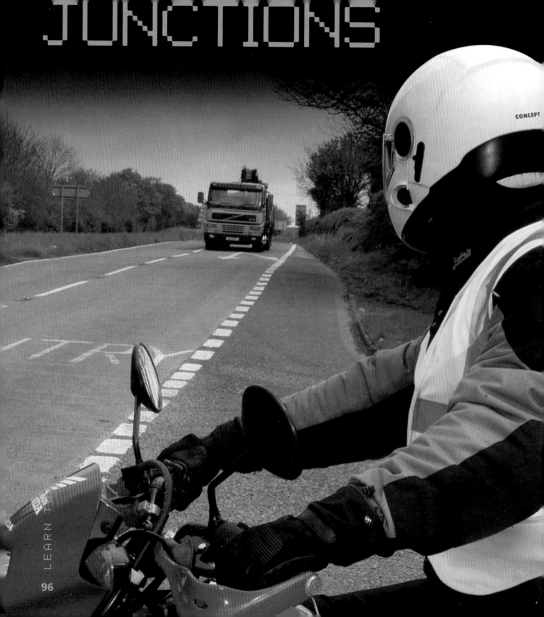

LEARN TO

At a road junction two or more roads meet. Traffic has to merge and with this comes the risk that mistakes may lead to collisions. It's a fact that many serious accidents involving motorcyclists occur at junctions when drivers of other vehicles fail to see them. This means that you need to take extra care at junctions, whatever the weather conditions or time of day or night. Always signal clearly and position your bike accurately to give a clear indication to other road users of what you intend to do. Make sure you are as visible as possible, and never assume that other drivers are aware of your presence.

06

PRIORITY

If no one knew who had priority where two roads meet the result would be chaos. To promote a smooth traffic flow, most junctions are organised so that traffic on the major road has priority and traffic on the minor road must wait until it is clear to proceed. Although there are few basic types of junctions, individual circumstances make each junction unique and they need to be negotiated with care. Assess each junction as you approach it by looking at such things as bends, visibility, obscured sightlines, the amount of traffic, road markings and signs.

types of junction

There are five main types of junction:

- T-junctions
- Y-junctions
- staggered junctions
- crossroads
- roundabouts.

priorities at junctions

Priorities at junctions are indicated by give way signs and markings, stop signs and markings, and traffic lights – or there may be no priority marked. Remember that even if you are on the road that has priority, you need to be ready to slow down or stop for vehicles which pull out in front of you, or for vulnerable road users such as cyclists or pedestrians who you may need to give priority to whatever the road signs say.

give way

A give way sign means you must stop at the line to give priority to traffic on the road you are joining. However, you do not need to stop if the road is clear and it is safe to proceed. A give way junction has double broken white lines across your half of the road, or a single broken white line at the entrance to a roundabout.

KNOW THE CODE HIGHWAY CODE RULE 146

Take extra care at junctions You should:

- watch out for cyclists, motorcyclists and pedestrians as they are not always easy to see
- watch out for pedestrians crossing a road into which you are turning. If they have started to cross they have priority, so give way
- watch out for long vehicles which may be turning at a junction ahead; they may have to use the whole width of the road to make the turn
- not assume, when waiting at a junction, that a vehicle coming from the right and signalling left will actually turn. Wait and make sure
- not cross or join a road until there is a gap large enough for you to do so safely.

VITAL SIGNS

STOP 100 yds

distance to stop line ahead

GIVE WAY 50 yds

distance to give way line ahead

GIVE WAY

give way to traffic on major road

side turning

T-junction (the road with priority is shown by the broader line)

stop and give way

roundabout

mini-roundabout

crossroads

staggered junction

stop sign

A stop sign is used instead of a give way sign where reduced visibility means it would be dangerous to proceed through a junction without stopping at all times. You must come to a complete halt at the line and check that the road is clear before proceeding. A stop junction has a single continuous white line across your side of the road. This type of line also shows where you should stop at traffic lights, level crossings, swing bridges and ferries.

uncontrolled junctions

On minor roads some junctions may not have road signs or markings. This means all vehicles approaching the junction have equal priority. Slow down, look for traffic coming from all directions and be prepared to stop and give way if necessary.

box junctions

Box junctions are designed to prevent the junction being blocked by queuing traffic. It is illegal to enter the area of yellow criss-cross lines marked on the road at a box junction unless your exit road is clear. But remember the important exception to this rule: you *can* enter a box junction when you want to turn right and your exit road is clear but you are prevented from proceeding by oncoming traffic or right-turning vehicles in front of you.

traffic lights

At junctions controlled by traffic lights the priorities change with the lights. See p79 to remind yourself of the sequence and meaning of traffic lights.

At a give way sign (left), if the junction is clear you may ride across it without coming to a halt; but at a stop sign (right) you must by law do just that – come to a complete standstill before moving off again

approaching junctions

All junctions should be approached using the observation-signal–manoeuvre and position-speed-look routines described on p65. In good time as you approach the junction:

- look all around including taking rear observation
- make a signal if it would assist other road users
- check your position on the road and adjust it if necessary
- check your speed and adjust it if necessary
- select the appropriate gear
- take one last good look all around, including rear observation into your blind spot, to check it is safe to proceed
- make the manoeuvre if it is safe to do so.

road markings at junctions

This marking appears on the road just before a give way sign

Give way to traffic on a major road

Stop line at stop sign

Give way to traffic from the right at a roundabout

Give way to traffic from the right at a mini-roundabout

Stop line at signals or police control

Stop line for pedestrians at a level crossing

KNOW THE CODE

HIGHWAY CODE RULE 150

Box junctions These have criss-cross yellow lines painted on the road. You MUST NOT enter the box until your exit road or lane is clear. However, you may enter the box and wait when you want to turn right, and are only stopped from doing so by oncoming traffic, or by other vehicles waiting to turn right.

JUNCTIONS

EMERGING FROM JUNCTIONS

When you emerge from a junction you may have to join traffic which is heavy or fast-moving. If making a right turn there is the additional hazard of crossing the path of oncoming vehicles. This is a potentially dangerous situation and you must exercise careful judgement and continually monitor what is happening all around you.

Careful all round observation is essential when you are emerging from a road junction

emerging left from a junction

Follow this general procedure:

- ➡ take rear observation as you approach the junction
- ➡ if other road users would benefit from a signal give it in good time
- ➡ position your bike to the left of the road, about one metre from the kerb
- ➡ slow down and be prepared to give way or stop at the junction
- ➡ look in all directions before pulling out. Check for bicycles or motorcycles which may be passing on your nearside
- ➡ pull onto the main road, cancel your indicator, take rear observation to check for following traffic and accelerate to a safe speed for the road you have joined.

When stopping at a junction make sure that you pull right up to the give way or stop line (above). Do not stop short of the line (below) or you will restrict your view out of the junction

emerging right from a junction

Carry out the same procedure, but position your bike as near to the centre of the road as possible (although if the road is narrow, you must leave enough space for other vehicles to turn into the junction). Take extra care when pulling out as you have to give way to traffic coming from both directions.

maximising your vision

Sometimes you will find that your view
out of a junction is obscured, for instance
by parked vehicles. If this is the case, stop
at the junction and then edge carefully
forward until you can get a good view
down the road in both directions.

Large vehicles may also obscure your
view. Before pulling out in front of a bus or
lorry, ask yourself if there might be a hidden
car or motorcycle overtaking it. Remember
that other motorcyclists and cyclists are
particularly vulnerable at junctions because
they are smaller and harder to see.

Take care if a vehicle approaching from
your right is signalling as though it intends
to turn into the road from which you are
emerging. Do not pull out until you are
absolutely certain that this what it is going
to do - the driver may intend pulling into
the side of the road after the junction,
or may simply have left on the indicator
by mistake.

staggered junctions

This is where two minor roads join a major
road not quite opposite each other. When
you are on a minor road and wish to pass
across the major road you should usually
treat this as two manoeuvres: first join the
major road, then make a second turn into
the minor road. If the junctions are very
close together you may proceed across
the major road in one manoeuvre, but
check carefully that the road is clear in
both directions.

When approaching a staggered junction
on the major road you should treat it with
caution. Be prepared to slow down and give
way to emerging vehicles.

Y-junctions

At a Y-junction the minor road meets the
major road at an angle. When turning right
at a Y-junction you may need to pull up
at a right angle to the major road to give
yourself a clearer view to your left.

*Where parked vehicles obstruct your view out of
a junction, edge cautiously forward until you can
see if the road is clear for you to pull out*

turning right onto a dual carriageway

Crossing a dual carriageway needs extra care because of the high speed of traffic. There are two types of right turn onto a dual carriageway:

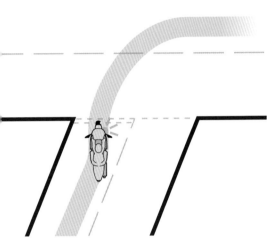

Pulling up at a right angle to the major road at a Y-junction makes it easier to get a clear view in both directions

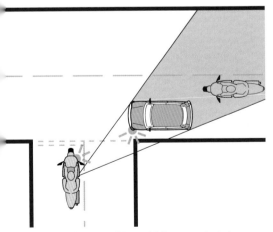

Be alert for overtaking vehicles – particularly other motorcycles – which can easily be hidden from view behind another vehicle at a junction

➡ where there is a waiting area within the central reservation

You should cross the road in two stages. First, check that the road to your right is clear of oncoming traffic and ride into the waiting area. Stop here and check if the road is clear to the left before joining the carriageway. You must not not join the right-hand lane and expect approaching traffic to pass you on the left. Wait until both lanes are clear so you are able to cross safely to the left-hand lane.

Always check before carrying out this manoeuvre that there is enough space for your motorcycle to fit into the central reservation without obstructing traffic already on the dual carriageway.

➡ where there is no waiting area within the central reservation

You must cross the dual carriageway in a single manoeuvre. This calls for careful observation in both directions before pulling out.

Where there is a central reservation wide enough to wait in, split a right turn across a dual carriageway into two separate manoeuvres

06

TURNING INTO SIDE ROADS

Careful observation is needed when turning into a minor road. Try not to concentrate your attention on the danger from just one direction – for instance, oncoming traffic when you are turning right – as you may overlook other hazards, such as another motorcycle overtaking you, or pedestrians crossing the road you are turning into.

turning left

Follow this general procedure:

- ➡ take rear observation as you approach the junction
- ➡ if other road users would benefit from a signal give it in good time
- ➡ position your bike to the left of the road, but don't move too far into the gutter or following drivers may think you are pulling up, not turning left
- ➡ slow down, then select the appropriate gear. Your speed must reflect how sharp the corner is and how clearly you can see round it. Remember that a vehicle could be parked just round the corner out of sight, or an oncoming vehicle may be in the middle of the road passing parked cars
- ➡ look all round. Check your mirrors again, and look over your left shoulder in case a cyclist or motorcyclist is passing on your nearside. Check that the road you are turning into is clear. You must stop and give way to any pedestrians who are crossing the road
- ➡ turn the corner, making sure you stay well on your side of the road
- ➡ cancel your indicator, take rear observation to check for following traffic and accelerate to a safe speed for the road you are now on.

Keep close in when turning left, but don't cut round so tightly that you risk clipping the kerb

TEST TIPS

DO

- ➡ take care to check that the road you are riding into is clear before starting to turn
- ➡ judge your positioning carefully when turning right on a road which has no centre line

DON'T

- ➡ swing to the left before turning right, or swing out to the right before making a left turn
- ➡ forget to check over your right shoulder immediately before making a right turn into a side road.

KNOW THE CODE

HIGHWAY CODE RULE 158

Turning left Use your mirrors and give a left-turn signal well before you turn left. Do not overtake just before you turn left and watch out for traffic coming up on your left before you make the turn, especially if driving a large vehicle. Cyclists and motorcyclists in particular may be hidden from your view. Do not cut in on cyclists. When turning:

- ➡ keep as close to the left as is safe and practical
- ➡ give way to any vehicles using a bus lane, cycle lane or tramway from either direction.

Do not cut in on cyclists

Continuous observation is vital when turning right. As well as checking for oncoming traffic, look for vehicles overtaking you and hazards – such as pedestrians – in the road you are turning into

turning right

Follow this general procedure:

- ➡ take rear observation as you approach the junction
- ➡ if other road users would benefit from a signal give it in good time
- ➡ position your bike towards the centre of the road, keeping as close as you can to the white line. This helps other road users see what you are intending to do, and also lets following traffic pass on your nearside while you are waiting to turn. If there is a waiting area marked on the road for traffic turning right, follow the road markings into this
- ➡ slow down and be prepared to stop if you need to give way to oncoming traffic or if the entrance of the road you are turning into is blocked
- ➡ look out for vehicles waiting to turn right from the road you are riding into – they may try to pull out ahead of you
- ➡ check your mirrors and look over your right shoulder just before turning, in case a vehicle is overtaking you. Be particularly alert for other motorcycles
- ➡ do not start to turn unless you are sure you can enter the side road and will not be forced to stop in a dangerous position halfway across the main road
- ➡ if you have to wait for some time for oncoming traffic to clear, don't forget to repeat your rear observation just before starting to move
- ➡ take care not to cut the corner as you make the turn
- ➡ cancel your indicator, take rear observation to check for following traffic and accelerate to a safe speed for the road you are now on.

Never cut a corner like this as you risk colliding with a vehicle emerging from the junction

Move over to the white line when waiting to turn to allow other vehicles to get past on your inside

When waiting to make a right turn, don't turn the handlebars before you are ready to move off. If you were hit from behind while waiting in the middle of the road with your front wheel already turned, the impact could push you across the road into the path of oncoming traffic

VITAL SIGNS

no motorcycles

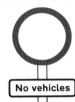

No vehicles

no vehicles except bicycles being pushed

no entry for vehicular traffic

no left turn

no motor vehicles

no right turn

The above signs all mean that you must not ride into a road. Sometimes there will be a plate giving exceptions – for instance, you may be able to enter outside certain hours, or if you need to gain access to a property in the road.

However, you may enter a road showing this sign, which means 'no motor vehicles except motorcycles without sidecars'

no U-turns

no through road

109

CROSSROADS

At a crossroads there are two T-junctions opposite each other. Serious collisions can occur at crossroads when one vehicle crosses in front of another travelling at high speed. Take special care when you are on a major road and see a crossroads ahead. Slow down and be prepared to give way in case a driver proceeds straight across without seeing you.

turning right

When turning right at a crossroads at the same time as an oncoming vehicle wants to turn right across you, you have two choices:

➡ **turn right side to right side**

This is the safer option. It has the advantage of giving you a clear view of approaching traffic.

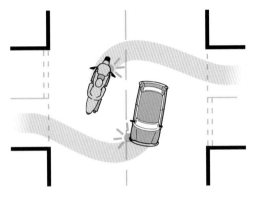

➡ **turn left side to left side**

This method can be useful when turning against a long vehicle, or where the side roads are slightly offset. But because the other vehicle is passing in front of you, it blocks your view of oncoming traffic, so take extra care.

Sometimes there are road markings which direct which course you should take. Where there are no markings, watching the course of the other vehicle and establishing eye contact with its driver may help you decide.

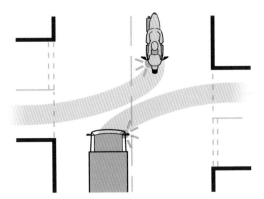

emerging

When you are emerging from one minor road at a crossroads and another vehicle is waiting to emerge from the minor road opposite, what you should do depends on the circumstances:

➡ if you are turning right and the other vehicle is turning left or going ahead, you should wait for the other vehicle to proceed before you emerge, otherwise you would be cutting across its path

➡ if you are turning left or going ahead you should proceed with caution in case the other vehicle emerges and cuts across your path

➡ if you are turning right and the other driver is turning right, neither of you has priority and you should proceed with extra care.

In practice you will find that many road users are unfamiliar with the priorities described above. It is usually helpful to establish eye contact with the other driver to help determine what they intend to do. The other driver may gesture you to come out first – but do so only if you are completely certain that their meaning is clear and it is safe to do so. You should not wave or flash at someone across a crossroads – it could be dangerous if they pull out without checking for themselves that the road is clear.

Extra caution is needed when emerging from a crossroads at the same time as another vehicle

Roundabouts are designed to allow vehicles to merge smoothly and so keep the overall traffic stream flowing. A rider who is looking well ahead and anticipating traffic movements may be able to traverse a string of roundabouts safely and smoothly without once having to come to a complete halt. But negotiating roundabouts correctly does demand a high degree of concentration, anticipation and accurate signalling.

roundabout safety

Fewer serious crashes occur on roundabouts than at crossroads. That's because roundabouts slow down the traffic flow so when accidents happen they tend to be less severe. But the give and take nature of roundabouts means that these minor shunts are more common – and, of course, they can have more serious consequences for the motorcyclist than for a driver coccooned in a car. Careful observation, anticipation and signalling are needed to stay out of trouble.

Take care when anticipating what other road users intend to do on roundabouts. Some drivers have strange ideas about the correct lane or signalling to use, others don't bother signalling at all and some may simply be lost and unsure of which exit to take. So look out for vehicles:

- ➲ turning right without indicating
- ➲ indicating right but going straight on
- ➲ using the right-hand lane to go straight ahead even if the left lane is clear
- ➲ making a U-turn at the roundabout.

Take extra care also around cyclists, horse riders and long vehicles, all of which may take an unusual course at roundabouts.

Signal clearly at roundabouts to let other road users know which direction you intend to take

At roundabouts you should look carefully for warning signs that the road surface may be slippery. Tyre rubber can accumulate on the road at roundabouts, and diesel can spill from trucks when they corner with a full tank of fuel. There's also likely to be a lot of paint on the road, and poorly sited metal inspection covers: all these can make the road treacherous for motorcyclists, especially in wet conditions.

negotiating roundabouts

As you approach the roundabout, scan all the approach roads to spot vehicles which may arrive there at the same time as you do. Aim to make progress by adjusting your speed so you can join the traffic flow, but be prepared to stop and give way if necessary. Use the observation-signal-manoeuvre routine on the approach to a roundabout, and always look over your left shoulder before taking your exit road in case someone is trying to pass on your left.

113

lanes and signalling

On some roundabouts, particularly larger roundabouts with multiple exits, white arrows painted on the approach road indicate which lane you should get into for the exit you intend to take. Where there are no arrows or signs indicating which lane to take, follow these guidelines:

Turning left:
- indicate left as you approach
- take the left-hand lane
- keep left on the roundabout
- continue to indicate left until you have exited the roundabout.

Turning right:
- indicate right as you approach
- take the right-hand lane
- keep right on the roundabout
- after passing the exit before the one you intend to take, indicate left
- continue to indicate left until you have exited the roundabout.

Going straight ahead:
- do not indicate on approach
- take the left-hand lane
- keep left on the roundabout
- after passing the exit before the one you intend to take, indicate left
- continue to indicate left until you have exited the roundabout.

It is also acceptable to use the right-hand lane when going straight ahead if the left-hand lane of the roundabout is blocked, for instance by vehicles turning left. In this case you should stay in the right-hand lane as you ride through the roundabout. Don't forget to check over your left shoulder before moving over towards your exit, in case a vehicle is coming up on your nearside.

It is perfectly legal to carry out a U-turn by going all the way round a roundabout, but other road users may not be expecting you to do this so take special care and signal your intentions clearly.

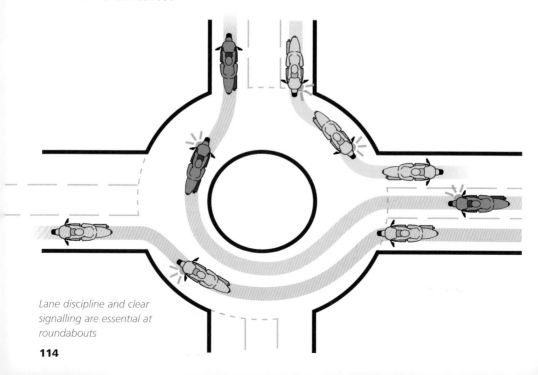

Lane discipline and clear signalling are essential at roundabouts

Where there are mini-roundabouts close together, you must treat them as separate junctions

Get into the correct lane for your exit as soon as possible on the approach to a roundabout

Avoid riding alongside large vehicles on roundabouts as they may need to take up more than one lane to make their turn

mini-roundabouts

Treat mini-roundabouts in the same way as larger roundabouts. You must ride around, not over, the white central circle for two reasons: firstly, because that's the law, and secondly, because such an expanse of white paint can be dangerously slippery when wet. Do however watch out for other road users who may cut straight across mini-roundabouts without slowing down.

When turning right at a mini-roundabout you should indicate right as you approach but the small size of the roundabout means it is usually not practical to indicate left before exiting.

Some junctions consist of a series of mini-roundabouts. Treat each separately and give way if necessary as you approach each one in turn.

TEST TIPS

DO

➡ give special caution to cyclists: they can find it difficult to pull across the traffic stream and may stay in the left-hand lane even when they want to turn right

➡ take extra care in the wet, as the road surface on roundabouts can become polished and slippery, increasing the risk of a skid if you brake or accelerate harshly

DON'T

➡ creep forward when waiting to join the roundabout. Drivers on the roundabout may think you are about to pull out in front of them. It could also lead to someone driving into the back of your bike because they think you are pulling onto the roundabout

➡ neglect to take proper rear observation, including a check over your left shoulder before exiting the roundabout.

07
ON THE ROAD

When riding you have to deal with constantly changing situations. In a single journey you could find yourself negotiating busy city back streets, cruising on an empty motorway, tackling a twisting country lane and queuing in head to tail traffic at roadworks. You need to be ready to adapt your riding style to meet these changing conditions, and be aware of the specific hazards you are likely to encounter in different situations on the road.

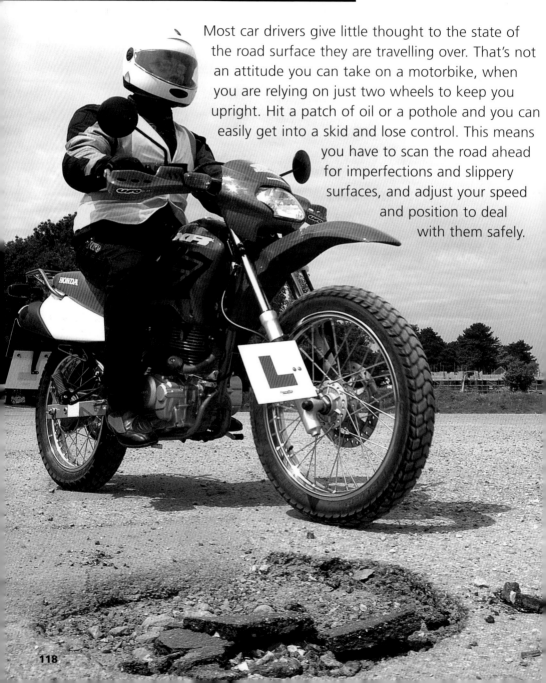

Most car drivers give little thought to the state of the road surface they are travelling over. That's not an attitude you can take on a motorbike, when you are relying on just two wheels to keep you upright. Hit a patch of oil or a pothole and you can easily get into a skid and lose control. This means you have to scan the road ahead for imperfections and slippery surfaces, and adjust your speed and position to deal with them safely.

poor road conditions

Many roads are in a poor state of repair. Look out for potholes so you can slow down well in advance and steer around them. Avoid having to swerve to avoid obstacles at the last second – on a poor road surface this is itself likely to provoke a skid.

Take into account seasonal factors, such as winter mud and autumn leaves, and reduce your speed, particularly when cornering.

Weather conditions have a significant effect on tyre adhesion (this is covered in chapter 10). Remember that as well as the more obvious dangers of icy conditions, hot weather can make tarmac roads soft and affect braking and cornering, and rain after a hot spell can make it slippery where rubber coats the surface of the road, especially at junctions and roundabouts.

If you do find you are riding on a slippery surface, don't brake abruptly: instead ease off the throttle and lose speed gradually to reduce the risk of skidding.

road repairs

Rough surfaces encountered at roadworks need to be negotiated with caution. After resurfacing, loose chippings may be left on the road and these will greatly reduce tyre grip. Reduce your speed and take care when braking, accelerating and changing direction.

Look out also for chippings thrown up by other vehicles. Keep well back from the vehicle in front to avoid injury or damage to your bike, and always keep your visor down or goggles on through roadworks.

Also keep your eyes peeled for tar banding – the shiny black lines left around road repairs. These become dangerously slippery when wet.

metal surfaces

Items made of metal such as inspection covers (manholes) and tram lines are likely to be slippery, especially in wet conditions, and you should avoid riding over them wherever possible.

road markings

Although the road markings painted on the road serve an important purpose they have the unfortunate property of getting slippery when wet. Try not to brake, accelerate or change direction when passing over road markings, and avoid taking a course which means both your wheels pass over road markings at the same time.

diesel spills

Diesel can spill from a truck when it corners with a full fuel tank, as the fuel sloshes about and overflows. The resulting slick of oil is hazardous for riders in any weather, and on a wet road it can be as slippery as black ice. Take care wherever diesel spills are likely, especially at junctions, roundabouts and bends. Look out for the rainbow-coloured sheen on a wet road which indicates the presence of a diesel spill; if you see this, slow down but don't brake or steer harshly or you could provoke a skid.

Oil patches are also left by buses while stationary at bus stops, and can be slippery in wet weather. Slow down and ease out away from the kerb while passing bus stops to reduce the risk of a skid.

VITAL SIGNS

falling or fallen rocks

uneven road

loose chippings

SLOW WET TAR

temporary hazard at roadworks

ON THE ROAD

BENDS

A major element in the enjoyment of riding is the agility and responsiveness of a motorbike on a twisting road. Many bikes have impressive cornering abilities, but you should never forget that ultimately all that gets your bike round a bend is the contact of two patches of tyre tread – no bigger than your handprints – on the tarmac.

cornering

Road signs and markings give advance warning to slow down when you approach a bend, but not all sharp bends have warning signs. Remember that the bend sign not only warns you to slow down, it also shows you which direction the road turns.

On a right-hand bend, position your bike a little nearer to the kerb to improve your view through the bend. But avoid moving towards the centre of the road at the start of a left-hand bend: this could put you in danger from oncoming traffic, particularly if an oncoming vehicle cuts the corner.

If you need to change down a gear do this before you enter the bend. Lean with the bike through the bend, and apply a little power to maintain a constant speed. Once the bend starts to open out and your bike returns to the upright, progressively apply more power and build back up to an appropriate speed.

speed and grip

The golden rule when riding through a bend is that you must be able to stop, on your side of the road, in the distance you can see to be clear. Most bends are blind – your view through them is obscured by hedges or walls. At every bend ask yourself what might be hidden from your view halfway round. A horse rider? Stationary traffic? A fallen branch? Some riders get into the habit of cornering a little too fast because experience tells them that most of the time there is nothing hidden round a bend. Until one day their luck runs out and they have a serious accident.

Corner at a speed that keeps you well within the grip of your tyres on the road. On a damp or greasy road the amount of grip you have is greatly reduced. If you try to take a corner too fast, the tyres will start to slide, putting you in danger of skidding off the road or into the path of another vehicle.

Remember that it is much more difficult to carry out emergency braking while cornering, so you will not be able to stop as quickly as if you can while riding on a straight road. Always avoid harsh braking while cornering or you may provoke a skid.

Take into account the camber of the road when cornering. Camber is the slope built into a road to allow rainwater to drain off it, and most roads slope downwards from the centre to the kerbs. On an adverse camber – such as when taking a right-hand bend on a steeply cambered road – your tyres will start to lose grip at a lower speed.

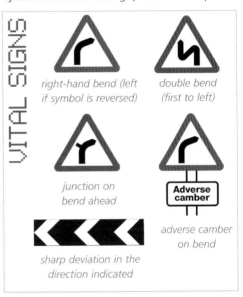

VITAL SIGNS

right-hand bend (left if symbol is reversed)

double bend (first to left)

junction on bend ahead

Adverse camber

adverse camber on bend

sharp deviation in the direction indicated

Slow down when approaching a bend and be ready to stop in the distance you can see to be clear

07
ON THE ROAD
HILLS

On hills you have to take into account the force of gravity. Going uphill, a motorbike needs more power to maintain its speed, so you may have to change down the gearbox. Downhill, the bike will pick up speed and you may need to use the brakes and select a lower gear to restrain it. Hills affect the feel of the controls: harder braking is needed to slow a bike going downhill, and in a high gear it may lose speed up a steep hill even with the throttle fully open.

hill warnings

Steep hills often have warning signs shown as a percentage: 25% indicates a steep one-in-four gradient, where the road rises one metre for every four metres travelled horizontally; 10% means a less severe one-in-ten slope.

In hilly country look out for crests and dips in the road: taking a crest at speed can make your bike unstable, while dips in the road can hide other vehicles and make overtaking hazardous.

riding uphill

You will need to apply more power when climbing a hill, and your motorbike will slow more quickly than when riding on the level. When approaching an uphill gradient don't wait until the engine starts to labour before changing down. Anticipate the need for more power and select the appropriate gear before the bike starts losing momentum.

Look out for slow-moving heavy vehicles going uphill. If you want to overtake, remember that your bike will feel more sluggish than on the level, and you will need more space to get past safely.

On motorways look out for special crawler lanes provided for the use of slow vehicles on uphill sections.

riding downhill

You need to prevent your bike picking up unwanted speed when going downhill. Making use of engine braking by engaging a lower gear to help slow the bike gives more control than relying on the brakes alone. The steeper the descent, the lower the gear you should select: as a rule of thumb, you should use the same gear to go down a hill as you would to come up it.

Always apply the brakes carefully when riding downhill as harsh use may provoke a skid, especially if the road is wet or slippery.

Leave extra space between your bike and the vehicle in front when going downhill, as you will need a greater distance to stop in an emergency. On very steep hills an escape lane is sometimes provided, filled with loose gravel which will bring a vehicle to a halt if its brakes fail.

When riding downhill change down the gears for extra engine braking, which makes it easier to control your bike than relying on the brakes alone

VITAL SIGNS

steep hill upwards (1-in-5 gradient)

steep hill downwards (1-in-10 gradient)

lane for slow-moving vehicles (uphill)

escape lane on steep hill (downhill)

Riding in a built-up area poses an extra challenge because of the sheer number of hazards. You are sharing the road with vulnerable road users such as cyclists, pedestrians and children, there are numerous traffic signs and speed limits to observe, and your view of the road ahead is often obscured by parked vehicles. It means that extra concentration, anticipation and observation is required to ride safely.

speed

Because they are so hazardous, town streets have low speed limits – usually 30mph. Remember that there is no requirement for 30mph repeater signs to be displayed on roads which have street lighting. Where buildings are less dense a 40mph limit is often posted, while in town centres 20mph zones are becoming common.

Take special care:

- on busy high streets where people may not have their mind on traffic
- in zones with a 20mph speed limit where there are pedestrians or children playing
- near schools, especially around school opening and closing times. Roads outside schools can become chaotic when parents are dropping off and picking up their children so slow down and give way to manoeuvring vehicles. Parking or stopping to drop off passengers is not permitted where road markings indicate a school entrance.

traffic calming

Physical obstructions such as humps, chicanes and constrictions are becoming more common in urban streets. Their purpose is to slow down traffic in residential areas, and discourage drivers from using 'rat-runs' – short cuts through backstreets.

Ride at a slow and steady speed through these areas. Don't accelerate and then brake harshly between speed humps, and don't try to overtake a slower-moving vehicle. Not all humps are of uniform size so be prepared to slow to a walking pace to pass over them without discomfort.

congestion charging

Riding a scooter or motorcycle is a great way to get around town. In London it can also be much cheaper than driving a car because motorcyclists are exempt from the congestion charge which is levied on vehicles entering central London between 7am and 6.30pm, Monday to Friday (excluding Bank Holidays).

The 'twist-and-go' ease of scooter riding makes them an increasingly popular choice for city dwellers

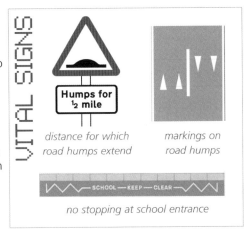

VITAL SIGNS

Humps for ½ mile

distance for which road humps extend

markings on road humps

SCHOOL — KEEP — CLEAR

no stopping at school entrance

Take special care in residential zones which have a 20mph speed limit and traffic calming measures

COUNTRY ROADS

Country roads may look open, traffic free and safe, but appearances can be deceptive. That country bend could hide a horse and rider, a slick of mud left by a tractor, or a sudden sharp turn onto a narrow hump bridge. Although you should make progress where it is safe to do so on country roads, always be ready to encounter slow-moving vehicles, cyclists and pedestrians.

narrow lanes

On country roads wide enough for only one vehicle, be prepared to pull over where there is a passing place to let an oncoming vehicle through, or to let a following vehicle overtake. If the passing place is on your right-hand side then wait opposite it. Never park in a passing place.

Use extreme caution when approaching a blind bend on a single-track road. In this situation you should be able to stop in half the distance you can see to be clear, which allows space for any approaching vehicle to stop too.

special hazards

Take care when overtaking slow-moving agricultural vehicles as the driver may have difficulty seeing or hearing you.

Look out for horse riders and cyclists, and for pedestrians who may be approaching on your side of the road.

Animals – both domestic and wild – are another hazard you may encounter on country roads (see p164).

Leaves, mud and hedge clippings on the road can all be hazardous for motorcyclists. Take heed of the unofficial signs that farmers put up as a warning when agriculture vehicles are depositing large quantities of mud on the road.

Be prepared to stop and give way to oncoming vehicles when riding on narrow county roads

Look out for slow-moving agricultural vehicles – and for the slippery mud they leave on the road

VITAL SIGNS

agricultural vehicles

hump bridge

opening or swing bridge ahead

quayside or river bank

KNOW THE CODE

HIGHWAY CODE RULE 132

Country roads Take extra care on country roads and reduce your speed at approaches to bends, which can be sharper than they appear, and at minor junctions and turnings, which may be partially hidden. Be prepared for pedestrians, horse riders and cyclists walking or riding in the road. You should also reduce your speed where country roads enter villages.

DUAL CARRIAGEWAYS

On dual carriageways the lanes in either direction are separated by a central reservation. Riding on a dual carriageway is similar to riding on a motorway, with a speed limit of 70mph unless otherwise signed, but there can be extra hazards such as slow-moving vehicles and right turns across the carriageway which would not be encountered on a motorway.

joining a dual carriageway

At many dual carriageway junctions you join by using a slip road. The purpose of the slip road is to let vehicles build up speed so they can merge smoothly with the traffic on the main carriageway.

As you ride onto the slip road try to assess the speed at which traffic in the inside lane of the dual carriageway is moving and accelerate to match it. Use the observation-signal-manoeuvre routine, signal right to show that you intend moving across from the slip road and glance over your right shoulder just before you join the main carriageway to make sure there is nothing in your blind spot.

Don't expect traffic to make space for you and be prepared to use the full length of the slip road to merge safely. You should not have to stop and wait at the end of the slip road unless traffic on the main dual carriageway is very slow moving.

Where there is no slip road you join the dual carriageway as you would a normal road at a stop or give way junction. Be sure to take into account the higher speed of vehicles on the dual carriageway before moving out.

leaving a dual carriageway

Where there is a long slip road at the exit to a dual carriageway you can use this to lose speed. But some slip roads are short and end in a sharp bend, so be prepared to start losing speed before you leave the main carriageway. Where no slip road is provided you should start signalling and slowing early to give following traffic plenty of warning that you are turning off.

When joining from a slip road you must be prepared to give way to vehicles already on the dual carriageway. Always check your blind spot before moving across into the inside lane

Exit slip roads may be short and busy so watch your speed when leaving a dual carriageway

TEST TIPS

DO
→ use the length of the slip road to build up your speed to match that of traffic on the dual carriageway
→ show good lane discipline and stay in the inside lane unless overtaking

DON'T
→ get too close to vehicles you intend to overtake. Remember the two-second rule
→ leave it till the last moment before returning to the left-hand lane when you see that the dual carriageway is about to end.

right turns

Keep in the left lane of the dual carriageway unless you are overtaking slower-moving traffic or turning right. If you want to carry out a right turn, you need to consider the high speed of traffic and start planning your turn at an early stage. Take rear observation and signal well in advance, and consider a gentle pressure on the brakes at an early stage to signal to following traffic that you are slowing. Position your bike accurately inside the turning bay in the central reservation, and take care to check that the road you are entering is clear before turning across the right-hand carriageway.

Take extra care when overtaking large vehicles as you may be obscured in the driver's blind spot

dual carriageway ends

When you see the 'dual carriageway ends' sign, check your speed because, unless signposted otherwise, the speed limit is about to drop back from 70mph to 60mph – the national speed limit for single carriageway roads. If you are overtaking, make sure you get back into the left-hand lane in good time before the dual carriageway ends. Be alert for other vehicles cutting past to pull in front of you at the last moment, and leave plenty of room from the vehicle in front so they have space to pull in safely.

Keep in the left-hand lane of the dual carriageway except when overtaking or making a right turn

Finish overtaking and return to the inside lane in good time when you see the dual carriageway ends sign

overtaking

On dual carriageways you need to plan your overtaking manoeuvres well in advance and give clear signals in good time because other vehicles may be coming up fast behind you.

1 Carry out the observation-signal-manoeuvre routine and look down the road to check for hazards in front of the vehicle you will be overtaking. Let the indicator flash at least three times before you start to move out to give other road users time to respond to your signal. Take a final glance over your right shoulder before changing lanes to check for vehicles in your blind spot.

2 When you have confirmed it is safe to do so, pull across into the right-hand lane of the dual carriageway. This should be carried out as a smoothly flowing manoeuvre – don't steer harshly or change lanes abruptly. (Remember that on a dual carriageway you may overtake only on the right, unless traffic is moving slowly in queues and your queue is quicker than the one in the right-hand lane).

3 Accelerate and overtake briskly, always keeping within the speed limit. Avoid lingering in the blind spot of the vehicle you are overtaking where the driver may not be able to see you, especially when you are overtaking a large vehicle.

4 Don't cut in sharply once you're past the front of the vehicle you've overtaken – you mustn't leave it with less than a two-second separation distance once you've pulled back in. Take rear observation to make sure you've left enough room before pulling back into the inside lane.

07
MOTORWAYS

You aren't permitted to ride on motorways until you get your full motorcycle licence (and no bike under 50cc is allowed on the motorway) but the theory test includes lots of questions about motorways, so don't overlook this section. Motorways are useful for covering long distances quickly, but using them demands discipline and responsibility. Although motorways are statistically the safest of all roads, because of their higher speeds and volume of traffic, when accidents do occur they are often serious ones.

planning your journey

Always make sure you are prepared before setting out, because long high-speed journeys put an extra strain on both motorbike and rider. Check your bike's lights, fluid levels and tyre pressures.

Many motorbikes have a limited range so keep an eye on signs advising distances to service stations and make sure you have enough fuel to avoid running out before the next one. If you do break down, recovery from a motorway is expensive so it pays to be a member of a recovery service.

lane discipline

Keep in the left-hand lane unless you need to overtake slower-moving vehicles. Where there is a stream of slower-moving traffic, don't weave in and out of the left-hand lane. It's better to stay in the middle lane until the left-hand lane clears (but do keep an eye on your mirrors and be prepared to move over to let faster-moving vehicles pass).

Use the outer lane to overtake when the inner and middle lanes are occupied with slower traffic, but again be ready to move back as soon as it is clear to do so.

If a vehicle which is clearly exceeding the speed limit comes up behind you, never try to make it slow down or hold it up: pull over at the first safe opportunity and let it overtake. If you are held up by a slower vehicle, never try to intimidate your way past: wait patiently until it pulls over.

Large goods vehicles, buses, coaches and vehicles towing a trailer or caravan are not allowed to use the outer lane of a motorway, so take care not to block their progress by neglecting to pull back into the left-hand lane as soon as you are able to do so.

anticipation

Anticipating what is happening far ahead is vital when riding at high speed on the motorway. Leave at least a two-second following distance from the vehicle in front – more in wet weather or poor visibility. Keep looking well ahead and ease off the throttle if you see brake lights in the distance. Be ready to slow down or stop if you see hazard warning lights flashing ahead. Don't be distracted if you see an accident in the opposite carriageway: concentrate on what's happening ahead of you.

junctions

As you approach a junction be prepared for vehicles exiting the motorway to cut across in front of you at the last moment.

There is usually a slip road joining the motorway immediately after you pass an exit. Anticipate that vehicles may be joining here. If there is space to do so then pull into the middle lane to give vehicles joining the motorway room to move across from the slip road into the inside lane.

It is illegal (except in an emergency) to ride into the triangular area of chevrons within a solid white line which separates a motorway slip road from the main carriageway

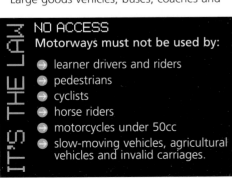

stopping

Stopping is permitted on a motorway only in an emergency, or if you are directed to stop by a sign with flashing red lights or by the police (Highways Agency traffic officers also work alongside police officers on motorways to manage incidents and keep traffic moving and it is an offence not to comply with any directions they give.) The hard shoulder is reserved for emergency use only – If you need to take a break then ride on to the next exit or service station.

joining and leaving

When joining a motorway, use the slip road as when joining a dual carriageway. Once you have joined, keep in the left-hand lane until you have adjusted to traffic conditions.

Motorway exits are marked with signs at one mile and half a mile, and then countdown markers at 300, 200 and 100

KNOW THE CODE

HIGHWAY CODE RULES 229-32

Motorway signals

229. Motorway signals are used to warn you of a danger ahead. For example, there may be an accident, fog, or a spillage, which you may not immediately be able to see.
230. Signals situated on the central reservation apply to all lanes. On very busy stretches, signals may be overhead with a separate signal for each lane.
231. Amber flashing lights. These warn of a hazard ahead. The signal may show a temporary maximum speed limit, lanes that are closed or a message such as 'Fog'. Adjust your speed and look out for the danger until you pass a signal which is not flashing or one that gives the 'All clear' sign and you are sure it is safe to increase your speed.
232. Red flashing lights. If red lights on the overhead signals flash above your lane (there may also be a red 'X') you MUST NOT go beyond the signal in that lane. If red lights flash on a signal in the central reservation or at the side of the road, you MUST NOT go beyond the signal in any lane.

yards (270, 180 and 90m) before the slip road. Don't pull across to the exit at the last moment, but aim to be in the left-hand lane by the half-mile warning sign. Where other traffic might benefit from a signal, start indicating left at the 300 yard marker. Take special care when entering service stations as slip roads can be shorter than normal.

If you go past your junction by mistake you must continue to the next junction to turn around.

Keep an eye on your speedometer after leaving a motorway, as it may seem you are riding more slowly than you really are.

bad weather

Because of the high traffic speeds it is essential to make yourself visible on the motorway. Use your headlight at all times.

In wet conditions, beware of spray thrown up from the road, particularly as you overtake large vehicles. Look out also for the effect of crosswinds on exposed stretches.

Fog patches are a special danger on motorways as you may enter them at high speed without warning. Reduce your speed in conditions where fog patches may be likely to form and take heed of fog warning signs, even if it is clear where you are.

ATM schemes

Active Traffic Management (ATM) schemes are in place on some motorways to reduce congestion. They use variable mandatory speed limits to promote a more constant traffic flow and reduce delays. In congested conditions the hard shoulder comes into use as an extra traffic lane. Emergency refuge areas are provided every 500m and should be used in the event of a breakdown, whether or not the hard shoulder is open to traffic. When the ATM is operating, speed limits are shown in red circles on electronic overhead signs: a speed limit shown above the hard shoulder means it is open to traffic; a red cross means the hard shoulder should be used in emergencies only.

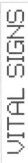

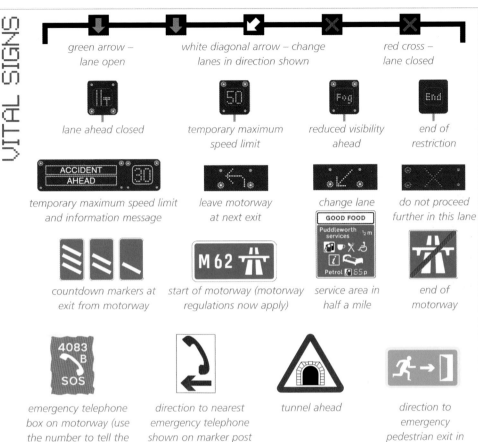

green arrow – lane open

white diagonal arrow – change lanes in direction shown

red cross – lane closed

lane ahead closed

temporary maximum speed limit

reduced visibility ahead

end of restriction

temporary maximum speed limit and information message

leave motorway at next exit

change lane

do not proceed further in this lane

countdown markers at exit from motorway

start of motorway (motorway regulations now apply)

service area in half a mile

end of motorway

emergency telephone box on motorway (use the number to tell the operator your location)

direction to nearest emergency telephone shown on marker post on hard shoulder

tunnel ahead

direction to emergency pedestrian exit in tunnel

tunnels

Take extra care by observing all road signs and signals on the approach to a tunnel. Always use your dipped headlight in a tunnel, and if you are wearing sunglasses stop and remove them before you enter it.

Leave a generous separation distance from the vehicle in front, especially if you have to stop in a tunnel in congested traffic. Follow any instructions given on variable message signs.

Breaking down in a tunnel can be particularly hazardous. If you break down in a tunnel, switch off the engine, put on your hazard warning lights (if fitted) and telephone for help.

If fire breaks out and you cannot continue out of the tunnel, pull over, switch offf the engine and put the bike on its stand. Try to extinguish the fire with your own extinguisher or an emergency fire extinguisher situated in the tunnel, but if you cannot put it out or in the case of a serious fire developing, make your way to the nearest emergency exit and safety.

135

Roadworks are an occupational hazard for any road user, and the delays they cause can be frustrating. For safety's sake, stay calm and follow all signs to the letter. You may have to merge with other traffic where lanes are closed off, follow a deviation over an uneven temporary road surface, and give way to workmen and machinery crossing in front of you. Take particular care on motorway contraflows.

WHEN RED LIGHT SHOWS WAIT HERE

WN54 ZRC

roadwork precautions

- take care when you see a 'roadworks ahead' sign, and look out for more signs
- temporary speed limits posted at roadworks are mandatory and you must obey them, even if there is no work taking place
- if one or more lanes are closed, carry out the observation-signal-manoeuvre routine and get into the correct lane in good time. Leave plenty of space and be alert for vehicles cutting across at the last moment
- when queuing in lines of traffic, obey merge-in-turn signs where posted
- use the hard shoulder if signs direct you
- be prepared to stop where traffic at roadworks is controlled by a stop-go board, a police officer or temporary traffic lights. At roadworks with temporary traffic lights, you must obey the lights even if the road ahead appears to be clear
- do not enter areas cordoned off by cones
- try not to be distracted by work going on around you, but be prepared to give way to works vehicles or staff
- slow down for ramps, rough road surfaces or loose chippings
- at the end of motorway roadworks there may be a national speed limit sign or an end of roadworks sign: both indicate that the speed limit has returned to 70mph
- where the pavement is closed due to street repairs, look out for pedestrians walking in the road.

contraflows

On motorway contraflows vehicles from both directions share the same carriageway. Lanes are separated by temporary red and white marker posts, and may be narrower than usual. You may need to select a lane some way in advance if you intend leaving at the next junction. Make sure you:

- reduce speed in good time and obey any speed limit signposted
- get into an appropriate lane early
- keep a generous separation distance.

VITAL SIGNS

roadworks

manually operated temporary stop and go signs

roadworks one mile ahead

lane restrictions at roadworks ahead

temporary lane closure

one lane crossover at contraflow roadworks

Mandatory reduced speed limit ahead

end of roadworks and any temporary restrictions

When minor roadworks are carried out on motorways and dual carriageways these signs may be shown on the back of a slow-moving or stationary works vehicle blocking a traffic lane. The four amber lamps flash in alternate horizontal pairs. Pass the vehicle in the direction shown by the arrow. Where a lane is closed there will be no cones to separate it off

07

ON THE ROAD

PARKING

When you need to park your motorcycle
you must make sure you find a safe and
legal place. Parking regulations can be
complicated, so if you plan to leave your
bike check road markings and signs to
make sure that it is permitted. Sadly,
motorcycles are a popular
target for thieves, so invest
in an effective security
device and make sure
you use it every time you
leave your bike.

MOTORCYCLES

where to park

When looking for somewhere to leave your motorbike, try to use a secure off-street parking site. If you have to park in the street use a marked parking bay wherever possible. When parking on the road, always dismount on your nearside, away from passing traffic. Do not park on the pavement unless there are signs which specifically permit this.

You must by law switch off the engine and headlight (and foglight if fitted) when leaving your bike on the roadside, even just for a couple of minutes.

parking at night

When leaving your motorbike at night, remember the following rules:

- you are not allowed to leave your motorbike facing against the direction of traffic flow on a road at night
- motorbikes must display parking lights when parked on a road (or a lay-by on a road) with a speed limit over 30mph
- motorbikes may be parked without lights on a road (or a lay-by on a road) with a speed limit of 30mph or less as long as they are at least ten metres away from any junction, close to the kerb and facing in the direction of the traffic flow, or in a recognised parking place or lay-by
- trailers must not be left on a road at night without lights.

signs and markings

Whenever you park your motorbike, check signs and road markings to ensure you are legally entitled to do so.

On a clearway you may not stop at any time. On an urban clearway, you may stop only to set down or pick up a passenger.

Double yellow lines along the edge of the road mean no waiting at any time (although in places such as seaside towns this restriction may be eased out of season). A single yellow line indicates no waiting during the times shown on the nearby yellow plate. If no days are shown on the plate, then the restrictions are in force every day including Sundays and bank holidays.

You may stop on yellow lines for a short time to load and unload, or to let a passenger on and off, unless yellow lines on the kerb and accompanying black and white plates indicate that no loading is allowed.

Red routes have been introduced in some cities to improve the traffic flow. These have red lines in place of yellow lines along the side of the road. You must not stop even to unload or drop off passengers on a red route except in marked bays or at the times indicated by accompanying signs.

disabled parking

Disabled parking spaces are reserved for disabled motorists displaying the blue or orange disabled badge. Leave extra space if you park next to a car displaying a disabled badge. The driver may need room to get a wheelchair alongside the car.

IT'S THE LAW

NO PARKING

It is illegal to stop or park on:

- the carriageway or hard shoulder of a motorway (except in an emergency)
- a pedestrian crossing (including the area marked by zig-zag lines)
- a clearway
- an urban clearway, or a bus stop clearway within its hours of operation (except to pick up or set down passengers)
- a road marked with centre double white lines (except to pick up or set down passengers)
- a bus, tram or cycle lane during its hours of operation
- a cycle track
- red routes, unless otherwise indicated by signs
- school entrance markings.

parking hazards

Parking areas are full of hazards such as manoeuvring vehicles, pedestrians walking to and from their cars and excited children running around. The golden rule is to ride dead slow. Observe what is going on all around and look out for children running out from between parked cars. Show courtesy when parking – don't leave your bike so close to another vehicle that it will be difficult for its driver or passengers to get in or out.

beat the bike thief

A motorcycle is vulnerable to theft: even if it can't be started, the determined thief can haul it into a van and make off with it. To keep your bike safe:

- if you have a garage always keep your bike locked inside it overnight
- if you don't have a garage, park your bike where a thief would draw attention to himself. Leave it under a lamp post on the main road and not in a dark side street where the thief could work uninterrupted
- lock your bike and remove the key, even if you are leaving it for just a few seconds outside your home or at a petrol station

- always ensure the steering column lock is engaged by twisting the handlebar until it clicks
- fit an additional lock whenever you leave your bike. There are locks available that fit on the front brake disc or forks to immobilise the front wheel, but these won't stop a determined thief lifting your bike into a van. A better option is a lock and chain that can be used to fasten your bike to an immovable object. Be sure to take out any slack so the chain doesn't rest on the ground where it could be attacked with a hammer, and don't thread it through a removable part of your bike. Stow the lock and chain safely when not in use – never ride with it carried around your waist or shoulder
- choose a model of motorbike that has an engine immobiliser and alarm, and make sure they are always activated when leaving your bike
- look after your motorbike keys. Don't leave them near the front door at night where they are vulnerable to theft by an intruder.

Take extra care in car parks: ride very slowly and look out for cyclists, pedestrians and children

Get a lock and chain and use it to secure your motorbike whenever you leave it parked

VITAL SIGNS

no stopping
(clearway)

no waiting

no stopping at times shown
(except to set down or pick up
passengers)

controlled
parking zone
(pay at meter at
times shown)

end of
controlled
parking zone

distance to
parking place
ahead

vehicles may
park fully on
the verge or
footway

parking place
for solo
motorbikes

parking
restricted to
permit holders

direction
to parking
place

direction to
park and ride
site

No loading at
any time

no loading at
times shown

no waiting
at any time

no waiting at times
shown

loading allowed only
at times shown

parking limited as
indicated by sign

no stopping
at any time

no stopping
at times shown

waiting limited as
indicated by sign

loading bay

parking space reserved
for vehicles named

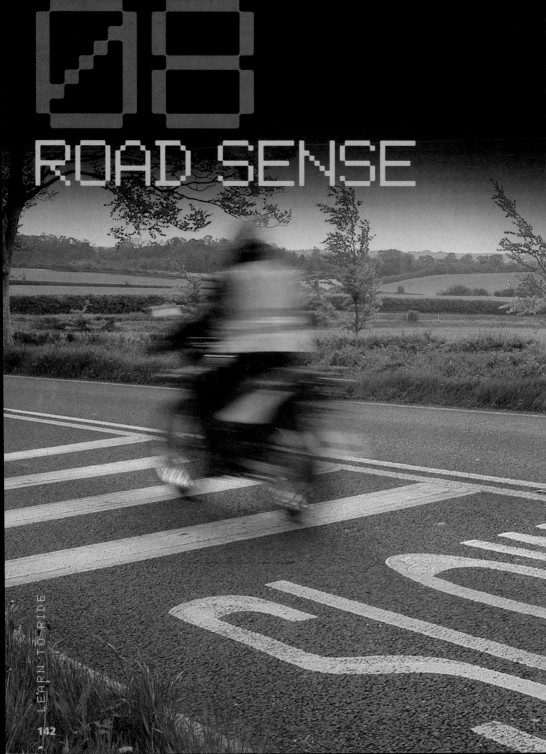

08

ROAD SENSE

Every second you are riding your motorbike, you need to concentrate one hundred per cent. Not only do you need to observe what is happening on the road all around you, you need to think hard about what you're seeing, identifying hazards and assessing what sort of risk they represent. That way you will be able to anticipate dangers before they happen, instead of reacting to them at the last moment. You must also watch your speed on the road: speeding is both illegal and responsible for many serious road accidents involving motorcyclists.

08

HAZARD PERCEPTION

SLOW DOWN

One reason why inexperienced riders have a higher accident rate is that they take more time to recognise a hazard as it is developing on the road ahead. Hazard perception is tested in a special video-clip based exam that forms part of the theory test. Get into the habit of trying to identify potential hazards as you ride and ask yourself what action you need to take to deal with them safely.

what is a hazard?

A hazard is simply any potential danger you encounter on the road which may cause you to change your speed or direction.

There are three types of hazard:

➡ static hazards

These are stationary features such as bends, junctions, traffic lights and crossings. They are the easiest type of hazard to recognise, as they do not change as you approach them, but you often have to deal with them while concentrating on what other road users – such as pedestrians using a zebra crossing – are doing as well

➡ moving hazards

These may be pedestrians, cyclists, animals, horse riders, cars and large vehicles as well as other motorcyclists. Each type of road user is likely to react differently to situations on the road, and you need to understand why this is in order to anticipate how they are likely to react and share the road safely with them

➡ road and weather hazards

Rain, ice or snow, mud or loose gravel on the road all make it more likely that harsh steering, braking or acceleration will cause a skid. Bright sunshine can dazzle you, and darkness makes it harder to spot hazards. Fog dangerously reduces visibility and high winds are especially hazardous to motorcyclists as well as cyclists and high-sided vehicles.

prioritising hazards

Hazards on the road don't come neatly one at a time. It's important to assess how serious each hazard is so you can decide which one takes priority. For instance, a parked car on a wide road with no oncoming traffic is a minor hazard. But if you spot that there is a driver sitting in the car and exhaust fumes show that the engine is running, then it becomes a more serious hazard, and you must anticipate that the driver might pull out in front of you.

The sooner you recognise a hazard, the sooner you are able to take the action needed to negotiate it safely. If ever you have to take emergency action to avoid a collision on the road, ask yourself whether you could have recognised and anticipated the hazard earlier, and what steps could you take to avoid the same thing happening again in the future.

145

Effective observation is a vital skill that you need to develop. You can only react to hazards that you see, and the sooner you see a hazard, the more time you will be able to give yourself to deal with it safely.

looking or seeing?

If you let your attention wander you may find you are looking at hazards without really seeing them. It is surprisingly easy to ride straight past a road sign without taking in what it means. It's important to train your sense of observation so you really are seeing and thinking about everything on the road around you.

scanning

Keep your eyes moving, so you are seeing what is happening in all directions. Scan to the left and right of the road, then shift the focus of your eyes into the far distance. By looking well ahead of the vehicle in front you can see any hazards that it may have to react to, and anticipate in advance when you will need to slow down. Don't wait till you see the brake lights of the vehicle in front come on before starting to take action.

Use effective rear observation so you are aware at all times of what is happening behind you too, and be sure to carry out the observation-signal-manoeuvre routine every time you encounter a hazard.

improve your view

- following too closely behind the vehicle in front can drastically reduce your view. Keep well back, especially when you are behind a large vehicle, so you can see around it
- scan to your left and right as you approach a crossroads or roundabout to see if you can spot other vehicles which will arrive there at the same time you do
- look at rows of trees or lamp posts along the road ahead to see if they curve to indicate a bend in the road
- look underneath parked cars to spot the feet of pedestrians who may be about to cross the road
- don't rely just on your eyes. In fog or where high hedges or walls obscure a junction, listen for the sound of approaching vehicles.

Keep your eyes constantly moving and shifting focus from the foreground into the far distance

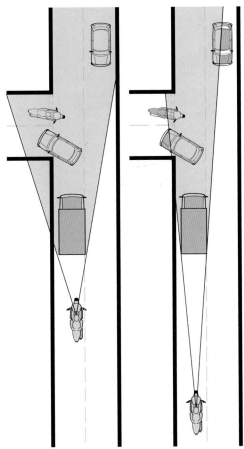

Keeping well back from the vehicle in front can dramatically improve your view and give you earlier warning of any hazards ahead

08 ANTICIPATION

Some people think that a good rider is one who has the quick reactions to get out of trouble. This isn't true. The good rider is the one who anticipates trouble and avoids getting into it in the first place. Constantly ask yourself 'what if?' as you drive along the road. What if that pedestrian walks onto the zebra crossing? What if that taxi does a U-turn? What if that driver waiting to pull out hasn't seen me? If you always anticipate the worst that may happen, you won't be taken unawares when it does.

anticipating hazards

Hazards on the road come in all sorts, shapes and sizes. The situations pictured opposite illustrate the sort of questions you need to ask yourself in order to anticipate what hazards might develop on the road ahead.

Approaching a pedestrian crossing
Scan the pavements on either side of the road and ask yourself whether any pedestrians may be about to use the crossing ahead

Approaching a busy junction
Ask yourself if the drivers waiting to join the road ahead of you have seen you. Slow down and be prepared to stop if one pulls out

Approaching a school entrance
Extra care is needed at school opening and closing hours in term time. Ask yourself if there are likely to be children about whenever you approach a school

Car following slow truck on motorway
Ask yourself if the driver is likely to pull out in front of you in order to overtake the slow truck, with or without giving a signal beforehand

Stationary vehicle on hard shoulder
Ask yourself whether this vehicle may start to move out without warning, or if the driver may open the door and jump out without looking. This situation needs particular care as most of your attention is focused on joining the motorway

 VITAL SIGNS

stationary traffic is likely ahead (always make sure that you can stop in the distance you can see to be clear)

danger ahead

reduce speed warning shown beneath some signs

08 CONCENTRATION

Riding is a serious business. If you walk along a footpath not concentrating on where you're stepping, you may trip on a fallen branch and stub your toe. It's irritating but no disaster. But if you're riding along daydreaming about your next holiday, and you fail to anticipate a car pulling out in front of you, then the outcome could be devastating.

staying alert

To maintain your concentration:

- never ride when you are feeling distracted or emotional. Delay setting out until you have calmed down, or take a cab instead
- keep your eyes on the road. At 70mph you are travelling over 30 metres (100ft) every second – so if you glance away for just three seconds, you have covered nearly 100 metres (330ft) without looking where you are going
- if you need to consult a map, find a safe place to pull over. Never try to read a map and ride at the same time
- if you need to use a mobile phone, stop and park in a safe place first
- don't ride when you are tired or unwell – even a cold can seriously impair your ability to concentrate
- never ride when under the influence of alcohol or drugs.

fatigue

Tiredness is a major cause of death on the road. Don't start a journey if you are already feeling tired. Monotonous roads, such as motorways, can increase boredom and make it harder to concentrate. If you start to feel drowsy and lose concentration you should:

- pull over as soon as you can into a lay-by or service area (but not the hard shoulder of a motorway) and take a break
- have a drink high in caffeine, such as two cups of strong coffee.

You can reduce the risk of becoming seriously sleepy while you are riding by:

- avoiding long journeys during your body's natural sleep periods (the early hours of the morning and just after lunch)
- taking regular breaks during a long journey. Stop for at least 15 minutes for every two hours you are on the road
- not riding a long distance after a poor or interrupted night's sleep.

warm and dry

You'll start to lose concentration if you get cold or wet. Always wear adequate clothing for the prevailing conditions and be prepared to meet bad weather on your journey.

Noise can also affect your concentration. Wearing ear plugs to reduce sound levels is a good idea, both to help you concentrate better and to prevent your hearing from being damaged.

Getting cold and wet can badly affect your ability to concentrate, so always wear appropriate clothing

Take regular breaks when riding long distances to avoid getting tired and losing concentration

Most motorbikes are capable of rapid acceleration which can quickly take you above the speed limit. Many could easily double the maximum speed permitted on the motorway. With so much power on tap it takes discipline to keep your speed under control. But using speed safely is one of the most vital riding skills. The stark truth is that if you have to stop in an emergency and you are riding too quickly then you will crash. The higher your speed, the more serious that crash will be.

speed limits

You must always keep your speed below the maximum speed limit for the road and vehicle you are driving. These general rules govern the speed limit for motorcycles on most roads:

- the national speed limit on single carriageway roads is 60mph
- the national speed limit on dual carriageways and motorways is 70mph
- the speed limit on roads with street lighting is 30mph.

These speed limits apply at all times if there are no speed limit signs indicating otherwise. There will not necessarily be signs to remind you that one of these speed limits is in force.

These limits are overridden if there are signs which indicate a specific speed limit, such as 40mph on a road with street lighting or 50mph on a dual carriageway. Where other speed limits apply there will be regular speed limit repeater signs placed along the road.

national speed limits

Type of vehicle	Built-up area	Single carriageway	Dual carriageway	Motorway
Cars & motorcycles	30	60	70	70
Cars & motorcycles towing a trailer	30	50	60	60
Buses & coaches	30	50	60	70
Goods vehicles * 60 if articulated or towing a trailer	30	50	60	70*
Goods vehicles (exceeding 7.5 tonnes maximum laden weight)	30	40	50	60

safe speeds

Speed limits represent the maximum speed permitted. They are not targets to be achieved at all costs. There are many occasions where it is not safe to ride as fast as the speed limit. For instance, when riding past children running along the pavement, or where parked cars obscure your vision on either side, 30mph could be recklessly fast.

In busy town centres (above) or on narrow country lanes (below) you may need to keep your speed well below the speed limit to stay safe

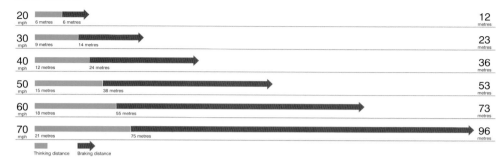

20 mph	6 metres 6 metres	12 metres
30 mph	9 metres 14 metres	23 metres
40 mph	12 metres 24 metres	36 metres
50 mph	15 metres 38 metres	53 metres
60 mph	18 metres 55 metres	73 metres
70 mph	21 metres 75 metres	96 metres

Thinking distance   Braking distance

stopping distances

The diagram above gives typical stopping distances from varying speeds. There are a number of important points to bear in mind when you are considering these stopping distances:

- it takes a long way to come to a complete halt even from a low speed – 23m is needed from just 30mph
- it takes time to react and put on the brakes before you even start to slow down. At 40mph you will travel 12m during the time it takes you to react. This assumes that it takes you about 0.7 seconds to react before braking, a time that could easily treble if you aren't concentrating
- stopping distance doesn't increase uniformly with speed: double your speed from 30mph to 60mph, and you need not twice but three times the distance in which to stop
- these are stopping distances on a dry road in good weather: in the wet, allow twice the distance to stop; on icy roads, ten times further may be needed
- a motorbike with worn brakes or tyres may take much further to stop, particularly on a wet road, even if the tyre tread depth is still above the legal minimum
- if you are carrying a load, or a pillion passenger, or have a sidecar, the extra weight will increase your stopping distances

- don't expect your bike to brake as effectively as the car you're following. This is partly down to physics – four wheels give more braking grip than two – and partly because the car is likely to be fitted with anti-lock brakes which can be more effective in an emergency than the non-ABS brakes fitted to most bikes
- always remember the rule which cannot be repeated too often: you must always be able to stop in the distance you can see to be clear.

how fast?

Sometimes your senses can trick you into thinking you are riding more slowly than you really are. A speed of 40mph feels much slower on an open road than it does through an avenue of trees, because the objects flashing past on the edge of your vision give you a sensation of speed. This means it is particularly difficult to judge your speed when the reference points around you are obscured, for instance at night or in foggy weather.

Take particular care to monitor your speed at times when you may feel you are going more slowly than you really are, such as:
- at night or in poor visibility
- on long, open stretches of road, especially motorways
- when you enter a speed limit after a spell of fast riding on the open road
- when riding an unusual motorbike, particularly if it is quieter and more powerful than the one you are used to.

Don't race up to hazards and brake at the last moment: anticipate them and lose speed smoothly

It's good riding to make progress when it is safe to do so, but you must stay within the speed limit

minimum speed limits

Minimum speed limits aren't common, but are sometimes posted on roads where it is important to keep traffic flowing smoothly.

acceleration sense

Never accelerate towards a hazard. If you spot brake lights coming on ahead, or see advance warning for a give way sign, ease off the throttle. The sooner you start to lose speed as you approach a hazard, the more time you give yourself to deal with it. Accelerating up to a hazard and braking at the last moment also wastes fuel and causes unnecessary brake wear.

making progress

Speeding is bad for safety, but conversely you do need to make progress on the road, to keep traffic flowing and avoid holding up other road users. Where it is safe to ride at the indicated speed limit, then it is good practice to do just that.

other vehicles

Remember that other vehicles are not necessarily permitted to travel as quickly as you are. Make allowance for this and don't get frustrated when you are following, for instance, a car towing a caravan at 50mph on an A-road – it's going as fast as the law allows.

maximum
speed limit

national speed
limit applies

end of 20
mph zone

maximum speed
limit within traffic
calming scheme

minimum
speed limit

end of minimum
speed limit

area with traffic
enforcement cameras

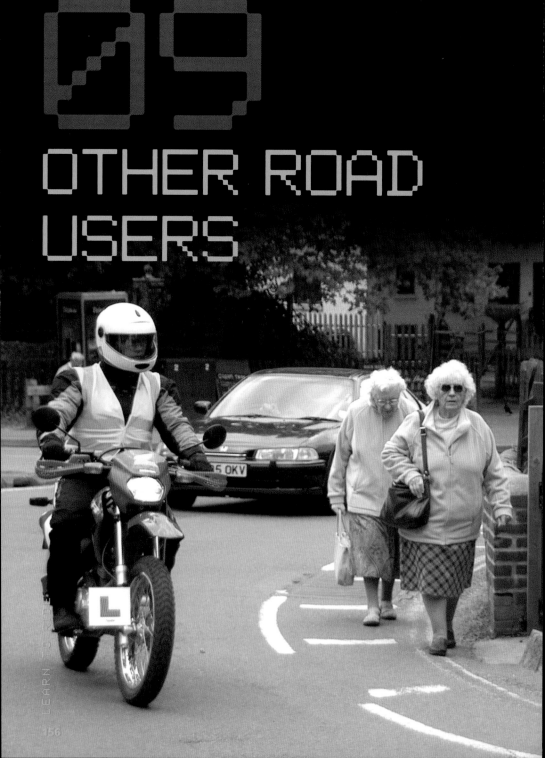

09

OTHER ROAD USERS

Other road users may view road conditions differently to you as a motorcyclist, and this can affect how they react. So try to put yourself in their position to anticipate what they are about to do. Are those pedestrians hurrying to get home through blinding rain likely to look as they cross the road? Will the cyclist swerve to avoid that broken drain cover? How will that nervous-looking horse react as you approach? You should never forget that your motorcycle is a potentially lethal weapon and it is your responsibility to look out for the safety of more vulnerable road users.

PEDESTRIANS

For a pedestrian a speeding motorbike is a potentially lethal missile. You simply cannot take risks where pedestrians are around. That means slowing down when there are people on the pavement and always being prepared to give way to pedestrians crossing the road.

vulnerable people

Take special care around pedestrians who may fail to be aware of your presence, such as:

- the elderly, who can find it harder to judge the speed of an approaching bike
- children, who may run into the road unexpectedly
- blind and deaf pedestrians, who may be unaware of your approach. If a person is holding a white stick, or leading a guide dog on a harness, it means they are blind. If the white stick has a red band around it, they are deaf as well. There are guide dogs for the deaf too, and these usually wear a burgundy-coloured coat
- wheelchair users. Be patient when a wheelchair user needs to cross the road, and don't obstruct them by parking your bike where the kerb is lowered to allow wheelchair access.

pedestrian crossings

Pedestrian crossings are points designed to allow pedestrians to cross the road in safety. Always be prepared to stop when approaching a crossing, and take special care if your view as you approach the crossing is obscured by queuing traffic or badly parked vehicles.

Treat pedestrians using a crossing courteously. Consider giving a slowing down arm signal as you approach to let waiting pedestrians know you are stopping, but do not beckon them to cross – this may be dangerous if other vehicles are approaching. Wait patiently while they are crossing, especially for elderly or disabled pedestrians who may not be able to get across before the lights change.

Never park your bike on a crossing or in the area marked by zig-zag lines. When approaching a crossing in a slow-moving queue, hold back so you do not stop where you would obstruct the crossing. It is illegal to overtake the moving vehicle nearest to a pedestrian crossing or a vehicle which has stopped to give way to pedestrians at the crossing.

Look out for powered vehicles used by disabled people. These small vehicles travel at a maximum speed of 8mph. When used on a dual carriageway they must by law have a flashing amber light, but on other roads you may not be given any such warning of their presence

Pedestrians don't always use crossings, so ride with extra care wherever there are people on foot

HIGHWAY CODE RULE 5

KNOW THE CODE

Organised walks Groups of people should use a path if available; if one is not, they should keep to the left. Look-outs should be positioned at the front and back of the group, and they should wear fluorescent clothes in daylight and reflective clothes in the dark. At night, the look-out in front should carry a white light and the one at the back a red light. People on the outside of large groups should also carry lights and wear reflective clothing.

Approach zebra crossings with caution and be prepared to stop and give way to pedestrians

zebra crossings

Be ready to slow down or stop as you approach a zebra crossing. You must by law give way when someone has stepped on to a crossing, but you should also be prepared to stop and let waiting pedestrians cross. Scan the pavements as you approach for anyone who looks like they might want to cross and slow down well before you get to the crossing. If a pedestrian does not cross immediately, be patient and remain stationary until they do. Be prepared for pedestrians to change their mind halfway across and walk back in front of you.

Where the zebra crossing is divided by a central island you should treat each half as a separate crossing.

pelican crossings

Pelican crossings are controlled by lights. Unlike normal traffic lights, these have a flashing amber phase in between red and green. When the amber light is flashing, you must give way to pedestrians who are on the crossing. If there are no pedestrians on the crossing when the amber light is flashing, you may proceed across it with caution. If pedestrians are still crossing after the lights have changed to green you should continue to give way to them.

Pelican crossings which go straight across the road are one crossing, even when there is a central island. This means you must wait for pedestrians who are crossing from the other side of the island. However, if the crossings are staggered on either side of the central island they should be treated as separate crossings.

Pelican crossings (above), toucan crossings and puffin crossings are all controlled by traffic lights

Take care around children: you must by law obey the signals given by a school crossing patrol

toucan crossings

Cyclists as well as pedestrians are permitted to use a toucan crossing. They are operated by push buttons and follow the normal traffic light sequence, with no flashing amber phase. Take care when preparing to move off when the lights turn green, in case a pedestrian has left it late to cross or an elderly person is crossing slowly.

school crossings

You must stop when a school crossing patrol shows a stop for children sign. Always be courteous to school crossing patrols.

There may be a flashing amber signal below a school crossing sign as a warning at times that children are crossing the road ahead. Ride very slowly until you are clear of the area. Be cautious also when passing a stationary bus showing a school bus sign. You may have to give way to children running across the road to and from the bus.

puffin crossings

These have automatic sensors which detect when pedestrians are on the crossing and delay the green light until they have safely reached the other side. Like the toucan crossing, puffins have a normal traffic light sequence with no flashing amber.

VITAL SIGNS

pedestrian crossing

elderly people (or blind or disabled as shown) crossing road

stop at school crossing patrol

Patrol

school crossing patrol ahead

No footway for 400 yds

no footway (there may be pedestrians walking in the road)

HORSE RIDERS

Horses are easily alarmed and unpredictable. When you encounter a horse rider on the road, slow right down and be prepared to stop. Don't become irritated with horse riders for slowing your journey – they aren't riding on the road for the fun of it, but usually have no other option to get to and from local bridleways.

passing horses

Treat all horses as a potential hazard. Slow to a walking pace as you approach a horse rider and give them plenty of space. Be prepared to stop and wait if other vehicles are approaching, as you will need to move well onto the other side of the road to pass a horse rider. Never try to squeeze by when a vehicle is coming the other way. Remember that horses are easily startled and may shy into the middle of the road if surprised by something – even just a rustling crisp packet – in the hedge.

Slow right down when passing horse riders and always leave them plenty of space

avoid noise

The extra noise of a motorbike can alarm horses, so don't rev your engine or accelerate harshly in their vicinity. Never sound your horn while approaching a horse. If the horse looks skittish, stop and turn off your engine until it has gone by.

Caution is also needed in wet weather when your tyres make more noise, and you need to avoid startling the horse by splashing it with spray.

inexperienced riders

Be particularly careful when horses are being ridden by children, or where there is a line of inexperienced riders. Riders may be in double file when escorting a young or inexperienced horse rider. Look out for signals from horse riders, and always heed a request to slow down or stop.

Take special care when you encounter horse riders who may be young or inexperienced

right turns

Take care when following a horse and rider at the approach to a right-hand turn or roundabout. The rider may signal right but stay on the left of the road at the approach to the turn, so slow down and be prepared to stop and wait to let the rider cross the road in front of you and make the right turn.

HIGHWAY CODE RULE 191

Horse riders Be particularly careful of horses and riders, especially when overtaking. Always pass wide and slow. Horse riders are often children, so take extra care and remember riders may ride in double file when escorting a young or inexperienced horse rider. Look out for horse riders' signals and heed a request to slow down or stop. Treat all horses as a potential hazard and take great care.

ANIMALS

Animals – both wild and domestic – are
unpredictable and represent a serious hazard
when they stray onto the road. Observe signs
warning of animals, and keep your speed down,
especially where there are no fences to keep
cattle, sheep or ponies off the road.

domestic animals

In country areas, especially moorland, there may be no fences keeping cattle, sheep and horses from straying onto the road. Exercise great caution in these areas and keep your speed down, especially at night or in misty conditions. Where there are animals on or near the road, ride past them at a walking pace. Do not sound your horn, flash your lights, or rev your engine loudly as this may cause them to panic. Bear in mind that if an animal such as a sheep crosses the road in front of you then several others may follow it, and that young animals will run to their mother if they feel threatened, even if that means darting in front of you.

Sometimes sheep or cattle have to be led across the road. If your way is blocked by a herd of animals, stop, switch off your engine and wait until they have left the road.

wild animals

Colliding with a large wild animal like a deer could be potentially life threatening both to it and you. Keep your speed down wherever there is likely to be wildlife near the road, and slow down when you see warning signs. Take special care at dawn and dusk when deer are most active.

Cattle grids are often placed at the entrance to areas of open country: vehicles can cross them but cattle cannot. Slow right down when riding across a grid as they can be loose and the metal will be slippery when wet

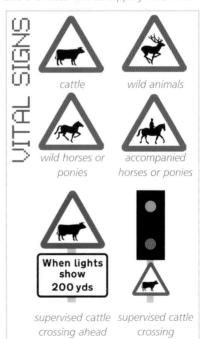

VITAL SIGNS

cattle

wild animals

wild horses or ponies

accompanied horses or ponies

When lights show 200 yds

supervised cattle crossing ahead

supervised cattle crossing

CYCLISTS

If you have ever cycled on a busy road you'll know how intimidating it is when vehicles speed by leaving only a couple of feet to spare. Cyclists have every much right to use the road as motorcyclists, so treat them with courtesy, and be conscious of their extra vulnerability.

overtaking cyclists

Leave as much room when overtaking a cyclist as you would when overtaking a car. Remember that a cyclist may swerve to avoid something you may not see, such as a pothole or rubbish in the road. Never try to squeeze past a cyclist when another vehicle is coming towards you, and slow right down when passing a cyclist on a narrow road.

Be prepared for cyclists to do the unexpected. Although most cyclists are responsible road users, remember that no training is needed to ride a bicycle and riders of any age are allowed to use the road. Situations where you should be particularly alert for cyclists include:

- **slow-moving traffic**
  Cyclists may try to filter through narrow gaps where even motorcyclists have to queue, so when moving slowly in traffic check your nearside mirror before pulling into the kerb or turning left
- **junctions and roundabouts**
  Cyclists can find it daunting to pull across the road to turn right in busy traffic, and may feel safer keeping to the left when turning right at a roundabout. Be cautious whenever you see a cyclist looking over their shoulder as they could be about to turn right. Give them time and space to do so safely
- **left turns**
  Never overtake a cyclist just before a left turn so you have to cut in front to make the turn. Slow down and hold back until the cyclist has passed the turning
- **country lanes**
  In rural areas you may encounter slow-moving cyclists around any bend
- **at night or dusk**
  Cyclists may not be showing lights, or their lights may be hard to spot among other vehicle lights
- **windy weather**
  In strong winds cyclists may find it hard to keep a straight course and you should leave more space when overtaking.

Always leave take care when approaching cyclists and plenty of space when overtaking them

VITAL SIGNS

cycle route ahead

no cycling

route for cycles only

route for pedestrians and cyclists

recommended route for cycles

with-flow cycle lane

KNOW THE CODE — HIGHWAY CODE RULE 119

Cycle lanes These are shown by road markings and signs. You MUST NOT drive or park in a cycle lane marked by a solid white line during its times of operation. Do not drive or park in a cycle lane marked by a broken white line unless it is unavoidable. You MUST NOT park in any cycle lane whilst waiting restrictions apply.

LARGE VEHICLES

Drivers of large articulated vehicles demonstrate some impressive skills as they thread their vehicles through narrow streets and reverse into tight spaces. But LGV drivers can't work miracles, and there are times when they need extra space and consideration from other road users.

caution needed

Situations where you need to take extra care around large vehicles include:

- **left turns**: a long vehicle may need to pull onto the right side of the road to be able to make a sharp left turn without cutting the corner. Don't overtake until it has completed the manoeuvre
- **roundabouts**: a long vehicle may not be able to keep entirely inside its own lane markings on a tight roundabout. Don't pull alongside it or you may get squashed
- **low bridges**: a high lorry or bus may have to pull into the middle of the road to squeeze under a low bridge. Slow down and be prepared to stop at a bridge with a height restriction
- **overtaking**: it can be difficult to see past large vehicles to overtake. Keep well back to improve your view, and look down the nearside of the vehicle as well as the offside. Remember you will need extra space to overtake a long vehicle. Be cautious about overtaking a truck after it crests a hill – it may pick up speed quickly as it starts heading downhill
- **blind spots**: you may be hidden in the driver's blind spot while riding past a truck or coach, particularly if it's a left-hand drive vehicle. Remember – if you cannot see the driver's eyes in their offside mirror, they cannot see you. Don't linger in this blind spot: get past trucks on multi-lane roads briskly. You will also be hidden from the driver's view if you get too close behind a large vehicle, so always maintain a generous separation distance
- **bad weather**: in the wet take care to avoid being blinded by spray thrown up by large vehicles. Be careful when passing high vehicles in windy weather as wind gusting around them may cause your bike to wobble alarmingly.

VITAL SIGNS

no goods vehicles over maximum weight shown in tonnes

risk of grounding

markers displayed on a vehicle with an overhanging load

low bridge – beware of oncoming high vehicles in middle of road

vehicles more than 13 metres long must display these warnings to the rear. The vertical markings are also required to be fitted to builders' skips left in the road

KNOW THE CODE

HIGHWAY CODE RULE 196

Large vehicles may need extra road space to turn or to deal with a hazard that you are not able to see. If you are following a large vehicle, such as a bus or articulated lorry, be prepared to stop and wait if it needs room or time to turn.

BUSES

One thing you know for certain when you are following a bus is that it's soon going to stop to let down or pick up passengers. Keep well back so when the bus does pull in you are not held up behind it but are in a position to see beyond and overtake it if it is safe to do so.

bus stops

Exercise great care when passing a stationary bus as passengers getting on or off may walk into the road without checking for traffic. Take care even when a bus has stopped on the other side of the road: passengers may run across to get on it, and oncoming vehicles may pull onto your side of the road to overtake it.

As you approach a bus at a bus stop try to assess whether it is about to move off. If there is a long queue waiting, it will probably be stopped for a while; if no-one is queuing, it may have loaded its passengers and be ready to leave. Be ready to slow down and give way to a bus which indicates that it wants to pull out.

Take care and position your motorcycle towards the middle of the road when riding past a bus stop as oil deposits can make the road surface there slippery.

Do not park at or near a bus stop.

bus lanes

These are special lanes at the side of the road which only buses (and taxis or cycles if indicated) are permitted to use. Check if there is a sign showing times of operation because the lane may be restricted to rush

Slow down and give way when you see a bus at a bus stop with its right-hand indicator flashing

hours only; outside the times indicated, you are allowed to ride in the lane. Where there are no signs it means the lane is reserved for buses 24 hours a day.

If you have to turn across a bus or cycle lane to enter a side road or driveway, always give way to vehicles using it.

VITAL SIGNS

school bus: take extreme care passing a stationary school bus as children may run from or towards it without looking

bus lane on road at junction ahead

with-flow bus lane ahead

other vehicles may use this bus lane outside the times shown

no buses (over eight passenger seats)

bus lane road markings

bus stop road markings

buses and cycles only

contra-flow bus lane

TRAMS

Trams or Light Rapid Transit (LRT) systems have been established in several cities. They are an environmentally efficient public transport system which runs on electricity and helps to reduce noise and traffic congestion in town. For a motorcyclist trams represent a special hazard: not only do you have to look out for the trams, which move quickly and quietly, and cannot steer to avoid you, but you also have to take care to avoid losing control on bumpy and slippery tram lines.

tram lanes

Do not enter a lane reserved for trams and indicated by white lines, yellow dots or a different colour or texture of road surface.

Always give way to trams and do not try to overtake a moving tram – wait until it is stationary at a tram stop. Take care where a tram track crosses from one side of the road to the other and where the road narrows and the tracks come close to the kerb. Where a tram line crosses the road, treat it in the same way as a railway level crossing.

Tram lines are a special hazard for cyclists and motorcyclists. They can be slippery when wet so where possible avoid riding on them and do not brake or steer as you cross them.

traffic signals

Tram drivers usually have their own traffic signals. These may give a different instruction to the signal for other road users, and a tram may be permitted to move when other vehicles are not. Diamond-shaped road signs give instructions to tram drivers only.

tram stops

Follow the route indicated by signs and road markings where the tram stops at a platform, either in the middle or at the side of the road. Do not ride between a tram and the left-hand kerb when it has stopped to pick up passengers at a stop with no platform. Look out for pedestrians, especially children, running to catch a tram which is at or approaching a stop.

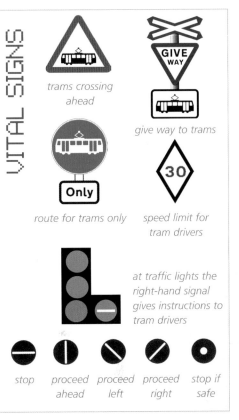

VITAL SIGNS

trams crossing ahead

give way to trams

route for trams only

speed limit for tram drivers

at traffic lights the right-hand signal gives instructions to tram drivers

stop | proceed ahead | proceed left | proceed right | stop if safe

IT'S THE LAW — TRAM RULES

It is illegal to:
- park your motorcycle where it would get in the way of trams or where it would force other drivers to do so
- ride in a lane reserved for trams
- ride between the left-hand kerb and a tram which has stopped to pick up passengers.

Extra care is needed near a tramway, especially where trams are stopping or crossing the road

LEVEL CROSSINGS

Level crossings are situated where a railway line crosses the road. Trains approach them at high speed, which means accidents involving vehicles on a crossing are serious ones. Never take risks when approaching a level crossing, and make sure you do not get stranded on a level crossing when a train is approaching. Only ride onto a crossing if you can see the exit is clear on the other side, and never stop or park on or near the crossing.

controlled crossings

Most crossings have traffic light signals with a steady amber light, twin flashing red stop lights and an audible alarm for pedestrians. They may have full, half or no barriers. Never try to zig-zag around half-barriers or ride over a crossing without barriers when the lights show.

When a train approaches, the amber light will show, followed by the red lights. If the amber light comes on after you have passed the stop line you should keep going. Otherwise, stop and wait at the line. Turn off your engine as you may be waiting for a few minutes. If a train goes by and the red lights continue to flash, or the alarm changes tone, you must carry on waiting as this means another train is approaching. Only cross when the lights go out and the barriers open.

Some crossings do not have warning lights. In this case you should stop and wait at the barrier or gate when it begins to close, and wait until it opens again before crossing.

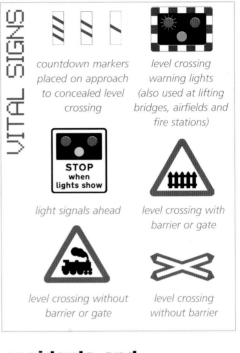

VITAL SIGNS

countdown markers placed on approach to concealed level crossing

level crossing warning lights (also used at lifting bridges, airfields and fire stations)

light signals ahead

level crossing with barrier or gate

level crossing without barrier or gate

level crossing without barrier

user-operated crossings

These crossings have stop signs and small red and green lights. Only cross if the green light is on, and wait when the red light shows. To cross, open the gates or barriers on both sides of the crossing, check that the green light is still on and ride quickly across. Then pull up well clear of the crossing, walk back and close the gates or barriers.

If there are no lights, stop, look both ways and listen before you cross. If there is a railway telephone, use it to contact the signal operator to make sure it is safe to cross. Inform the signal operator again when you are clear of the crossing.

open crossings

These require special care as they have no gates, barriers, attendant or traffic lights (but do have a give way sign). Look both ways, listen and make sure there is no train coming before crossing.

accidents and breakdowns

If your motorcycle breaks down or you have an accident on a level crossing you should get yourself and any passengers or occupants of other vehicles clear of the crossing immediately.

If there is a railway telephone then use it to tell the operator what has happened. Follow any instructions you are given. If there is time before a train arrives then try to move your bike clear of the crossing. If the alarm sounds, or the amber light comes on, leave the bike and get clear of the crossing immediately.

EMERGENCY VEHICLES

It's easy to panic when you see an emergency vehicle bearing down on you with lights flashing and siren blaring. In this situation it's important to stay calm and do your best to help the driver of the emergency vehicle get past quickly and safely.

warning lights

In an emergency, drivers of police, fire and ambulance vehicles are permitted to use flashing blue lights and sirens. They are also exempt from certain road regulations and may lawfully exceed the speed limit and drive through red traffic lights.

Certain other organisations, including mountain rescue, coastguard, mines rescue, bomb disposal, blood transfusion, lifeboat and medical transplant services are also permitted to drive under blue lights. A doctor answering an emergency call may display a flashing green beacon.

(A flashing amber beacon indicates a slow-moving vehicle.)

giving way

When you see an emergency vehicle it's important to keep your cool and not simply slam on the brakes. This will only make it more difficult for the driver to get by quickly. Look ahead and find a safe space where you can pull over, and signal clearly to let the driver of the emergency vehicle know what you are doing.

If you see an emergency vehicle coming from the other direction, pull over to make room for it to drive on your side of the road

Stop in a safe place and give way when you see or hear an emergency vehicle approaching

if it needs to. If you are approaching a junction and can hear the emergency vehicle but are uncertain where it is coming from, hold back till you can see it.

Remember that several vehicles may attend the same emergency. Don't pull straight out after letting an emergency vehicle pass without checking there isn't another one following it. It makes sense anyway to pause for a few moments after having an emergency vehicle rush by to calm yourself before continuing your journey.

stop – police

You must by law stop your motorbike if signalled to do so by a police officer. The officer will usually signal you to stop by flashing their vehicle headlights and indicating and pointing to the left. Stop in the first safe place you come to, then switch off your engine. Stay calm and courteous, listen carefully to what the officers have to say, and be prepared to produce your documents for inspection (if you are not carrying your documents with you, you may be required to produce them at a police station of your choice within seven days).

177

10
ADVERSE
CONDITIONS

Riding is easiest – and most enjoyable – in clear, bright weather on dry roads. Once night falls, or it starts to rain, or the thermometer drops below zero, the hazards start to multiply alarmingly. You need to slow down, concentrate harder and sharpen your anticipation skills to stay safe. Unlike a car driver you are exposed to the elements, and a cold, wet, miserable rider trying to get home as quickly as possible can make poor judgements that compromise safety. Recognise that in bad weather it can be best to avoid riding altogether. If you wake up to icy roads or torrential rain, ask yourself whether your journey is really worth risking an accident to accomplish, and stay at home instead until conditions improve. There's no shame in taking the course that many riders follow and restricting your motorcycling to the summer months, using alternative modes of transport in winter.

RIDING AT NIGHT

Riding at night can feel strange and a little unnerving at first. Get your first experience of night riding in clear weather on quiet roads you know well. In busy traffic, drivers may find it hard to pick out your headlight from so many other distracting lights, so take extra care to check that drivers have seen you before crossing their path, and always wear reflective clothing at night.

night vision

On unlit roads at night, what you can see is limited to the range of your headlight. Reduce speed to compensate, and never ride so fast that you are unable to stop within the distance your headlight shows to be clear.

Keep your helmet visor spotlessly clean for night riding as smears and dirt can blur the lights of other vehicles. A scratched visor also causes dazzle at night, so replace yours as soon as it shows signs of deterioration. Never wear sunglasses, or use a tinted visor or goggles at night.

If you find riding at night particularly difficult this can be a sign that your eyesight needs checking, so see an optician.

using lights

By law you must use your headlight at night (except on town roads with a 30mph speed limit and street lighting) and whenever visibility falls below 100 metres (328ft). But because a motorbike is more easily overlooked than larger vehicles, it is strongly advisable to keep your dipped headlight lit at all times, even in bright daylight. Wear bright, clothing too, with reflective strips that show up at night.

Use the headlight's main beam setting whenever you ride on unlit roads at night. But remember that main beam will dazzle oncoming drivers, so dip your headlight when you see another vehicle approaching. Road users such as cyclists or pedestrians will also be dazzled by main beam so dip your headlight for them too.

Just before you dip your headlight look along the left-hand verge to check that there is nothing on the road ahead. Immediately the oncoming vehicle has passed, switch back to main beam. If there is a stream of traffic approaching you will need to leave your headlight dipped until the road clears.

Main beam headlights can cause discomfort for drivers in vehicles you are following, so switch to dipped beam when you approach a vehicle ahead.

overtaking at night

Exercise great caution when overtaking at night. Switch to main beam as soon as you have pulled past the vehicle you are overtaking so you get the maximum view of the road ahead. Beware of bends and dips in the road ahead which may hide an oncoming vehicle.

If another road user wants to overtake you, help them see the road ahead by keeping your headlight on main beam while they are preparing to overtake, and dip it only as the overtaking vehicle comes level with you.

avoiding dazzle

- don't stare at oncoming headlights, or you may be dazzled. Look slightly towards the left-hand side of the road. Slow down and if necessary stop if you cannot see
- anticipate when your vision may be reduced by oncoming lights. When a car approaches round a bend, slow down in advance if you think that you may be dazzled by its lights
- if an oncoming vehicle is blinding you with main beam headlights, give a short flash of main beam to remind the driver that they need to dip their lights. But never try to retaliate by leaving your light on main beam as this will leave both of you dangerously dazzled
- when you are carrying a pillion passsenger the altered weight distribution can cause your headlight beam to rise so it dazzles oncoming traffic even when dipped. If necessary adjust the headlight angle to compensate.

noise at night

Remember that people are trying to sleep at night so avoid revving your engine.

It is illegal to use your horn in a built-up area between 11.30pm and 7.00am, except in an emergency. Flash your headlight instead if you need to give a warning.

ADVERSE CONDITIONS

BAD WEATHER

Bad weather makes riding more difficult in many ways. Winter is a time to be especially cautious on the road, as it brings a number of hazards including icy roads, snow, fog, heavy rain and high winds. When bad weather threatens check the forecast before leaving and if possible postpone your journey until conditions improve.

riding in winter

Make sure you and your bike are prepared for wintry conditions before setting out. You need to:

➔ get your battery checked, especially if your bike has an electric starter

➔ inspect your tyres to ensure they have plenty of tread: to be sure of staying safe on winter roads you need at least double the legal 1.0mm minimum

➔ keep your headlight and indicators clean

➔ wear plenty of warm clothing under a proper weatherproof motorcycling suit

➔ use sunglasses or an approved tinted visor in bright weather, as during the winter the sun is low in the sky and is particularly likely to dazzle you.

In bad wintry conditions, if possible stay off the roads. If you do have to make a journey, keep to main roads which are more likely to be gritted to keep them free of ice. Remember that falling snow is likely to build up on your headlight and indicators and obscure them, so stop frequently to wipe them clear.

Be extremely cautious in freezing conditions. You need to slow right down, steer and brake very gently and leave a much greater stopping distance – up to ten times further than normal.

Be alert for ice forming on roads whenever you ride on a winter evening with clear skies. Look for signs of frost forming on verges or parked cars. Take special care where the road is exposed, such as on motorway bridges, because ice often forms here first.

Beware of rain falling in freezing conditions and forming black ice, which is particularly treacherous because it is invisible. If it is very cold and the road looks wet but you cannot hear the usual noise caused by tyres on a wet road, black ice may

Snow makes the roads extremely hazardous, so unless you have no choice postpone your journey and stay at home until conditions improve

be the cause. Slow down, and keep in as high a gear as possible.

As the air temperature rises, look out for areas where ice may linger, such as shady patches behind trees or buildings, and dips in the road where pockets of cold air settle.

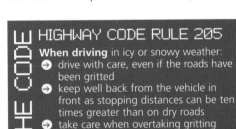

KNOW THE CODE: HIGHWAY CODE RULE 205

When driving in icy or snowy weather:

➔ drive with care, even if the roads have been gritted

➔ keep well back from the vehicle in front as stopping distances can be ten times greater than on dry roads

➔ take care when overtaking gritting vehicles, particularly if you are riding a motorcycle

➔ watch out for snowploughs which may throw out snow on either side. Do not overtake them unless the lane you intend to use has been cleared

➔ be prepared for the road conditions changing over relatively short distances.

wet weather

Riding is more dangerous when it's raining for several reasons:

➡ reduced vision

Rain makes it more difficult to see, and other road users may find it harder to see you too. When the roads are wet the reflections from wet surfaces can make it harder to see unlit objects.

Your visor and goggles become obscured by raindrops, and they may mist up too. Carry a cloth and when necessary stop and use it. It's a good idea to use an anti-misting spray on your visor and also on your mirrors.

➡ slippery roads

Water on the road acts as a lubricant which reduces tyre grip, making it easier to skid and lose control. Emergency braking distances are increased in the wet, even if your bike has anti-lock brakes. On wet surfaces it's even more important than usual to anticipate the need to brake and make sure any braking is done while your bike is upright and moving in a straight line. Reduce your speed and increase your separation distance from the vehicle in front, leaving at least a four-second gap. Be careful when cornering, especially where the road surface is worn or greasy, such as on roundabouts. Be vigilant for hazards such as manhole covers and road markings, which become dangerously slippery when wet. Where possible steer around such hazards and avoid taking a cornering line which will cause your tyres to pass over them. Look out for the rainbow film on the road which indicates a slippery patch of spilt diesel.

➡ spray

In wet weather vehicles send up spray from their tyres which can drastically reduce your vision. Keep well back from other vehicles, particularly large vehicles which can throw up huge quantities of spray, and take special care when overtaking.

➡ standing water

Aquaplaning can occur on standing water when tyres surf on the water and lose their grip. The higher your speed on a wet road, the more likely you are to aquaplane, so slow down in conditions where aquaplaning is likely. Try to anticipate where puddles of standing water are likely to form in dips in the road and slow down well in advance. If you feel your bike begin to aquaplane don't attempt to steer or brake as this could cause loss of control. Ease off the throttle, and as the bike loses speed the tyres will regain contact with the road surface. If you do experience aquaplaning, check your tyres as the better condition the treads are in, the more effectively they resist aquaplaning.

If your visor mists up while riding, stop as soon as possible and clean it with a soft cloth

VITAL SIGNS

Ice

risk of ice

slippery road

Ride through a ford only if you are certain the water level is low enough to allow safe passage

⊜ flooding

You may have to ride through water either where the road has flooded, or at a ford (where a river runs across the road). If possible, try to take a route which avoids any flooded roads, as riding through deep water can cause your engine to stall if water blocks the exhaust, and if water enters the engine it can cause serious damage.

Fords may be slippery and uneven with loose gravel. There may be a strong current which could throw you off balance. They may get much deeper than usual after heavy rain or in winter and become unsafe to cross. Never attempt to ride through water unless you are certain how deep it is. Watch another vehicle make the attempt first, or check the depth on the gauge located beside many fords. If the water is too deep, turn round and find another route.

When you ride through standing water, try to choose the shallowest route. This is usually the middle of the road, because the camber makes the edges slope away.

Proceed slowly and steadily in a low gear and keep the engine revs high by slipping the clutch if necessary (this helps prevent water entering the exhaust).

Once out the other side, ride slowly while applying the brakes gently to make sure they are dry and working properly.

KNOW THE CODE HIGHWAY CODE RULE 202

Wet weather In wet weather, stopping distances will be at least double those required for stopping on dry roads. This is because your tyres have less grip on the road.

In wet weather

➡ you should keep well back from the vehicle in front. This will increase your ability to see and plan ahead

➡ if the steering becomes unresponsive, it probably means that water is preventing the tyres from gripping the road. Ease off the accelerator and slow down gradually

➡ the rain and spray from vehicles may make it difficult to see and be seen.

Riding in fog is hazardous, so slow down and leave plenty of extra time to complete your journey

Be careful when riding with the sun low in the sky, as it can dazzle you and obscure other vehicles

fog

Fog is a major road hazard. Serious motorway pile-ups occur because road users go too fast and too close in foggy conditions. If you can avoid making your journey, stay off the road when it is foggy.

If you do have to ride in fog:

- leave more time for your journey as you will have to reduce your speed
- make sure your lights – including your foglight (if fitted) – are clean and working properly
- check your visor or goggles are clean, and carry a cloth in case you need to demist them during the journey
- use your dipped headlight, plus foglight (if fitted) when visibility falls below 100 metres (328 ft). Avoid using your headlight on main beam as the light reflecting back off the fog can make it harder to see. Don't leave a foglight switched on once visibility has improved – this is illegal, it makes your brake light less easy to see and it dazzles and annoys other road users
- always make sure you can stop in the distance you can see to be clear. With all usual reference points obscured by thick fog it can be harder to gauge how quickly you're travelling, so keep an eye on your speedometer
- don't overtake unless you can be absolutely sure nothing is coming
- when waiting to emerge at a junction it can help to listen for the sound of approaching vehicles which may not be visible till the last moment. Use your brake light while stationary at the junction to give an extra warning to vehicles approaching from behind, and consider using your horn as a signal before pulling out
- keep to the centre of your lane; riding along the central lane marking to find your way in thick fog is extremely dangerous; keeping to the gutter is also hazardous as you could suddenly encounter hazards such as pedestrians or a parked car
- beware of other vehicles which may not have switched on their lights despite the reduced visibility
- remember that in dense fog the reflective studs separating lanes on a motorway can help you tell which lane you are in:

  red studs to left, white studs to right mean you are in the left-hand lane

white studs to both left and right
mean you are in a middle lane
white studs to left, amber studs right
mean you are in the right-hand lane
green studs to left
mean you are passing a slip road

- avoid parking your bike on the road on a foggy day. If you have to do this, then leave the parking lights on
- be alert to the possibility of encountering unexpected fog patches. Slow down in conditions where fog might occur, and anticipate that fog may form on higher ground, or in valleys on cold winter mornings. Always slow down on the motorway when you see a fog warning sign, even if it is clear where you are.

high winds

Motorcycles are particularly vulnerable to windy conditions. Keep your speed down and take particular care where crosswinds may gust across the road, such as on exposed open sections of road, and as you pass gaps in fences, hedges or buildings. In windy weather expect to encounter fallen branches or even trees in the road.

Take care around other vehicles which are vulnerable to high winds, such as high-sided vehicles, caravans and trailers, and when overtaking other motorcyclists and cyclists who could be blown in front of you by a fierce gust. Choose a sheltered place to pass high-sided vehicles, and as you pass anticipate that you may need to correct your steering to compensate for eddying wind currents.

hot weather

Although most bikers would agree that warm, sunny weather is best for motorcycling, it can bring its own problems. A full set of protective clothing can get uncomfortably warm in summer, but never be tempted to compromise your safety by riding with legs or arms uncovered or in skimpy footware.

Glare from the sun can make riding tiring and compromise your vision. Use an approved tinted visor, or sunglasses (if you need corrective lenses to ride, make sure your sunglasses are made up to match your prescription). When riding with the sun setting behind you, be aware that oncoming drivers may find it harder to see you, although from your perspective you can still see clearly. Use your dipped headlight to make yourself more visible.

When it's very hot the road surface becomes soft, reducing the grip of the tyres, so take extra care particularly when steering and braking.

Be cautious also when it rains after a period of dry weather: the water can combine with the film of grease, rubber and oil deposited on the road to make the road surface treacherous.

KNOW THE CODE
HIGHWAY CODE RULES 207-8

Windy weather High sided vehicles are most affected by windy weather, but strong gusts can also blow a car, cyclist or motorcyclist off course. This can happen at open stretches of road exposed to strong cross winds, or when passing bridges or gaps in hedges.

In very windy weather your vehicle may be affected by turbulence created by large vehicles. Motorcyclists are particularly affected, so keep well back from them when they are overtaking a high-sided vehicle.

SKIDDING

Skidding is more likely in bad weather, but it's important to understand that in the majority of cases when a motorbike skids the fundamental cause is bad riding. Most skids occur only because the bike is being ridden too fast for the conditions, or control is compromised by harsh steering, braking or acceleration. Ride smoothly and sensibly at all times and you will dramatically reduce your risk of experiencing a skid.

avoiding skids

Skids can be avoided by never asking your bike to do more than it can with the grip available from its tyres in the prevailing road conditions. Skidding is more likely:

➜ in bad weather when roads are damp, flooded, icy or snow-covered
➜ on poor surfaces such as loose chippings
➜ where there are slippery features on the road such as road markings, tar banding and metal inspection covers
➜ if you have worn tyres

Wherever there is an increased risk of skidding you must:

➜ slow down
➜ increase your stopping distance, so if the vehicle in front of you stops unexpectedly you have enough space to brake to a halt without skidding
➜ take extra care when approaching a bend which may be slippery
➜ be gentle and progressive when changing direction, accelerating and braking.

skidding when accelerating

If you accelerate too harshly when moving off, especially on a slippery road, the rear wheel will spin and the rear of the bike may slide sideways. High-performance bikes may skid at higher speeds if the throttle is opened too abruptly.

To counteract a skid caused by harsh acceleration, ease off the throttle and steer in the same direction that the bike is sliding. If you experience wheelspin on a slippery or icy road, use a higher gear for moving off and riding at low speed.

Traction control systems are becoming more common on motorcycles. These detect electronically when the rear wheel is starting to spin and reduce the power going to it. This reduces the risk of skidding under acceleration. However, it is still best to use the throttle smoothly to ensure that traction control never needs to intervene.

skidding when braking

If you brake hard on a slippery surface the wheels may lock up. Because of forward weight transfer under braking, the rear wheel has less grip and locks up more readily. If you feel the rear wheel locking up, release the brake pedal and reapply it more gently and progressively.

If the front wheel locks up, keep a firm grip on the handlebars, release the brake lever and reapply it more gently and progressively.

If your motorcycle has ABS fitted it will prevent the wheels locking up under braking (see p59). But even ABS can't work miracles on greasy or icy roads. You still need to allow a much longer stopping distance than you would if you were riding on dry tarmac.

Whenever road conditions are poor, anticipate the effect it is likely to have on your bike's braking performance. Slow down for hazards earlier, make more use of engine braking, and when you use the brakes do so smoothly and progressively.

Be extra cautious when heading downhill on a slippery road. Engage a lower gear and approach the incline slowly, as you may find it particularly difficult to slow down without risking a skid.

skidding when cornering

A skid can be provoked by a sudden change of direction (such as a swerve to avoid something in the road) or by leaning over too far while cornering.

If the rear wheel loses grip during cornering the rear of the bike will swing to the outside of the curve. If you feel the rear starting to slide, ease off the throttle or brake, and steer in the direction that the rear of the bike is sliding. Keep your feet on the footrests, as putting a foot on the ground is more likely to make you lose balance.

189

11
YOU AND
YOUR BIKE

As a motorcyclist you have legal responsibilities. You must ensure that you have a valid signed driving licence, that you are insured for the bike you are riding, and that it is properly registered and taxed. It is also your responsibility to keep your bike properly maintained in a roadworthy condition at all times. You must take care that it is never overloaded, and if you carry a pillion passenger you must make sure they understand what they must and must not do while they are on your bike. You should also take whatever steps you can to minimise the impact of your bike on the environment.

There are a number of documents required to keep you and your bike legal on the road. You must by law produce your driving licence and counterpart, a valid insurance certificate and (if appropriate) a valid MOT certificate if requested to do so by the police. If you can't produce these documents on the spot, you will be asked to take them to a police station of your choice within seven days. You must also ensure your motorcycle is taxed and the tax disc clearly displayed.

driving licence

You must have a valid signed driving licence which allows you to ride your category of motorcycle.

The photocard driving licence consists of a photo ID card and a counterpart. You must be able to show both parts if you are asked to produce your licence by a police officer. You must by law inform the Driver and Vehicle Licensing Agency (DVLA) if you change your name or address – there is a section on the licence to fill in and return to the DVLA to do this.

All motorcyclists have regular contact with the Driver and Vehicle Licensing Authority, which administers driving licences and registrations. You can contact them at DVLA, Swansea SA6 7JL (or www.dvla.gov.uk). For drivers in Northern Ireland, the equivalent organisation is Driver and Vehicle Licensing Northern Ireland, County Hall, Castlerock Rd, Coleraine BT51 3TB (www.dvlni.gov.uk)

registration document

Every motorcycle has its own registration document (sometimes called a logbook or V5) which lists identification details including the name and address of its registered keeper, the make, model, engine size and number, and year of first registration.

You must by law notify the DVLA if you change any of the details listed on the V5, including your name or your permanent address. When a motorcycle is sold, both buyer and seller must complete the top part of the V5 and the seller must forward this immediately to the DVLA (for a V5 issued before March 27, 1997, the buyer must fill in the change of keeper section and send it to the DVLA).

The V5 is not proof of ownership of a motorcycle – which is something worth bearing in mind when you are buying a second-hand bike privately.

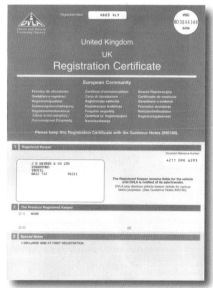

You must notify the DVLA of any changes to your motorcycle on the registration document (V5)

193

insurance certificate

You are legally required to be insured for the bike you ride. There are three types of motor insurance:

- **third party insurance** is the minimum legal requirement. It means that if you injure or cause damage to the property of a third party (that is, another person), your insurance will cover the cost of their repairs and medical treatment – but you will receive nothing for your own injuries or damage to your own motorcycle
- **third party, fire and theft insurance** means that in addition to having third party cover you will be compensated if your motorcycle is stolen or if it is damaged by fire
- **comprehensive insurance** means that your costs, as well as those of any third party, will be covered if you have an accident, even if it is your own fault. Comprehensive is the most expensive sort of insurance cover but it is well worth the extra cost.

If you intend to carry a pillion passenger check that the terms of your insurance cover permits this; some policies give a discount if you agree not to carry a pillion.

Always check that you are properly insured before riding another person's bike; most policies give a reduced level of cover or no cover at all when you are not on your own bike.

When you take out motorcycle insurance you will be given a detailed policy document, plus an insurance certificate which acts as legal confirmation of your insurance cover (you may initially receive a cover note, which is legally recognised as a substitute for your certificate until this is sent to you).

You must always inform your insurer of any changes to your circumstances, or modifications to your motorcycle, otherwise you may invalidate your insurance policy.

You will need to produce your insurance certificate when taxing your motorcycle and at its MOT.

Many factors influence the cost of motorcycle insurance. You will pay more:

- to insure a high-performance bike
- if you live in a high-risk area such as an inner city
- if you are a younger rider
- if you get penalty points on your licence – insurance is particularly difficult to get after a drink-driving conviction.

You may cut your insurance premium by:

- avoiding accidents – every year that you don't claim on your insurance earns you a no-claims bonus, which knocks a percentage off your insurance premium (usually up to a five-year maximum). If you have to make a claim you lose a year's no-claims bonus, and your next premium may also rise
- opting for a higher excess (this is an amount you have to pay when you make a claim. If you have an excess of £100, it means you have to pay the first £100 of any claim you make).

riding abroad

If you take your motorcycle overseas, be sure to carry with you all necessary documentation, including your full valid UK driving licence, the registration document and MOT certificate (if applicable). If the bike is on hire or lease you need written authorisation that you are permitted to ride it. Check also with your insurance company that you are fully covered.

Unless it is fitted with a europlate (which show the letters GB below the Euro symbol) you must affix a GB sticker to the rear of your bike. You should also fit headlight convertors so your lights do not dazzle other road users when riding on the right-hand side of the road. Be alert for different speed limits and laws – in most European countries it is a legal requirement for motorbikes to use their headlight at all times.

For further advice and information on motoring laws overseas, see the Haynes book **Driving Abroad** *by Robert Davies*

Vehicle Excise Duty

This is better known as road tax. You must by law clearly display a tax disc on the left-hand side of any motorcycle which is used or parked on the public road (on a motorcycle with sidecar, the disc must be displayed on the left-hand side of the handlebars or on the left-hand side of the sidecar). You can apply for a tax disc at a post office. You will need to take along your motor insurance certificate, MOT certificate (if applicable) and either the DVLA road tax reminder form V11, or the registration document (V5). Applications can be made from the 15th day of the month in which the current tax is due to expire.

Tax discs are available for one year for bikes up to 600cc, and for either six months or one year for larger-engined bikes. The cost varies depending on the engine size, in the following classes:

- 150cc and under
- 151cc to 400cc
- 401cc to 600cc
- 601cc and over.

If you intend to keep your motorcycle off the road you must use the road tax reminder form (V11) to make a Statutory Off Road Notification (SORN) declaration at the post office. This must be renewed annually if the bike is kept off the road for more than a year.

Motorcycles first registered before 1973 are exempt from road tax but must still display a current nil tax disc.

MOT certificate

All motorcycles, mopeds and scooters must take an MOT test three years after the date they were first registered. The MOT test checks that the bike is safe to use on the road, and that exhaust noise and emissions are within specified limits. Items examined include suspension, steering, brakes, lighting, tyres, indicators and horn.

If your bike passes you will be given an MOT certificate which shows the bike's registration number and chassis number. This is valid for one year. You can get your bike tested up to one month before its current MOT expires, and the new certificate will still run from the original expiry date. You need to produce your MOT certificate when renewing your road tax disc.

Remember that an MOT certificate shows only that the items examined were found to be satisfactory on the day the test was carried out – it is no guarantee of roadworthiness, and possession of a current MOT is no defence against a charge of riding an unroadworthy motorcycle.

You are breaking the law if you ride a motorcycle without a current MOT certificate when it requires one (the only exception is if you are riding it to an MOT test which you have already booked). If you ride a motorcycle without a current MOT it could invalidate your insurance cover.

There is an automatic £80 fine for failing to display a valid tax disc; in addition your motorcycle may be wheelclamped, or seized and scrapped

The consequences of breaking the law on the road can be severe. Serious offences result in automatic disqualification or even a jail sentence – up to ten years for causing death by dangerous driving. Being convicted of even a minor motoring offence is an unpleasant and expensive experience. It's worth remembering that it is easy to avoid ever coming into conflict with the law, simply by riding in a safe, sensible and responsible manner.

PENALTY TABLE

IT'S THE LAW

OFFENCE	Imprisonment	Fine	Disqualification	Penalty points
			MAXIMUM PENALTIES	
Causing death by dangerous driving	10 years	Unlimited	Obligatory 2 years minimum	3–11 (if exceptionally not disqualified)
Dangerous driving	2 years	Unlimited	Obligatory	3–11 (if exceptionally not disqualified)
Causing death by careless driving under the influence of drink or drugs	10 years	Unlimited	Obligatory 2 years minimum	3–11 (if exceptionally not disqualified)
Careless or inconsiderate driving	–	£2500	Discretionary	3–9
Driving while unfit through drink or drugs or with excess alcohol; or failing to provide a specimen for analysis	6 months	£5000	Obligatory	3–11 (if exceptionally not disqualified)
Failing to stop after an accident or failing to report an accident	6 months	£5000	Discretionary	5–10
Driving when disqualified	6 months (12 months in Scotland)	£5000	Discretionary	6
Driving after refusal or revocation of licence on medical grounds	6 months	£5000	Discretionary	3–6
Driving without insurance	–	£5000	Discretionary	6–8
Speeding	–	£1000 (£2500 for motorway offences)	Discretionary	3–6 or 3 (fixed penalty)
Traffic light offences	–	£1000	Discretionary	3
No MOT certificate	–	£1000	–	–

motoring offences

Some examples of motoring offences and their maximum penalties are shown in the table above. For serious offences, the courts can impose a range of penalties including imprisonment, a fine, disqualification and endorsing the offender's driving licence with penalty points. Minor offences, such as speeding slightly in excess of the limit, may be dealt with by a fixed penalty fine and licence endorsement which can be settled without a court hearing.

penalty points

Under the penalty point system, a motorcyclist who breaks the law has their licence endorsed with points, the number depending on the severity of the offence. A rider who accumulates 12 or more penalty points within a three-year period will be disqualified for a minimum of six months.

For every offence which carries penalty points the court has a discretionary power to order the licence holder to be disqualified. This may be for any period the court thinks fit, but is usually between one week and a few months. For serious offences there is a mandatory period of disqualification – 12 months in the case of drink-driving. Serious or repeat offenders may face longer periods of disqualification, and in some cases the offender has to take and pass an extended motorcycle test before being allowed back on the road.

New Driver Act

Special rules apply to all riders and drivers for the first two years after passing their driving test. If they get six or more penalty points on their licence as a result of offences they commit before the two years are over (including any they committed before passing their test) their licence is revoked. Riders revert to learner status and must reapply for a provisional licence and retake CBT and theory and practical tests to regain their full licence.

197

YOUR BIKE

MAINTENANCE

Your motorcycle needs regular attention to function safely and efficiently. Running a bike with worn or wrongly inflated tyres, or which is low on oil or brake fluid, is dangerous and illegal. Although it can be satisfying and save money to carry out your own routine maintenance, if you have any doubts about tackling a job yourself take the bike to your dealer instead. You will be asked questions about basic safety checks as part of your practical test (see p232). Your answers should refer specifically to the bike you are riding, so consult your own bike's handbook in addition to the advice in this section.

regular checks

Every time you ride your bike you should ensure that it is roadworthy, with lights, brakes and tyres in good condition. Its lights and numberplate must by law be kept clean. Be alert for any indications that a mechanical fault is developing, for instance:

- poor braking performance suggesting a fault in the braking system – get the bike checked as soon as possible
- a smell of petrol or burning rubber. Stop and investigate immediately to avoid any risk of fire
- loud or unusual knocking or rubbing noises. Any noise indicates that wear is taking place and it needs to be checked
- poor handling which may point to worn steering or shock absorbers.

refuelling

Check your fuel level whenever you start a journey and anticipate when you may need to fill up. Many bikes have a fuel gauge with a warning light that comes on when the tank is getting low, but if yours does not you will have to remove the petrol filler cap to check how much fuel remains. Resetting the trip

If your bike has a two-stroke engine it needs a special lubricant in addition to unleaded petrol

meter after refuelling will help you to judge when you need to stop and refill.

Some bikes have a reserve fuel supply. When the main tank runs dry the engine splutters and loses power, and you need to turn the fuel tap to the reserve position to restore fuel supply. Clearly, losing power could be dangerous during manoeuvres such as overtaking, so it's always preferable to fill up before the main tank runs dry.

When you visit a fuel station, remember that petrol is highly flammable. Smoking is strictly forbidden on fuel station forecourts. You must also never use a mobile phone in the vicinity of a fuel station.

There are two types of motorcycle engine:

- a two-stroke engine runs on a mixture of petrol and oil, typically in a 20:1 ratio (see your handbook for the ratio recommended for your bike). You will either need to add two-stroke oil directly to the fuel tank when refuelling, or, more usually these days, add it to a separate oil tank where it feeds automatically into the engine.
- a four-stroke engine does not need extra oil. Modern bikes run on unleaded fuel, and if your bike is fitted with a catalytic converter you must not use leaded fuel or you will damage it.

horn

Test the horn at regular intervals, but do so where it will not affect other road users and remember that it is illegal to sound the horn while your bike is stationary on the road.

lights

Check regularly that all the lights, including brake light and indicators, are working properly. The indicators should flash between one and two times per second. Make sure your headlight beam is properly adjusted so it doesn't dazzle other road users. You may need to adjust the beam when you carry a pillion passenger or a heavy load on the rear of your bike.

Check regularly that all the lights are working, including indicators and brake light

Controls such as the clutch which are operated by a cable need to be lubricated to work smoothly

brakes

Check brake pads and shoes regularly for wear and replace as necessary. Two types of braking system are commonly fitted:

● **mechanically operated**

These need regular adjustment to allow for stretching of the brake cables and wear of the brake pads or shoes. Cables and pivots also need oiling regularly to ensure they move freely

● **hydraulically operated**

These use pipes filled with brake fluid to work the brakes. If the brake fluid is allowed to run low then braking efficiency can be seriously impaired and an accident may result. Look out for brake fluid weeping from joints and couplings, and check flexible hoses regularly for damage. Never let the fluid in the brake fluid reservoir drop below the minimum mark. Get a garage to investigate if there is any loss of fluid. Brake fluid becomes contaminated with age and must be replaced at the intervals stated in your bike's service schedule.

clutch

As with the brakes, the clutch may be mechanically or hydraulically operated. If cable-operated, inspect the cable regularly for fraying or chafing, adjust it if the amount of free play exceeds that specified in the handbook and keep it oiled so it moves freely. If hydraulic, check for leaking joints and couplings, damaged flexible hoses and monitor the fluid level in the reservoir.

throttle

The throttle should operate smoothly and return to the fully closed position when released. Check that throttle cables (many bikes have two, an accelerator and a decelerator) are not chafing or fraying and that they aren't stretched when turning the handlebars from lock to lock. Keep them lubricated to prevent stiff operation caused by friction inside the casing.

battery

Most batteries are sealed and need no maintenance other than keeping the terminals secure, clean and greased. If there is a filler cap, remove it and check the fluid level – it should just cover the plates in each cell. Use distilled water to top up if necessary. Dispose of a battery only by taking it to a local authority site or garage.

Keep the drive chain correctly adjusted and make sure it never runs short of oil or it will wear rapidly

Any grinding or crunching sounds when you turn the handlebars must be investigated without delay

chain

It is important that the drive chain is in good condition, properly lubricated and correctly adjusted (around 3 to 4cm of slack is normal, but refer to your motorbike's handbook for the exact specification).

A loose or worn drive chain is potentially dangerous: it can cause a noisy rattle, affect gear changing and ultimately cause the rear wheel to lock, leading to an accident. After adjusting the drive chain tension, you should also check the alignment of the rear wheel.

Special lubricants are available for oiling the chain; it must not be allowed to run dry as this will cause rapid wear.

Some bikes use a shaft final drive in place of a chain. These have their own oil reservoir on the rear wheel hub. Make sure the bike is upright when you check the oil level. You must use the correct hypoid-type EP oil specified in the handbook.

steering

Before riding, check that the handlebars are free to move smoothly from full lock to lock without any control cables being stretched, trapped or pinched and without any snagging between moving and fixed parts.

If the steering head bearings become worn or out of adjustment, it may cause the bike to weave and wobble. Check for steering wear by turning the handlebars left and right with the bike stationary to make sure there is no grinding or crunching, or signs of excessive free play.

suspension

Shock absorbers must be in good condition or the bike's handling will be impaired. It's important to check for oil leaking from your front shock absorber as this could run onto your front tyre or brakes and cause an accident: if you see signs of an oil leak, don't ride the bike until it has been repaired.

wheels

With the motorbike on its centre stand, spin each wheel in turn and check that they are running true with no wobble from side to side. Look for cracks or other damage, and on spoked wheels check for loose or broken spokes. Always make sure your wheels are balanced after fitting a new tyre or having a puncture repaired.

The rear wheel needs to be precisely aligned behind the front or your bike could be unstable on bends and tyre wear will increase. Always recheck the wheel alignment to the manufacturer's specification after adjusting the drive chain or refitting the rear wheel.

engine oil

Check the engine oil regularly, especially before setting out on a long journey. If the engine runs short of oil expensive wear may result.

To check the oil level, first make sure the bike is level and upright on its centre stand. Your bike will be fitted with either a dipstick or a sight glass:

➔ **dipstick**: take out the dipstick, wipe it clean with a rag, reinsert it and then remove it again. Check that the oil is above the minimum marked on the stick.

➔ **sight glass**: first wipe the glass with a rag to make sure it is clean. The level should be between the minimum and maximum marks.

If necessary, undo the oil filler cap and add more oil of the grade recommended in the handbook (add a little at a time so you do not overfill, which could overpressurise the system and cause oil leaks). If changing your own oil, never pour old engine oil down the drain – take it to a local authority waste disposal site.

engine coolant

You should check whether your bike's engine is air-cooled or liquid-cooled.

If liquid-cooled, it is important not to let the coolant level fall below the minimum indicated on the coolant reservoir or the engine may overheat and be damaged. The engine cooling system is pressurised when hot, so never try to take off the filler cap straight after the engine has been running or you could be scalded. Don't add cold water to an overheated engine: let it cool down first. Ask a garage to investigate if you have to keep topping up the coolant level. Don't use water on its own in the cooling system. Anti-freeze should be added at the recommended concentration: this helps prevent corrosion as well as stopping the system from freezing in winter and causing expensive damage.

Check the engine oil at regular intervals – and always before setting out on a long journey

tyre care

Your tyres are your only contact with the road, so don't skimp on their maintenance or you could regret it. Get in the habit of glancing at your tyres every time you use your bike to check for obvious defects such as cuts or bulges.

At least every two weeks check that the tyres are correctly inflated to the pressures laid down in the handbook. Do this before a journey, when the tyres are cold, as warm tyres would give an inaccurate reading. Having underinflated tyres affects the braking and steering, and causes increased fuel consumption and tread wear. Overinflated tyres also affect steering and cause increased tread wear.

Tyre pressures may need increasing when carrying a pillion passenger or a heavy load, or when riding at sustained high speeds.

Replace any tyres which are worn or damaged. You must not use recut tyres or a tyre which:

➡ has a cut longer than 25mm or 10% of the width of the tyre, whichever is greater, and which is deep enough to reach the ply

➡ has a lump, bulge or tear

➡ shows exposed ply or cord

➡ has less than the legal minimum tread depth remaining. Tyres must have a tread depth of at least 1.0mm, forming a continuous band across at least three quarters of the width of the tyre and all the way around the tyre. Motorcycles under 50cc may have a tread depth of under 1.0mm, provided that the base of all the original tread grooves still show clearly. But you should regard these as the absolute legal minimum requirements. Worn tyres greatly reduce roadholding on damp, flooded or icy roads, and for safety's sake you should start thinking about replacing a tyre well before it approaches the legal limit, especially if you intend riding throughout the winter.

Excessive or uneven tyre wear may indicate that there is a fault with the brakes, wheel alignment or suspension.

When replacing a tyre, make sure you buy the correct type (this may vary between front and back wheels) and ensure it is fitted in the direction of travel as indicated by an arrow on the tyre. If your bike has tubed tyres fitted as standard, the tube should be replaced with each change of tyre.

Replacement tyres will not provide their usual level of grip when they are brand new, so ride carefully until the shiny surface has worn off them.

It's essential to check tyre pressures regularly to keep your bike safe on the road and to prevent unnecessary tyre wear and fuel consumption

203

LOADS AND PASSENGERS

There are a number of ways to make your motorcycle a more practical load carrier, including fitting a sidecar or trailer, but you must always take into account the effect of the extra weight. It is your responsibility to ensure that your bike is never overloaded, which could seriously affect its steering and handling. You also have responsibilities when carrying a pillion passenger, and must ensure that anyone you carry is fully aware of what they need to do to be safe while they are on your bike.

load carrying

If you want to carry items on your motorcycle you have several options:

➡ panniers

These come as either a pair of rigid boxes fixed to either side of the rear of the bike, or a bag which throws over the saddle. In either case, it is important that when loading panniers you make sure you distribute the weight evenly either side or your stability may be affected.

When using panniers it is important to make sure that the load is distributed evenly on both sides

➡ top box

This fastens onto a rack behind the seat. A top box is convenient to use, but there are disadvantages with carrying loads so high up on the bike. Avoid carrying heavy loads in a top box or you may cause instability, low-speed wobble and high-speed weave.

➡ tank bag

This fastens on to the top of the fuel tank. Be careful that a tank bag doesn't interfere with your control of the steering.

A top box is convenient to use, but avoid carrying too heavy a load in it or it can cause instability

➡ luggage rack

Items can be strapped straight on to the rear luggage rack. Make sure they are securely fastened and that there are no dangling straps that could get caught in the wheel or chain.

When carrying extra weight on your bike you may have to adjust its tyre pressures, suspension and headlight beam (see the section on pillion passengers overleaf, and check your handbook for advice specific to your bike).

Ride cautiously until you get used to the effect of the extra weight on your bike's handling. If it feels unbalanced, stop and rearrange the load more evenly.

Make sure any load is securely fastened with no dangling straps to get caught in the chain or wheel

pillion passengers

To carry a pillion passenger you must have a full licence for the category of motorcycle you are riding. Your bike must be fitted with rear footrests and a proper passenger seat, and you must not carry a child who isn't big enough to use the footrests and handholds safely.

The suspension and tyres have to work harder to cope with the extra weight of a passenger. The change in weight distribution can also raise the angle of the headlight. Check your handbook and follow the advice it gives on how to set up your bike for carrying a passenger. You may need to:
- inflate the tyres to a higher pressure
- adjust the rear shock absorber pre-load setting
- adjust the headlight aim to avoid dazzling oncoming drivers
- adjust your mirrors.

Make sure your passenger is properly attired, with:
- an approved, correctly fastened motorcycle helmet
- weatherproof, protective clothing, which is brightly coloured (and reflective if you are riding at night)
- no loose or dangling items such as a scarf which might get caught in the wheel or chain.

If your passenger has little or no experience of riding as a pillion, make sure you give instructions before setting out. Tell your passenger to:
- sit properly over the saddle – never ride side-saddle
- keep both feet on the footrests
- hold on securely to your waist, or to the passenger grab handle, if fitted
- lean with you when going round bends (but don't lean to the side to see ahead, which could affect your stability).

Carrying a pillion passenger requires extra care on your part. Your acceleration will be slower than you are used to with the extra weight on board, so take this into account when pulling out into a traffic stream or overtaking. Braking will be less effective, so leave extra space when following another vehicle. It will also be more difficult to balance, especially at low speeds, the steering will feel lighter, and the bike may lean more into corners than you expect. Be prepared too for the weight of your pillion passenger to be thrown forwards against you when you are braking.

Remember that you and only you are responsible for riding your motorbike. Don't ask your passenger to look behind or signal for you, and don't rely on your passenger to tell you the road is clear – always look and check for yourself.

Talk to your pillion passenger before setting off to make sure they know what is expected of them

sidecars

Motorcycle and sidecar outfits are a rare sight nowadays – for most people, the comfort, safety and convenience of a car is a better option.

If you wish to fit a sidecar you should first check with your dealer that your motorcycle is suitable. Sidecars must by law be fitted to the left side of the motorbike (except for bikes first registered before August 1 1981). The sidecar must be correctly fixed to the mounting points, and it must be properly aligned or the outfit will be hard to control and unsafe.

Riding with a sidecar attached requires special techniques:

- when steering, because the outfit can't be leaned into bends, it must be steered with a deliberate turn of the handlebars
- special care is needed on left-hand bends as the sidecar wheel may lift off the ground if they are taken too quickly
- under heavy braking the outfit will pull to the right unless the sidecar wheel has its own brake. The extra weight of the sidecar will increase stopping distances, so keep your speed down and leave longer following distances
- when parking on a hill, leave your motorcycle and sidecar in a low gear to prevent it rolling away.

A motorcycle and sidecar outfit has very different handling characteristics to a solo motorcycle

towing a trailer

A motorcycle is not ideally designed for towing a trailer, and if you need to transport larger loads a car may be a better option. However, it is quite legal to tow a trailer behind a bike, providing that:

- you have a full motorcycle licence
- the motorcycle's engine size is over 125cc
- the trailer is less than 1 metre wide
- there is less than 2.5 metres between the rear of the trailer and the motorcycle's rear axle
- the laden weight of the trailer is not greater than 150kg or two-thirds of the kerbside weight of the motorcycle (whichever is less)
- the motorcycle is clearly marked with its kerbside weight
- the trailer is clearly marked with its unladen weight
- the load in the trailer is securely fastened
- you tow no more than one trailer
- you do not carry a passenger in the trailer
- you obey the lower speed limits that apply to all vehicles towing trailers: 50mph on single carriageways, 60mph on dual carriageways and motorways
- you do not use the right-hand lane of a motorway that has more than two lanes.

Take **great** care when towing as your stopping distances will increase, the handling of your bike will be compromised, braking distances will be longer and you will need to leave more space when manoeuvring to take your greater width and length into account. If a trailer swerves or snakes when you are towing it, ease off the throttle and reduce your speed to bring it back under control.

Remember that a trailer must never be left on the road at night without lights.

In the last hundred years motor vehicles have
transformed the way we live. They allow us to
go where we want when we want, and to travel
long distances for work and leisure. The downside
is that this mobility has been achieved at a
considerable cost to the environment we live in.

environmental issues

The growth in traffic has had wide-ranging effects on the environment, including:

- depletion of natural resources such as oil reserves
- air pollution which causes health problems, damages historic buildings, and contributes to global warming
- road building which degrades the natural landscape
- traffic congestion
- noise pollution.

green riding tips

Follow these tips when riding, and not only will you minimise your impact on the environment, but you will also save money by reducing fuel consumption and wear and tear on your motorcycle.

keep your bike maintained
An unserviced engine can waste fuel and produce unnecessary emissions

stick to the speed limit
The higher your speed, the more fuel your bike uses. At 70mph fuel consumption is up to 30% higher than at 50mph

accelerate gently
Racing the engine in the lower gears wastes fuel

avoid short journeys
Short journeys on a cold engine cause a disproportionate amount of pollution. Walking or cycling these short journeys cuts pollution – and is better for your health

check tyre pressures
Wrongly inflated tyres can cause fuel consumption and tread wear to increase

travel light
Improve fuel consumption by not carrying unnecessary heavy items

plan your journey
Work out your best route in advance, make sure you know the way so you don't waste time and fuel by getting lost, and try to travel off-peak to avoid traffic congestion

cut the choke
Using the choke for longer than necessary wastes fuel – and can cause engine damage

use public transport
If more people took the train or bus, traffic congestion would be reduced

don't idle
Switch off your engine if you have to wait in a traffic queue, and never leave it idling while parked

anticipate
Planning ahead avoids the need for unnecessary braking and acceleration

choose an efficient motorcycle
A motorcycle fitted with a catalytic converter produces significantly cleaner exhaust emissions

ride sensibly off-road
If you ride off-road, respect the countryside, its livestock and wildlife

dispose of oil and batteries properly
Take them to a local authority site or garage for safe and environmentally-friendly disposal.

Avoid revving your engine unnecessarily, as this increases fuel consumption and mechanical wear

12
STAYING SAFE

Taking to the road is such an everyday thing to do that few people pause to think how dangerous it can be. Each of us has about a 1 in 200 chance of being killed in a road accident. For motorcyclists, lacking the protective cocoon of a car's bodyshell, the risks are even greater. And when riding you don't just put yourself at risk. A speeding bike can be a lethal weapon and every time you take to the road you have the capability to kill or maim. But crashes don't happen for no reason. In the overwhelming majority of road accidents human error is the cause. If you become a rider who always puts safety first, there is no reason why you should not enjoy an accident-free riding career.

DEFENSIVE RIDING

Riding a motorcycle is considerably more risky than driving a car: for motorcyclists the risk of being killed or seriously injured on the road is over 16 times greater than for car users. Many crashes involving motorcyclists are caused by riding inappropriately for the conditions; others result when other road users do not show enough awareness for motorcyclists. In either case, there are strategies you can follow to reduce your risk on the road.

causes of accidents

Motorcyclists tend to have different sorts of serious accident than other road users. In particular, motorcyclists have more crashes involving:

- excessive speed
- losing control on bends
- collisions at junctions
- manoeuvres that only motorcycles can perform, such as filtering between queues of traffic.

Accidents vary according to the age of the rider too. Young riders tend to have more crashes caused by poor judgement of other traffic, particularly at junctions. They are also likely to be overconfident in their own ability, liable to take unnecessary risks and to show off or act competitively when riding. If you are a young rider, you need to identify how these issues may influence you and address them before they affect your safety.

If you are coming to motorcycling after some years of driving, you also have some readjustments to make. As a rider rather than a car driver, you need to be much more aware of how weather conditions affect your safety. You also need to pay more attention to the quality of the road surface and anticipate how it will affect your ability to accelerate, brake and change direction.

Mature riders tend to ride more powerful bikes and are over-represented in crashes that don't involve another vehicle. These are likely to involve excessive speed or losing control on bends – even when road and weather conditions are good. If you want to find out what it's like to ride a high-performance motorbike at its limits, doing so on the public road is asking for trouble. Go to a track day at a racing circuit where you can ride quickly without putting anyone at unnecessary risk.

Riders are particularly at risk at junctions (above) where drivers sometimes seem to look without registering that a motorcyclist is there; filtering (below) is another hazardous manoeuvre and great care must be taken to anticipate the actions of other road users who may not be aware of you

defensive riding

You might think that the way to avoid accidents is to have highly developed bike control skills. This is actually not the case. The sort of abilities that make a good racer – quick reactions, the ability to corner a bike at its limits of grip, skid control and so on – are of little value when it comes to staying safe on the road. What really counts is having the right mental attitude. On the road good riders are those who put safety first. They always ride within their limits and do not let their emotions influence their behaviour.

Most car drivers expect to go through their driving career having the occasional knock resulting in a minor insurance claim. This attitude just doesn't work when you're riding a motorcycle. The kind of bump that results in a dented door on a car means a broken leg – or worse – for a rider. You must have an attitude of zero tolerance to risk. Train yourself to imagine the worst that might develop in any road scenario and plan your riding to neutralise the danger before it occurs.

Too many road users think no further ahead than the rear bumper of the vehicle in front. As a motorcyclist, you must make much better use of your anticipation skills to stay safe. Look as far up the road as you can see, and anticipate the events that will unfold around you two or three moves in advance – just as in a game of chess.

Recognise how your mood can affect your riding. If you've just fallen out with a friend, or are anxious because you're running behind schedule, this may cloud your judgement and make you aggressive towards other road users. It's important to realise when your mood is being affected and try to stay cool on the road at all times.

other drivers

Many car drivers are alert, conscientious and safety minded. Equally, there are those who put little active thought or effort into their driving. They drive on autopilot, minds busy with talking to their passenger or chatting on their mobile phone. When you are riding, as well as avoiding making your own mistakes, you need to anticipate and compensate for these drivers' mistakes too.

Most bike crashes involve a collision with another vehicle. Many of these happen at junctions where the driver simply fails to perceive that the bike is there – the 'sorry mate, I didn't see you' accident so familiar to riders. It's all too common for car drivers to fail to notice motorcyclists, even when they are in clear view. It is, of course, no comfort to be able to say from your hospital bed that the other driver was at fault. Take steps to prevent this sort of accident by:

- ➲ using visibility aids such as daytime running lights and high-visibility clothing
- ➲ never putting yourself in a situation where you are dependent on another person's reactions or alertness to stay safe
- ➲ never assuming that another road user has seen you. Always look for confirmation of what they are about to do before putting yourself in their path.

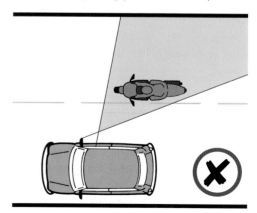

Don't ride in another driver's blind spot – always make sure you are clearly visible in their mirrors

bad habits

When a rider does something wrong and gets away with it they may do it again and again until it becomes a habit. They may get too close to the car in front on the motorway, or filter past queueing traffic at high speed. They keep doing this and getting away with it until it becomes part of their normal riding. Then one day the car in front slams on its brakes unexpectedly, or a queuing van changes lanes without warning.

To prevent yourself developing bad habits, you need to:

- be critical about your own riding. If you have to slam on the brakes to avoid another vehicle, or have a close shave when overtaking, ask yourself what you could do to avoid such a situation happening again in the future

- put your imagination to work when you are riding. Continually ask yourself 'what if?' What if a car pulls out of that driveway? What if there's a queue of stationary traffic round this bend? What if a child runs out between those two cars? If the answer is that there would be a nasty accident, then you're going too fast for the conditions and you need to slow down

- realise that riding is a skill which you can never stop trying to improve. Don't fall into the trap of getting two or three years' experience and thinking you have no room for improvement. The best riders – including professional police motorcyclists – recognise that however well trained they are, they are not perfect and are always working to improve their riding. Consider taking an advanced riding course such as that offered by the Institute of Advanced Motorists (see p237).

Always ask yourself 'What if' as you ride: for instance, 'What if there is a broken down truck just around this blind bend? Could I stop in time?'

KNOW THE CODE

HIGHWAY CODE RULE 69

Daylight riding Make yourself as visible as possible from the side as well as the front and rear. You could wear a white or brightly coloured helmet. Wear fluorescent clothing or strips. Dipped headlights, even in good daylight, may also make you more conspicuous.

There are some 27 million vehicles on our congested roads, and whenever you get on your motorcycle you need to interact with other road users. As in any other sphere of life, you can't expect these people to think or act exactly like you do – but you should make it your aim to get along with them courteously and harmoniously.

staying calm

Losing your cool on the road can seriously impair your ability to ride safely. If you find yourself getting angry or impatient with other road users:

- recognise that when on the road you are not able to communicate with other people face to face and this prevents you from reacting to them as you would normally. In your daily life you meet all sorts of people, and even when they seem difficult you make an effort to get along with them and create a pleasant atmosphere. Aim to do the same when you are on the road

- remember that if someone seems to be getting in your way, it's almost certain they're not doing it on purpose. Other people get distracted, or lose their way, or make a mistake – just as we do ourselves on occasion

- don't get into stressful situations where you're more likely to lose control over your emotions. Plan your journey in advance and leave plenty of time so you don't find yourself running late and getting tense

- recognise that getting upset over someone else's bad driving serves no useful purpose. You can't control how other people behave on the road, so let them get on with it and concentrate on what you *can* control – your own riding. If you think someone is driving dangerously, let them get on their way and have their accident somewhere else, not near you

- remind yourself that however important your appointment may be, it's not worth having a crash because you're rushing to get there on time

- never use hand signals or your horn or lights to rebuke another road user. It will have no positive effect whatsoever, but it could provoke them to retaliate, putting you and other road users at risk

- be patient with elderly drivers who seem slow and hesitant behind the wheel. They may hate driving and share your wish that they weren't on the road, but for many older people without access to public transport driving is their only way of staying in touch with friends and family and getting to the shops

- give learner drivers and riders plenty of space to do something unpredictable, and don't hassle a learner who is holding you up – they may just get more nervous and take even longer to move out of your way

- always take particular care around children, whether they are on foot or riding bicycles, and anticipate that they may act unpredictably and not follow the rules of the road.

KNOW THE CODE

HIGHWAY CODE RULE 125

Be considerate Be careful of and considerate towards other road users. You should:

- try to be understanding if other drivers cause problems; they may be inexperienced or not know the area well

- be patient; remember that anyone can make a mistake

- not allow yourself to become agitated or involved if someone is behaving badly on the road. This will only make the situation worse. Pull over, calm down and, when you feel relaxed, continue your journey

- slow down and hold back if a vehicle pulls out into your path at a junction. Allow it to get clear. Do not over-react by driving too close behind it.

217

Motorcycles rarely break down unless they have been poorly maintained or abused. Never ignore any faults which your bike develops. Be alert for unusual noises or smells, and stop immediately to investigate. And consider joining a breakdown service: even if you are a competent home mechanic you will not want to try fixing your bike on the side of a busy road in bad weather, and the membership fee is worth paying for peace of mind alone.

safety first

If your motorbike breaks down, your first responsibility is to ensure that it is not causing a hazard for other road users. Try to get it right off the road if possible. If it is on the road, keep the parking lights on at night or in poor visibility. Put on the hazard warning lights if fitted.

Never stand between your broken-down bike and oncoming traffic, or stand where you might prevent other road users seeing your lights.

When riding, be prepared for the possibility of your bike suffering a breakdown. This can include:

➲ engine failure

If the engine cuts out while you are riding, it may be because the fuel supply needs switching to the reserve tank. Try to avoid this happening by filling up in good time before the tank runs dry.

➲ tyre blow-out

If a tyre deflates while you are riding, grip the handlebars firmly and allow the bike to roll gently to a stop at the side of the road. Try to avoid using the brakes or steering, which may cause you to lose control.

➲ overheating

If your engine overheats, stop and let it cool down before investigating further. Only when it is cool should you remove the filler cap and top up the coolant level if required.

➲ fire

Reduce the risk of fire by always stopping and checking for the cause if you smell petrol fumes while riding. If your bike catches fire, get everyone well clear and call the fire brigade.

motorway breakdowns

The motorway is a hazardous place to break down, so if your bike develops a fault, move to the inside lane and try to carry on to the next exit or service station. If you do have to stop on the motorway:

➲ pull on to the hard shoulder and stop as far to the left as possible. Keep your parking lights on at night or in poor visibility, and switch on hazard warning lights if fitted

➲ do not try to make even a simple repair

➲ phone the emergency services. Use an emergency phone rather than your own mobile, as this allows the police (in some areas, the Highways Agency) control operator to pinpoint your location. The direction of the nearest emergency telephone is given on marker posts situated every 100 metres along the hard shoulder. Face the oncoming traffic while you are using the phone so you can see danger approaching. The operator will ask you for the number of the telephone you are using, details of yourself and your motorbike, and whether you belong to a motoring organisation. Tell the operator if you are a woman on her own

➲ if you do decide to use your mobile phone to call for help, take note of the number on the nearest marker post as this can also help to identify your location

➲ wait near your motorbike on the embankment away from the carriageway and hard shoulder

➲ when you rejoin the carriageway, build up speed on the hard shoulder before pulling into a safe gap in the traffic

➲ If you (or another motorist) drop something on the motorway, don't attempt to retrieve it yourself: stop on the hard shoulder and use an emergency telephone to call the police

➲ If you see a vehicle with a 'help' pennant displayed, it indicates a disabled motorist who needs assistance.

ACCIDENTS

If you are involved in a road accident you must meet your legal obligations, and you should also try to gather as much information as possible for insurance purposes. Where you come across the scene of an accident involving other vehicles, you should stop to give assistance. It is useful to carry a basic first aid kit and take some training in how to use it in case you ever have to give emergency first aid to road casualties.

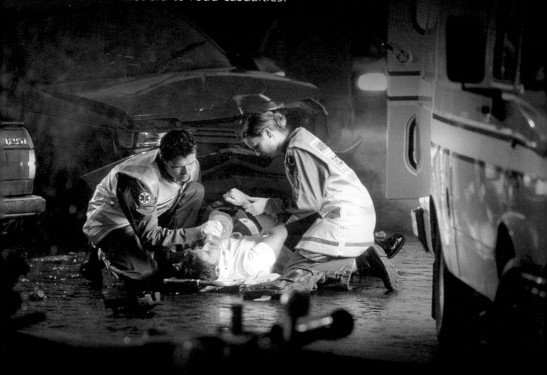

getting information

Even a minor accident may involve an insurance claim. You should gather as much information on the spot as you can. Draw a sketch map of the scene, and if you are carrying a camera take some photographs. Make a note of:

➲ the other driver's name, address and telephone number

➲ whether the driver owns the other vehicle

➲ the make, model and registration number of the other vehicle

➲ details of the other driver's insurance

➲ names and addresses of witnesses

➲ road and weather conditions

➲ what vehicles were doing at the time of the accident (such as whether their lights were on and if they were signalling)

➲ what other people say to you

➲ identification numbers of police officers attending the accident.

accident scenes

If other people have already stopped to give assistance, try not to let yourself be distracted by an accident scene. Where an incident has occurred on the other side of a motorway or dual carriageway, keep your attention on the road ahead as further accidents are often caused by 'rubbernecking' at accidents.

If you need to stop to give assistance:

➲ first stop and warn other traffic

➲ switch on your hazard warning lights if fitted

➲ make sure someone telephones for an ambulance if people are badly injured

➲ get people who are not injured clear of the scene

➲ place a warning triangle on the road at least 45 metres behind the crash scene

➲ switch off all engines

➲ make sure no one is smoking

➲ do not put yourself at unnecessary risk.

If your motorbike is involved in a accident, use the engine cut-off switch to turn off the engine and reduce the risk of fire breaking out

IT'S THE LAW — IN AN ACCIDENT

If you are involved in an accident which causes damage or injury to any other person, vehicle, animal or property, you must by law:

➲ stop

➲ give your own and (if different) your vehicle owner's name and address, and the registration number of your vehicle, to anyone having reasonable grounds for requiring them

➲ if you do not give your name and address at the time of the accident, report the accident to the police as soon as reasonably practicable, and in any case within 24 hours

➲ if another person is injured and you do not produce your insurance certificate at the time of the accident to a police officer or to anyone having reasonable grounds to request it, you must report the accident to the police as soon as possible (and in any case within 24 hours), and produce your insurance certificate for the police within seven days.

If any vehicle catches fire, stay well clear and call for the fire brigade to deal with it

first aid

Do not move injured people out of their vehicles unless you have to do so to protect them from further danger (moving them could aggravate a back injury). Do not remove a motorcyclist's helmet unless it is essential to clear their airway as it could make their injury worse. Casualties may be suffering from shock, so keep them warm and comfortable, give them constant reassurance and make sure they are not left alone. Do not give them anything to eat, drink or smoke. Stay at the scene until emergency services arrive. If a casualty is unconscious:

- first check their breathing. Clear any obstruction to the airway and loosen tight clothing. If breathing does not restart when the airway has been cleared, give mouth to mouth resuscitation. Lift the chin and tilt the head backwards. Pinch the casualty's nostrils and blow into the mouth until the chest rises. Repeat every four seconds until the casualty can breathe without assistance
- stop heavy bleeding by applying firm hand pressure over the wound, preferably using some clean material. Don't press on any foreign body in the wound. Secure a pad with a bandage or length of cloth. Raise the limb to lessen the bleeding, provided it is not broken
- douse any burns with cool liquid but do not remove anything sticking to the burns.

VITAL SIGNS

POLICE ACCIDENT

POLICE SLOW

temporary police warning signs at scene of accident or other danger

H A & E not 24 hrs

H No A & E

hospital with accident and emergency facilities

hospital without accident and emergency facilities

halfords **First Aid**

Carry a first aid kit and learn how to use it – it could save someone's life

hazard warning plates

hazard information panel displayed by tanker carrying dangerous goods (in this case flammable liquid)

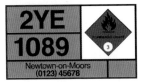

dangerous goods

Learn to recognise the markings displayed on vehicles carrying hazardous goods. If an accident involves a vehicle containing dangerous goods, it is essential that all engines are switched off and no one smokes. Do not use a mobile phone nearby. Keep well clear of the vehicle and stay away from any liquids, dust or vapours. Call the emergency services and give as much information as possible about the labels and markings on the vehicle.

diamond symbols indicating other hazardous substances include:

toxic substance

Keep at a safe distance if a tanker carrying a dangerous substance is involved in an accident

oxidising substance

non-flammable compressed gas

radioactive substance

spontaneously combustible substance

corrosive substance

panel displayed by vehicle carrying dangerous goods in packages

13
TAKING YOUR TEST

There are two parts to the motorcycle test. The first part is a theory test and the second a practical test. You cannot take (or book) your practical test until you have passed the theory test, and you must take your practical test within two years of passing the theory test. The theory test includes a multiple-choice examination, plus a separate hazard perception test based on video clips. The practical test involves riding for around 40 minutes while being followed by an examiner who will assess your riding. It includes an eyesight test and questions on vehicle safety checks and carrying a pillion passenger. The test is administered by the Driving Standards Agency (DSA) and you'll find useful information about applying for and taking theory and practical tests on their website: www.dsa.gov.uk.

The theory test consists of two elements. Firstly, a multiple-choice examination in which you have to answer correctly 30 out of 35 questions (all of which are listed, with answers, at the back of this book) on a touch-screen computer. Secondly, you have to identify the road hazards shown on 14 video clips by clicking a mouse button.

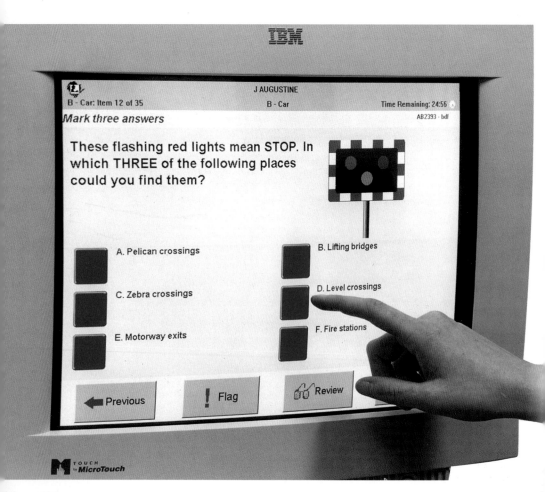

booking your test

You can book a theory test by postal application, telephone, or on the internet. The cost of the theory test is currently £20.50.

Weekday, evening and saturday test sessions are available as well as daytime appointments. If you need to cancel your theory test appointment, you must give at least three whole working days notice, or you forfeit your theory test fee. If you have hearing difficulties, dyslexia or light-sensitive epilepsy then let the DSA know at the time of making your booking and special arrangements will be made for you.

In Northern Ireland, driving tests are administered by the Driver and Vehicle Testing Agency (see *contact details* below). The tests follow the same format.

what to take with you

At the test centre you need to show:
- both parts of your photocard driving licence
- your appointment card or booking number.

If you have one of the older style driving licences which doesn't include a photograph, you will need to bring additional photographic identity, such as a passport or workplace identity card, or a photograph signed and dated by an authorised person such as an Approved Driving Instructor, teacher or doctor.

If you forget to bring the correct documents with you on the day, you won't be able to take your test and you will lose your fee.

Try to arrive in plenty of time for your theory test so that you don't feel rushed or stressed.

multiple-choice test

The theory test begins with a multiple-choice exam. To pass this you must answer at least 30 out of 35 multiple-choice questions correctly within the 40 minutes allowed (candidates with special needs can apply for additional time when they are booking their test).

You select your answers by touching the button on the screen beside the answer you want to select. You will be given the opportunity to practise this before starting the test.

If you think you have selected the wrong answer you can change it by touching the screen again. If you are unsure which answer is correct you can mark questions with a flag to help you go back to them. The system also prompts you to go back to questions you have not answered fully.

After the multiple-choice exam, you have a break of up to three minutes before taking the hazard perception test.

preparing for the multiple-choice test

The 35 questions in the multiple-choice test are selected from a bank of around 900. All these questions are listed, along with their answers, in the back of this book. You should not have to memorise all these questions in order to pass the test. All the information you need to pass the multiple-choice test is included in this book. If you read and make sure you understand all the preceding chapters, then you will know everything you need to answer any of the questions you may be asked.

CONTACT DETAILS

Driving Standards Agency (DSA)
Test and booking enquiries:
PO Box 280, Newcastle-upon-Tyne
NE99 1FP

Telephone: 0870 0101 372
Website: www.dsa.gov.uk

Driver and Vehicle Testing Agency (Northern Ireland)
Balmoral Rd, Belfast BT12 6QL

Telephone: 0845 600 6700
Website: www.dvtani.gov.uk

hazard perception test

Before you sit the hazard perception test you will be shown a short tutorial video demonstrating how it works.

The test consists of 14 video clips, each about one minute long, showing road situations involving other road users. You should press your mouse button as soon as you see a hazard which may require you to change speed or direction. The earlier you spot the potential danger and respond, the higher the score you receive. The video will not stop or slow down when you respond but a red flag appears at the bottom of the screen each time you press the mouse button to show your response has been recorded. You can click the right or left button on the mouse to show you have identified the hazard.

There are a total of 15 scoreable hazards: 13 clips contain one scoreable hazard and one clip contains two of them. You can score up to five marks for each hazard depending on how quickly you identify it. Unlike the multiple-choice test, in this section you are not able to go back or change your response. You will not lose points for identifying non-scoring hazards.

It is not possible to pass the test by clicking the mouse button continuously: this will score zero points.

You must score at least 44 out of 75 points to pass the hazard perception test.

preparing for the hazard perception test

The video clips you will see show real-life hazards of the sort you come across on the road every day. Test yourself whenever you are on the road, even as a passenger in a car, by scanning the road ahead and identifying potential hazards. Read through this book carefully, paying special attention to chapter 8 which deals with hazard perception, observation and anticipation. You may also find it useful to talk through some practice video sessions with an instructor.

pass or fail?

After completing both sections of the theory test you should receive your results, and feedback, within 30 minutes.

You must pass both the multiple-choice and hazard perception elements to pass your theory test. If you fail one element but pass the other, you still have to take the whole test over again.

If you have failed you can book another theory test straight away, but you must leave three clear working days before the date of your new test.

When you pass the theory test you will receive a pass certificate which is valid for two years. This means that if you don't pass your practical test within two years you will have to retake the theory test.

TEST TIPS

DO
➜ prepare properly beforehand by studying and making sure you understand the answers to all the theory questions listed in the back of this book
➜ listen carefully to all the instructions you are given before and during the theory test

DON'T
➜ arrive at the test centre late and feeling flustered
➜ forget to take along your driving licence and appointment card.

video clip example 1

The hazard is the school crossing patrol with children ready to cross the road. You should click on the mouse button as soon as you realise that the patrol might walk into the road to stop traffic in front of you and let the children cross

video clip example 2

The hazard is the small child on a bicycle who cycles across the road. You should click on the mouse button as soon as you realise that the child might ride across the road, causing the motorcyclist in front of you to brake

Taking the practical test isn't as daunting as you may think. But to make it go as smoothly as possible, you do need to get plenty of practice in first. Taking the test before you're properly prepared will certainly result in a costly and confidence-denting failure.

booking your test

You can book your practical motorcycle test by telephone, on 0870 0101 372, or on the internet at www.dsa.gov.uk.

The cost of the practical test is currently £51 when taken on a weekday. If you would prefer a saturday or weekday evening booking, then the cost is £60.

If you have hearing difficulties, dyslexia or any other disability which may affect your ability to take the test then you should let the DSA know at the time of booking.

If the date or time you are given for your practical test isn't suitable, or for any reason you need to postpone your test, you must give the DSA at least ten working days notice (not counting the day of the test and day of notification) or you will lose your fee.

what to take with you

When you arrive at the test centre you will need to show:
- your appointment card
- both parts of your signed photocard driving licence
- your theory test pass certificate
- your CBT certificate of completion (DL196).

If you have one of the older style driving licences without a photograph, you will need to bring additional photographic identity, such as a passport or workplace identity card, or a photograph signed and dated by an authorised person such as an Approved Driving Instructor, teacher or doctor.

If you forget to bring the right documents with you on the day, your test will be cancelled and you will lose your fee.

your test motorcycle

The motorcycle you intend to take your test on must be legally roadworthy and have a current MOT certificate (if applicable). It must be insured for you to ride and you will be asked to sign a declaration that your insurance is in order (you should contact your insurance company in advance to tell them you will be taking a motorcycle test on your bike).

If you are planning to take your test on a hired bike, you should check with the hire company that you are authorised to do so.

You must take your practical test on a motorcycle of the appropriate size, ie:
- **category P**: a moped with engine capacity under 50cc, weight under 250kg, and top speed of no more than 50 km/h (31mph)
- **category A1**: a motorcycle with engine capacity of 75cc to 125cc
- **category A**: a motorcycle with engine capacity of 121cc to 125cc and capable of 100km/h (62mph)
- **category A (Direct Access)**: a motorcycle with a power output of at least 35kW (46.6bhp).

Your test motorcycle must have a valid tax disc and L-plates (or D-plates, if taking your test in Wales) displayed front and rear. If it does not you won't be able to take your test and you will lose your fee.

If you pass your practical test on an automatic motorcycle your licence will be valid for automatics only.

Only physically disabled riders may take their test using a motorcycle and sidecar, and on passing their licence they will be restricted to motorcycle and sidecar outfits only.

coping with nerves

Of course you'll be nervous during your motorcycle test – everyone is. A reasonable degree of nervousness isn't necessarily a bad thing as it sharpens up your senses and concentration. But you will feel a lot happier if you have put in plenty of practice and have reached the stage where you are fluent and confident in your riding. Make sure on the day that you arrive for your test in good time to avoid any last minute panics. Look out all the documents you'll need the day before, and get an early night.

test procedure

The practical test lasts around 40 minutes. It begins with an eyesight examination. You must be able to read the current style of numberplate from a distance of 20 metres. You can wear spectacles or contact lenses to do so, but if so you must keep them on when you are riding. The examiner will select a parked vehicle probably a little further away than 20 metres and ask you to read the numberplate. If you cannot read it, the examiner will measure the distance exactly and ask you to repeat the test. If you still cannot read it, you have failed and your test will go no further.

After successfully completing the eyesight test, you will be asked two safety check questions.

Eyesight test: if what you see when asked to read a numberplate from a distance of 20 metres looks more like the picture above than the one below, you will fail your practical test on the spot

safety check questions

Candidates are required to answer two questions about motorcycle safety checks.

One of these is a 'tell me' question: you will be asked to tell the examiner how you would carry out a procedure, such as checking the engine oil.

The other is a 'show me' question: it requires you to show the examiner how you would carry out a safety check, such as inspecting the indicator lights to make sure they are working. You will not be asked to touch any hot engine parts, but you may have to switch on the ignition.

The questions you will be asked are set out below – you will be asked a combination of one of the 'tell me' questions plus one of the 'show me' questions.

Your answers should refer specifically to your motorcycle, so practise these maintenance checks on your bike and study its handbook before taking your test. See also pages 198–203 on bike maintenance.

If you fail to answer one or both of the safety check questions correctly it counts as one minor fault (see *fault assessment*, p235).

During your practical test you will be asked how you would carry out two vehicle safety checks, such as checking that your indicators are working

'tell me' questions

Q *identify where you would check the engine oil level and tell me how you would check that the engine has sufficient oil*

A indicate where to check the oil level, on the sight glass or dipstick. Explain that the sight glass should be clean before checking and that the oil level should be between the maximum and minimum marks. A dipstick should be removed and wiped clean, returned then removed again, before checking the level against the maximum and minimum marks

Q *identify where the brake fluid reservoir is and tell me how you would check that you have a safe level of hydraulic fluid*

A indicate the reservoir and explain how to check the brake fluid level against the maximum and minimum markings

Q *tell me how you would check the condition of the chain on this machine*

A explain that you would check for chain wear, correct tension and rear wheel alignment. Tension should be adjusted as specified in the motorcycle's handbook. The drive chain should be kept lubricated to ensure excessive wear does not occur

Q *tell me how you would check your tyres to ensure that they are correctly inflated, have sufficient tread depth and that their general condition is safe to use on the road*

A explain you would find the correct tyre pressure settings in the owner's manual. Pressures should be checked using a reliable gauge. Tread must be at least 1mm deep, forming a continuous band across at least three-quarters of the width of the tyre and all the way around it (on a bike over 50cc). There should be no lumps, bulges or tears in the tyre.

'show me' questions

Q *show me how you would check the operation of the front brake on this machine*

A wheel the machine forward and apply the front brake to test that it is working

Q *show me how you would check the operation of the brakes on this machine*

A check for excessive travel on the brake lever and the brake pedal and for unusual play or sponginess

Q *show me how you would check the operation of the engine cut out switch*

A operate the switch (without the engine being started)

Q *show me how you would check that the horn is working on this machine (off road only)*

A press the horn button to sound the horn (turn on the ignition first if necessary)

Q *show me how you would check that the lights, brake lights and reflectors are clean and working*

A operate the light switch (with the ignition turned on if necessary). Identify the lights, brake lights and reflectors and visually check that they are clean and working correctly

Q *show me what checks you would make on the steering movement before using the machine*

A check that the handlebars are free to move smoothly from full left lock to full right lock without any control cables being stretched, trapped or pinched and without any snagging between moving and fixed parts.

on the road

Once you have answered the safety check questions, you will proceed out on to the road. You must wear an approved safety helmet, properly fastened, during your test.

Your examiner will follow you round the test route, either on a motorcycle or in a car. Before starting off, you will be fitted with a radio receiver earpiece, and your examiner will give you instructions through this as you proceed round the test route.

You will be expected to keep riding ahead, unless the examiner specifically asks you to turn or traffic signs direct you otherwise. So if you receive no other instruction at a roundabout, take the exit straight ahead. If a road sign instructs you to turn left or right ahead, the examiner will expect you to obey this without being told to do so.

The test takes in a wide range of the riding situations covered in this book, although it excludes motorways. It includes the following special exercises:

➲ wheeling your motorbike

The examiner will ask you to put your bike on its stand. You will than be asked to take it off its stand and walk with it across the road in a U-turn, with the engine switched off.

➲ U-turn

You will be asked to move off from a parked position and turn round to face the opposite way within the width of the road. The examiner will check your balance and control, and that you carry out rear observation into your blind spot before starting the manoeuvre.

➲ angle start

You will be asked to pull up just behind a parked vehicle, then move off again at an angle. The examiner will be watching your balance and control and that you carry out full all-round observation for traffic coming from ahead and behind.

➲ slow ride

You will be asked to ride at a walking pace for a short distance.

➲ hill start

You will be asked to stop on an uphill gradient and move off again. You must take into account your bike's reduced acceleration and move off without obstructing other traffic.

➲ emergency stop

The examiner will demonstrate in advance the signal for you to stop. When the examiner makes this signal, pull up as in a real emergency (see p59). The examiner will check that the road behind you is clear before giving the signal, so you should not check your mirrors before performing the emergency stop.

The order in which you take these special exercises may vary. The examiner may not ask you to perform one of them (such as the hill start or angle start) if you have already done so while riding round the test route.

Remember that whenever you are asked to stop at the side of the road to perform an exercise the examiner will expect you to select somewhere safe and legal to stop.

At the end of your test the examiner will ask you a question about balance while carrying a pillion passenger.

Wheeling your bike is one of several special exercises included as part of the practical test

pillion questions

Your examiner will ask you a straightforward question on the topic of 'balance when carrying a passenger'. There is no set list of questions to revise, but typical questions you may be asked include:

➲ what problems could arise from carrying a pillion passenger?

➲ how should a passenger be carried on the pillion seat?

➲ how would the balance of the machine be affected if you carried a pillion passenger?

Refer to p206 where you will find full details about carrying a pillion passenger. Make sure you know:

➲ what you should tell an inexperienced pillion passenger they need to do when riding on a bike

➲ how the extra weight of a pillion passenger may affect the way your bike handles

➲ what adjustments you may need to make to your bike to compensate for the extra weight of a pillion passenger.

At the end of your test you will be asked a question about carrying a pillion passenger

fault assessment

The examiner assesses faults according to three categories:

➲ **dangerous faults**

This is when a fault committed during the test has resulted in actual danger. Committing one dangerous fault results in test failure. An examiner who considers that a candidate is riding dangerously may stop the test on the spot

➲ **serious faults**

This is when a potentially dangerous incident occurs, or the candidate reveals a habitual riding fault. Committing one serious fault results in failure

➲ **minor faults**

These are less serious faults. Accumulating more than 15 minor faults results in failure. Don't panic if you think you have made one or two minor faults, as very few candidates fail through making too many minor faults.

if you fail

Don't be too disheartened. If you failed your practical test first time that's no reason why you shouldn't go on to pass next time. The most common reason why applicants fail is lack of preparation. Have you really clocked up enough hours on the road? Have you ridden in a wide enough variety of traffic situations and become familiar with the whole range of hazards you are likely to encounter during the test?

The examiner will give you a statement of failure showing all the faults you have made, plus a short debrief, running through the reasons why you failed. Pay attention to the weak points revealed by your test, but don't concentrate only on the items where you failed, or you may find yourself getting out of practice in other areas.

If you've tried to prepare for the test on your own and failed, now would be a good time to consider signing up for some lessons

AFTER THE TEST

Those few seconds as you wait for the examiner's verdict at the end of your test will be as nerve-racking as any in your life. Being told you've passed comes as a massive relief. But passing doesn't mean you should stop thinking about learning to ride. Your career as a motorcyclist is only just beginning, and for a good rider the learning never stops.

UNIPART

passing your test

If you pass and have a photocard driving licence issued after March 1 2004, your examiner will ask if you want your full motorcycle licence issued to you automatically. If you do, the examiner will scan the details of your provisional licence and send them electronically to the DVLA. You will then be given a pass certificate to prove you have passed your test and the DVLA will send you a full licence by post within three weeks.

If you have an older licence, you will be given a pass certificate which you must exchange for a full licence within two years. Complete the declaration on your test pass certificate and send it together with your provisional driving licence (both photocard and counterpart sections) and the appropriate fee to the DVLA.

moving up

Now that you have a full licence you can use a motorway and carry a pillion passenger. Try both for the first time under good conditions, not when you're in a hurry, the weather is poor or the traffic heavy. Some extra training may help you to cope safely with these new situations.

If you passed the category A test on a 125cc motorcycle, you are restricted for two years to a bike with a maximum power output of 25kW (33bhp). Once the two years is up, you can ride any type of bike.

If you reach the age of 21 during the two years, you can elect to take a further test under the Accelerated Access scheme. Passing this qualifies you to ride any motorcycle.

If you passed your test under the Direct Access scheme you are immediately qualified to ride any bike.

For many riders, moving up to high-performance bike is a tempting prospect – but don't try to take on too much too soon. Top sports bikes are capable of astonishing acceleration and you need to build up your experience and bike handling skills over a number of years on less powerful machines before graduating to one of these.

Guard against overconfidence in the early months and years after passing your test. Motorcycling is a complex skill which takes a considerable time to master and you must never forget your vulnerabilty compared with road users in larger vehicles.

advanced riding

The best riders realise that they never stop learning. Treat your riding seriously and continuously assess how you are performing on the road. Take a regular look at the *Highway Code* to check you haven't forgotten anything or missed any revisions to the law.

Taking an advanced riding test makes excellent sense. The largest provider is the Institute of Advanced Motorists (*www.iam.org.uk*), which has a large number of enthusiastic motorcycle members. Preparing for an advanced test gives you a chance to assess how your riding has progressed since you passed your motorcycle test and weed out any bad habits that may have crept in – as well as to enjoy the company of a group of fellow motorcycling enthusiasts.

If you want to get the most out of your riding, consider going on to take an advanced test

14
THEORY
QUESTIONS

In your theory test you will have to answer correctly 30 out of 35 questions drawn from the following bank of around 800 questions. Test your knowledge by answering these questions and checking to see if you have answered correctly. If you don't understand one of the answers, go to the page number highlighted beside the question (eg **𝑖** p206) and read the relevant section again.

01 You are about to turn right. What should you do just before you turn?

Mark one answer **i** p64

a Give the correct signal
b Take a 'lifesaver' glance over your shoulder
c Select the correct gear
d Get in position ready for the turn

02 What is the 'lifesaver' when riding a motorcycle?

Mark one answer **i** p63

a A certificate every motorcyclist must have
b A final, rearward glance before changing direction
c A part of the motorcycle tool kit
d A mirror fitted to check blind spots

03 You see road signs showing a sharp bend ahead. What should you do?

Mark one answer **i** p121

a Continue at the same speed
b Slow down as you go around the bend
c Slow down as you come out of the bend
d Slow down before the bend

04 You are riding at night and are dazzled by the headlights of an oncoming car. You should

Mark one answer **i** p181

a slow down or stop
b close your eyes
c flash your headlight
d turn your head away

05 When riding, your shoulders obstruct the view in your mirrors. To overcome this you should

Mark one answer **i** p63

a indicate earlier than normal
b fit smaller mirrors
c extend the mirror arms
d brake earlier than normal

06 On a motorcycle you should only use a mobile telephone when you

Mark one answer **i** p151

a have a pillion passenger to help
b have parked in a safe place
c have a motorcycle with automatic gears
d are travelling on a quiet road

07 You are riding along a motorway. You see an accident on the other side of the road. Your lane is clear. You should

Mark one answer **i** p221

a assist the emergency services
b stop, and cross the road to help
c concentrate on what is happening ahead
d place a warning triangle in the road

08 You are riding at night. You have your headlight on main beam. Another vehicle is overtaking you. When should you dip your headlight?

Mark one answer **i** p181

a When the other vehicle signals to overtake
b As soon as the other vehicle moves out to overtake
c As soon as the other vehicle passes you
d After the other vehicle pulls in front of you

09 To move off safely from a parked position you should

Mark one answer **i** p64

a signal if other drivers will need to slow down
b leave your motorcycle on its stand until the road is clear
c give an arm signal as well as using your indicators
d look over your shoulder for a final check

10 Riding a motorcycle when you are cold could cause you to

Mark one answer **i** p26

a be more alert
b be more relaxed
c react more quickly
d lose concentration

11 You are riding at night and are dazzled by the lights of an approaching vehicle. What should you do?

Mark one answer **i** p181

a Switch off your headlight
b Switch to main beam
c Slow down and stop
d Flash your headlight

12 You should always check the 'blind areas' before

Mark one answer **i** p64

a moving off
b slowing down
c changing gear
d giving a signal

13 The 'blind area' should be checked before

Mark one answer **i** p64

a giving a signal
b applying the brakes
c changing direction
d giving an arm signal

14 It is vital to check the 'blind area' before

Mark one answer **i** p64

a changing gear
b giving signals
c slowing down
d changing lanes

15 Why can it be helpful to have mirrors fitted on each side of your motorcycle ?

Mark one answer **i** p63

a To judge the gap when filtering in traffic
b To give protection when riding in poor weather
c To make your motorcycle appear larger to other drivers
d To give you the best view of the road behind

16 In motorcycling, the term 'lifesaver' refers to

Mark one answer **i** p63

a a final rearward glance
b an approved safety helmet
c a reflective jacket
d the two-second rule

17 You are about to emerge from a junction. Your pillion passenger tells you it's clear. When should you rely on their judgement?

Mark one answer **i** p206

a Never, you should always look for yourself
b When the roads are very busy
c When the roads are very quiet
d Only when they are a qualified rider

18 You are about to emerge from a junction. Your pillion passenger tells you it's safe to go. What should you do?

Mark one answer **i** p206

a Go, if you are sure they can see clearly
b Check for yourself before pulling out
c Take their advice and ride on
d Ask them to check again before you go

19 What must you do before stopping normally?

Mark one answer **i** p64

a Put both feet down
b Select first gear
c Use your mirrors
d Move into neutral

ANSWERS

01 b	06 b	11 c	16 a
02 b	07 c	12 a	17 a
03 d	08 c	13 c	18 b
04 a	09 d	14 d	19 c
05 c	10 d	15 d	

241

20 You want to change lanes in busy, moving traffic. Why could looking over your shoulder help?

Mark two answers **i** p64

a Mirrors may not cover blind spots
b To avoid having to give a signal
c So traffic ahead will make room for you
d So your balance will not be affected
e Drivers behind you would be warned

21 You have been waiting for some time to make a right turn into a side road. What should you do just before you make the turn?

Mark one answer **i** p64

a Move close to the kerb
b Select a higher gear
c Make a 'lifesaver' check
d Wave to the oncoming traffic

22 You are turning right onto a dual carriageway. What should you do before emerging?

Mark one answer **i** p105

a Stop, and then select a very low gear
b Position in the left gutter of the side road
c Check that the central reservation is wide enough
d Check there is enough room for vehicles behind you

23 When riding a different motorcycle you should

Mark one answer **i** p33

a ask someone to ride with you for the first time
b ride as soon as possible as all controls and switches are the same
c leave your gloves behind so switches can be operated more easily
d be sure you know where all controls and switches are

24 Before you make a U-turn in the road, you should

Mark one answer **i** p52

a give an arm signal as well as using your indicators
b signal so that other drivers can slow down for you
c look over your shoulder for a final check
d select a higher gear than normal

25 As you approach this bridge you should

Oncoming vehicles in middle of road

Mark three answers **i** p90

a move into the middle of the road to get a better view
b slow down
c get over the bridge as quickly as possible
d consider using your horn
e find another route
f beware of pedestrians

26 In which of these situations should you avoid overtaking?

Mark one answer **i** p94

a Just after a bend
b In a one-way street
c On a 30mph road
d Approaching a dip in the road

27 This road marking warns

Mark one answer   **i** p94
- **a** drivers to use the hard shoulder
- **b** overtaking drivers there is a bend to the left
- **c** overtaking drivers to move back to the left
- **d** drivers that it is safe to overtake

28 Your mobile phone rings while you are travelling. You should

Mark one answer   **i** p151
- **a** stop immediately
- **b** answer it immediately
- **c** pull up in a suitable place
- **d** pull up at the nearest kerb

29 Why are these yellow lines painted across the road?

Mark one answer   **i** p77
- **a** To help you choose the correct lane
- **b** To help you keep the correct separation distance
- **c** To make you aware of your speed
- **d** To tell you the distance to the roundabout

30 You are approaching traffic lights that have been on green for some time. You should

Mark one answer   **i** p79
- **a** accelerate hard
- **b** maintain your speed
- **c** be ready to stop
- **d** brake hard

31 Which of the following should you do before stopping?

Mark one answer   **i** p64
- **a** Sound the horn
- **b** Use the mirrors
- **c** Select a higher gear
- **d** Flash your headlights

32 When following a large vehicle you should keep well back because this

Mark one answer   **i** p169
- **a** allows you to corner more quickly
- **b** helps the large vehicle to stop more easily
- **c** allows the driver to see you in the mirrors
- **d** helps you to keep out of the wind

ANSWERS

20 a,e	25 b,d,f	30 c
21 c	26 d	31 b
22 c	27 c	32 c
23 d	28 c	
24 c	29 c	

01 You are riding towards a zebra crossing. Pedestrians are waiting to cross. You should

Mark one answer **i** p160

- **a** give way to the elderly and infirm only
- **b** slow down and prepare to stop
- **c** use your headlight to indicate they can cross
- **d** wave at them to cross the road

02 You are riding a motorcycle and following a large vehicle at 40mph. You should position yourself

Mark one answer **i** p169

- **a** close behind to make it easier to overtake the vehicle
- **b** to the left of the road to make it easier to be seen
- **c** close behind the vehicle to keep out of the wind
- **d** well back so that you can see past the vehicle

03 You are riding on a country road. Two horses with riders are in the distance. You should

Mark one answer **i** p163

- **a** continue at your normal speed
- **b** change down the gears quickly
- **c** slow down and be ready to stop
- **d** flash your headlight to warn them

04 You are approaching a red light at a puffin crossing. Pedestrians are on the crossing. The red light will stay on until

Mark one answer **i** p161

- **a** you start to edge forward on to the crossing
- **b** the pedestrians have reached a safe position
- **c** the pedestrians are clear of the front of your motorcycle
- **d** a driver from the opposite direction reaches the crossing

05 You are riding a slow-moving scooter on a narrow winding road. You should

Mark one answer **i** p88

- **a** keep well out to stop vehicles overtaking dangerously
- **b** wave vehicles behind you to pass, if you think they can overtake quickly
- **c** pull in safely when you can, to let vehicles behind you overtake
- **d** give a left signal when it is safe for vehicles to overtake you

06 When riding a motorcycle your normal road position should allow

Mark two answers **i** p83

- **a** other vehicles to overtake on your left
- **b** the driver ahead to see you in their mirrors
- **c** you to prevent vehicles behind from overtaking
- **d** you to be seen by traffic that is emerging from junctions ahead
- **e** you to ride within half a metre (1 foot 8 ins) of the kerb

07 At a pelican crossing the flashing amber light means you MUST

Mark one answer **i** p160

- **a** stop and wait for the green light
- **b** stop and wait for the red light
- **c** give way to pedestrians waiting to cross
- **d** give way to pedestrians already on the crossing

08 You should never wave people across at pedestrian crossings because

Mark one answer *i* p159

- **a** there may be another vehicle coming
- **b** they may not be looking
- **c** it is safer for you to carry on
- **d** they may not be ready to cross

09 'Tailgating' means

Mark one answer *i* p88

- **a** using the rear door of a hatchback car
- **b** reversing into a parking space
- **c** following another vehicle too closely
- **d** driving with rear fog lights on

10 Following this vehicle too closely is unwise because

Mark one answer *i* p169

- **a** your brakes will overheat
- **b** your view ahead is increased
- **c** your engine will overheat
- **d** your view ahead is reduced

11 You are following a vehicle on a wet road. You should leave a time gap of at least

Mark one answer *i* p87

- **a** one second
- **b** two seconds
- **c** three seconds
- **d** four seconds

12 A long, heavily-laden lorry is taking a long time to overtake you. What should you do?

Mark one answer *i* p169

- **a** Speed up
- **b** Slow down
- **c** Hold your speed
- **d** Change direction

13 Which of the following vehicles will use blue flashing beacons?

Mark three answers *i* p177

- **a** Motorway maintenance
- **b** Bomb disposal
- **c** Blood transfusion
- **d** Police patrol
- **e** Breakdown recovery

14 Which THREE of these emergency services might have blue flashing beacons?

Mark three answers *i* p177

- **a** Coastguard
- **b** Bomb disposal
- **c** Gritting lorries
- **d** Animal ambulances
- **e** Mountain rescue
- **f** Doctors' cars

15 When being followed by an ambulance showing a flashing blue beacon you should

Mark one answer *i* p177

- **a** pull over as soon as safely possible to let it pass
- **b** accelerate hard to get away from it
- **c** maintain your speed and course
- **d** brake harshly and immediately stop in the road

ANSWERS

01 b	06 b,d	11 d
02 d	07 d	12 b
03 c	08 a	13 b,c,d
04 b	09 c	14 a,b,e
05 c	10 d	15 a

16 What type of emergency vehicle is fitted with a green flashing beacon?

Mark one answer   *i* p177

- **a** Fire engine
- **b** Road gritter
- **c** Ambulance
- **d** Doctor's car

17 A flashing green beacon on a vehicle means

Mark one answer   *i* p177

- **a** police on non-urgent duties
- **b** doctor on an emergency call
- **c** road safety patrol operating
- **d** gritting in progress

18 Diamond-shaped signs give instructions to

Mark one answer   *i* p173

- **a** tram drivers
- **b** bus drivers
- **c** lorry drivers
- **d** taxi drivers

19 On a road where trams operate, which of these vehicles will be most at risk from the tram rails?

Mark one answer   *i* p173

- **a** Cars
- **b** Cycles
- **c** Buses
- **d** Lorries

20 What should you use your horn for?

Mark one answer   *i* p68

- **a** To alert others to your presence
- **b** To allow you right of way
- **c** To greet other road users
- **d** To signal your annoyance

21 You are in a one-way street and want to turn right. You should position yourself

Mark one answer   *i* p85

- **a** in the right-hand lane
- **b** in the left-hand lane
- **c** in either lane, depending on the traffic
- **d** just left of the centre line

22 You wish to turn right ahead. Why should you take up the correct position in good time?

Mark one answer   *i* p83

- **a** To allow other drivers to pull out in front of you
- **b** To give a better view into the road that you're joining
- **c** To help other road users know what you intend to do
- **d** To allow drivers to pass you on the right

23 At which type of crossing are cyclists allowed to ride across with pedestrians?

Mark one answer   *i* p161

- **a** Toucan
- **b** Puffin
- **c** Pelican
- **d** Zebra

24 You are travelling at the legal speed limit. A vehicle comes up quickly behind, flashing its headlights. You should

Mark one answer   *i* p88

- **a** accelerate to make a gap behind you
- **b** touch the brakes sharply to show your brake lights
- **c** maintain your speed to prevent the vehicle from overtaking
- **d** allow the vehicle to overtake

25 You should ONLY flash your headlights to other road users

Mark one answer **i** p68

- **a** to show that you are giving way
- **b** to show that you are about to turn
- **c** to tell them that you have right of way
- **d** to let them know that you are there

26 You are approaching unmarked crossroads. How should you deal with this type of junction?

Mark one answer **i** p100

- **a** Accelerate and keep to the middle
- **b** Slow down and keep to the right
- **c** Accelerate looking to the left
- **d** Slow down and look both ways

27 You are approaching a pelican crossing. The amber light is flashing. You must

Mark one answer **i** p160

- **a** give way to pedestrians who are crossing
- **b** encourage pedestrians to cross
- **c** not move until the green light appears
- **d** stop even if the crossing is clear

28 The conditions are good and dry. You could use the 'two-second rule'

Mark one answer **i** p87

- **a** before restarting the engine after it has stalled
- **b** to keep a safe gap from the vehicle in front
- **c** before using the 'Mirror-Signal-Manoeuvre' routine
- **d** when emerging on wet roads

29 At a puffin crossing, which colour follows the green signal?

Mark one answer **i** p161

- **a** Steady red
- **b** Flashing amber
- **c** Steady amber
- **d** Flashing green

30 You are in a line of traffic. The driver behind you is following very closely. What action should you take?

Mark one answer **i** p88

- **a** Ignore the following driver and continue to travel within the speed limit
- **b** Slow down, gradually increasing the gap between you and the vehicle in front
- **c** Signal left and wave the following driver past
- **d** Move over to a position just left of the centre line of the road

31 A vehicle has a flashing green beacon. What does this mean?

Mark one answer **i** p177

- **a** A doctor is answering an emergency call
- **b** The vehicle is slow-moving
- **c** It is a motorway police patrol vehicle
- **d** The vehicle is carrying hazardous chemicals

32 A bus has stopped at a bus stop ahead of you. Its right-hand indicator is flashing. You should

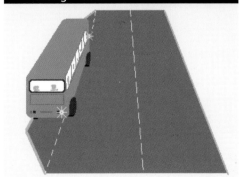

Mark one answer **i** p171

- **a** flash your headlights and slow down
- **b** slow down and give way if it is safe to do so
- **c** sound your horn and keep going
- **d** slow down and then sound your horn

ANSWERS

16 d	21 a	26 d	31 a
17 b	22 c	27 a	32 b
18 a	23 a	28 b	
19 b	24 d	29 c	
20 a	25 d	30 b	

01 A loose drive chain on a motorcycle could cause

Mark one answer `i` p201

- **a** the front wheel to wobble
- **b** the ignition to cut out
- **c** the brakes to fail
- **d** the rear wheel to lock

02 A wrongly adjusted drive chain can

Mark three answers `i` p201

- **a** cause an accident
- **b** make wheels wobble
- **c** create a noisy rattle
- **d** affect gear changing
- **e** cause a suspension fault

03 What is the most important reason why you should keep your motorcycle regularly maintained?

Mark one answer `i` p199

- **a** To accelerate faster than other traffic
- **b** So the motorcycle can carry panniers
- **c** To keep the machine roadworthy
- **d** So the motorcycle can carry a passenger

04 Your motorcycle has tubed tyres fitted as standard. When replacing a tyre you should

Mark one answer `i` p203

- **a** replace the tube if it is 6 months old
- **b** replace the tube if it has covered 6,000 miles
- **c** replace the tube only if replacing the rear tyre
- **d** replace the tube with each change of tyre

05 How should you ride a motorcycle when NEW tyres have just been fitted?

Mark one answer `i` p203

- **a** Carefully, until the shiny surface is worn off
- **b** By braking hard especially into bends
- **c** Through normal riding with higher air pressures
- **d** By riding at faster than normal speeds

06 When riding and wearing brightly coloured clothing you will

Mark one answer `i` p24

- **a** dazzle other motorists on the road
- **b** be seen more easily by other motorists
- **c** create a hazard by distracting other drivers
- **d** be able to ride on unlit roads at night with sidelights

07 You are riding a motorcycle in very hot weather. You should

Mark one answer `i` p26

- **a** ride with your visor fully open
- **b** continue to wear protective clothing
- **c** wear trainers instead of boots
- **d** slacken your helmet strap

08 Why should you wear fluorescent clothing when riding in daylight?

Mark one answer `i` p24

- **a** It reduces wind resistance
- **b** It prevents injury if you come off the machine
- **c** It helps other road users to see you
- **d** It keeps you cool in hot weather

09 Why should riders wear reflective clothing?

Mark one answer `i` p24

- **a** To protect them from the cold
- **b** To protect them from direct sunlight
- **c** To be seen better in daylight
- **d** To be seen better at night

10 Which of the following fairings would give you the best weather protection?

Mark one answer `i` p26

- **a** Handlebar
- **b** Sports
- **c** Touring
- **d** Windscreen

11 Your visor becomes badly scratched. You should

Mark one answer i p24

- **a** polish it with a fine abrasive
- **b** replace it
- **c** wash it in soapy water
- **d** clean it with petrol

12 The legal minimum depth of tread for motorcycle tyres is

Mark one answer i p203

- **a** 1mm
- **b** 1.6mm
- **c** 2.5mm
- **d** 4mm

13 When MUST you use a dipped headlight during the day?

Mark one answer i p181

- **a** On country roads
- **b** In poor visibility
- **c** Along narrow streets
- **d** When parking

14 Which of the following makes it easier for motorcyclists to be seen?

Mark three answers i p214

- **a** Using a dipped headlight
- **b** Wearing a fluorescent jacket
- **c** Wearing a white helmet
- **d** Wearing a grey helmet
- **e** Wearing black leathers
- **f** Using a tinted visor

15 Tyre pressures should be increased on your motorcycle when

Mark one answer i p203

- **a** riding on a wet road
- **b** carrying a pillion passenger
- **c** travelling on an uneven surface
- **d** riding on twisty roads

16 Your oil light comes on as you are riding. You should

Mark one answer i p43

- **a** go to a dealer for an oil change
- **b** go to the nearest garage for their advice
- **c** ride slowly for a few miles to see if the light goes out
- **d** stop as quickly as possible and try to find the cause

17 Motorcycle tyres MUST

Mark two answers i p203

- **a** have the same tread pattern
- **b** be correctly inflated
- **c** be the same size, front and rear
- **d** both be the same make
- **e** have sufficient tread depth

18 Riding your motorcycle with a slack or worn drive chain may cause

Mark one answer

- **a** an engine misfire i p201
- **b** early tyre wear
- **c** increased emissions
- **d** a locked wheel

ANSWERS

01 d	06 b	11 b	16 d
02 a,c,d	07 b	12 a	17 b,e
03 c	08 c	13 b	18 d
04 d	09 d	14 a,b,c	
05 a	10 c	15 b	

19 You forget to switch the choke off after the engine warms up. This could

Mark one answer **i** p34
- **a** flatten the battery
- **b** reduce braking distances
- **c** use less fuel
- **d** cause much more engine wear

20 When riding your motorcycle a tyre bursts. What should you do?

Mark one answer **i** p219
- **a** Slow gently to a stop
- **b** Brake firmly to a stop
- **c** Change to a high gear
- **d** Lower the side stand

21 A motorcycle engine that is properly maintained will

Mark one answer **i** p209
- **a** use much more fuel
- **b** have lower exhaust emissions
- **c** increase your insurance premiums
- **d** not need to have an MoT

22 What should you clean visors and goggles with?

Mark one answer **i** p24
- **a** Petrol
- **b** White spirit
- **c** Antifreeze
- **d** Soapy water

23 You are riding on a quiet road. Your visor fogs up. What should you do?

Mark one answer **i** p24
- **a** Continue at a reduced speed
- **b** Stop as soon as possible and wipe it
- **c** Build up speed to increase air flow
- **d** Close the helmet air vents

24 You are riding in hot weather. What is the safest type of footwear?

Mark one answer **i** p24
- **a** Sandals
- **b** Trainers
- **c** Shoes
- **d** Boots

25 Which of the following should not be used to fasten your safety helmet?

Mark one answer **i** p24
- **a** Double D ring fastening
- **b** Velcro tab
- **c** Quick release fastening
- **d** Bar and buckle

26 After warming up the engine you leave the choke ON. What will this do?

Mark one answer   ℹ️ p34

- **a** Discharge the battery
- **b** Use more fuel
- **c** Improve handling
- **d** Use less fuel

27 You want to ride your motorcycle in the dark. What could you wear to be seen more easily ?

Mark two answers   ℹ️ p24

- **a** A black leather jacket
- **b** Reflective clothing
- **c** A white helmet
- **d** A red helmet

28 Your motorcycle has a catalytic converter. Its purpose is to reduce

Mark one answer   ℹ️ p209

- **a** exhaust noise
- **b** fuel consumption
- **c** exhaust emissions
- **d** engine noise

29 Refitting which of the following will disturb your wheel alignment?

Mark one answer   ℹ️ p202

- **a** front wheel
- **b** front brakes
- **c** rear brakes
- **d** rear wheel

30 After refitting your rear wheel what should you check?

Mark one answer   ℹ️ p202

- **a** Your steering damper
- **b** Your side stand
- **c** Your wheel alignment
- **d** Your suspension preload

31 You are checking your direction indicators. How often per second must they flash?

Mark one answer   ℹ️ p199

- **a** Between 1 and 2 times
- **b** Between 3 and 4 times
- **c** Between 5 and 6 times
- **d** Between 7 and 8 times

32 After adjusting the final drive chain what should you check?

Mark one answer   ℹ️ p201

- **a** The rear wheel alignment
- **b** The suspension adjustment
- **c** The rear shock absorber
- **d** The front suspension forks

33 Your steering feels wobbly. Which of these is a likely cause?

Mark one answer   ℹ️ p201

- **a** Tyre pressure is too high
- **b** Incorrectly adjusted brakes
- **c** Worn steering head bearings
- **d** A broken clutch cable

34 You see oil on your front forks. Should you be concerned about this?

Mark one answer   ℹ️ p201

- **a** No, unless the amount of oil increases
- **b** No, lubrication here is perfectly normal
- **c** Yes, it is illegal to ride with an oil leak
- **d** Yes, oil could drip onto your tyre

ANSWERS

19	d	24	d	29	d	34	d
20	a	25	b	30	c		
21	b	26	b	31	a		
22	d	27	b,c	32	a		
23	b	28	c	33	c		

35 You have a faulty oil seal on a shock absorber. Why is this a serious problem?

Mark one answer *i* p201

a It will cause excessive chain wear
b Dripping oil could reduce the grip of your tyre
c Your motorcycle will be harder to ride uphill
d Your motorcycle will not accelerate so quickly

36 Oil is leaking from your forks. Why should you NOT ride a motorcycle in this condition?

Mark one answer *i* p201

a Your brakes could be affected by dripping oil
b Your steering is likely to seize up
c The forks will quickly begin to rust
d The motorcycle will become too noisy

37 You have adjusted your drive chain. If this is not done properly, what problem could it cause?

Mark one answer *i* p201

a Inaccurate speedometer reading
b Loss of braking power
c Incorrect rear wheel alignment
d Excessive fuel consumption

38 You have adjusted your drive chain. Why is it also important to check rear wheel alignment?

Mark one answer *i* p202

a Your tyre may be more likely to puncture
b Fuel consumption could be greatly increased
c You may not be able to reach top speed
d Your motorcycle could be unstable on bends

39 There is a cut in the sidewall of one of your tyres. What should you do about this?

Mark one answer *i* p203

a Replace the tyre before riding the motorcycle
b Check regularly to see if it gets any worse
c Repair the puncture before riding the motorcycle
d Reduce pressure in the tyre before you ride

40 You need to put air into your tyres. How would you find out the correct pressure to use?

Mark one answer *i* p203

a It will be shown on the tyre wall
b It will be stamped on the wheel
c By checking the vehicle owner's manual
d By checking the registration document

41 You can prevent a cable operated clutch from becoming stiff by keeping the cable

Mark one answer *i* p200

a tight
b dry
c slack
d oiled

42 When adusting your chain it is important for the wheels to be aligned accurately. Incorrect wheel alignment can cause

Mark one answer *i* p202

a a serious loss of power
b reduced braking performance
c increased tyre wear
d reduced ground clearance

43 What problem can incorrectly aligned wheels cause?

Mark one answer *i* p202

a Faulty headlight adjustment
b Reduced braking performance
c Better ground clearance
d Instability when cornering

44 What is most likely to be affected by incorrect wheel alignment?

Mark one answer *i* p202

a Braking performance
b Stability
c Acceleration
d Suspension preload

45 When leaving your motorcycle parked, you should always

Mark one answer *i* p140

a remove the battery lead
b pull it onto the kerb
c use the steering lock
d leave the parking light on

46 Why should you wear specialist motorcycle clothing when riding?

Mark one answer *i* p24

- **a** Because the law requires you to do so
- **b** Because it looks better than ordinary clothing
- **c** Because it gives best protection from the weather
- **d** Because it will reduce your insurance

47 You are parking your motorcycle. Chaining it to an immovable object will

Mark one answer *i* p140

- **a** be against the law
- **b** give extra security
- **c** be likely to cause damage
- **d** leave the motorcycle unstable

48 You are parking your motorcycle and sidecar on a hill. What is the best way to stop it rolling away?

Mark one answer *i* p207

- **a** Leave it in neutral
- **b** Put the rear wheel on the pavement
- **c** Leave it in a low gear
- **d** Park very close to another vehicle

49 You enter a road where there are road humps. What should you do?

Mark one answer *i* p125

- **a** Maintain a reduced speed throughout
- **b** Accelerate quickly between each one
- **c** Always keep to the maximum legal speed
- **d** Ride slowly at school times only

50 When should you especially check the engine oil level?

Mark one answer *i* p202

- **a** Before a long journey
- **b** When the engine is hot
- **c** Early in the morning
- **d** Every 6,000 miles

51 An engine cut-out switch should be used to

Mark one answer *i* p37

- **a** reduce speed in an emergency
- **b** prevent the motorcycle being stolen
- **c** stop the engine normally
- **d** stop the engine in an emergency

52 You service your own motorcycle. How should you get rid of the old engine oil?

Mark one answer *i* p202

- **a** Take it to a local authority site
- **b** Pour it down a drain
- **c** Tip it into a hole in the ground
- **d** Put it into your dustbin

53 You are leaving your motorcycle parked on a road. When may you leave the engine running?

Mark one answer *i* p139

- **a** If you will be parked for less than five minutes
- **b** If the battery is flat
- **c** When in a 20mph zone
- **d** Not on any occasion

ANSWERS

35 b	40 c	45 c	50 a
36 a	41 d	46 c	51 d
37 c	42 c	47 b	52 a
38 d	43 d	48 c	53 d
39 a	44 b	49 a	

54 What safeguard could you take against fire risk to your motorcycle?

Mark one answer **i** p219

- **a** Keep water levels above maximum
- **b** Check out any strong smell of petrol
- **c** Avoid riding with a full tank of petrol
- **d** Use unleaded petrol

55 Which of the following would NOT make you more visible in daylight?

Mark one answer **i** p23

- **a** Wearing a black helmet
- **b** Wearing a white helmet
- **c** Switching on your dipped headlight
- **d** Wearing a fluorescent jacket

56 It would be illegal to ride with a helmet on when

Mark one answer **i** p23

- **a** the helmet is not fastened correctly
- **b** the helmet is more than four years old
- **c** you have borrowed someone else's helmet
- **d** the helmet does not have chin protection

57 When may you have to increase the tyre pressures on your motorcycle?

Mark three answers **i** p203

- **a** When carrying a passenger
- **b** After a long journey
- **c** When carrying a load
- **d** When riding at high speeds
- **e** When riding in hot weather

58 Which TWO of these items on a motorcycle MUST be kept clean?

Mark two answers **i** p203

- **a** Number plate
- **b** Wheels
- **c** Engine
- **d** Fairing
- **e** Headlight

59 You should use the engine cut-out switch on your motorcycle to

Mark one answer **i** p37

- **a** save wear and tear on the battery
- **b** stop the engine for a short time
- **c** stop the engine in an emergency
- **d** save wear and tear on the ignition

60 You have adjusted the tension on your drive chain. You should check the

Mark one answer **i** p201

- **a** rear wheel alignment
- **b** tyre pressures
- **c** valve clearances
- **d** sidelights

61 A friend offers you a second-hand safety helmet for you to use. Why may this be a bad idea?

Mark one answer **i** p23

- **a** It may be damaged
- **b** You will be breaking the law
- **c** You will affect your insurance cover
- **d** It may be a full-face type

62 You are riding a motorcycle of more than 50cc. Which FOUR would make a tyre illegal?

Mark four answers **i** p203

- **a** Tread less than 1.6mm deep
- **b** Tread less than 1mm deep
- **c** A large bulge in the wall
- **d** A recut tread
- **e** Exposed ply or cord
- **f** A stone wedged in the tread

63 You should maintain cable operated brakes

Mark two answers   *i* p200

- **a** by regular adjustment when necessary
- **b** at normal service times only
- **c** yearly, before taking the motorcycle for its MoT
- **d** by oiling cables and pivots regularly

64 A properly serviced motorcycle will give

Mark two answers   *i* p209

- **a** lower insurance premiums
- **b** a refund on your road tax
- **c** better fuel economy
- **d** cleaner exhaust emissions

65 Which TWO are badly affected if the tyres are under-inflated?

Mark two answers   *i* p203

- **a** Braking
- **b** Steering
- **c** Changing gear
- **d** Parking

66 You must NOT sound your horn

Mark one answer   *i* p68

- **a** between 10 pm and 6 am in a built-up area
- **b** at any time in a built-up area
- **c** between 11.30 pm and 7 am in a built-up area
- **d** between 11.30 pm and 6 am on any road

67 The pictured vehicle is 'environmentally friendly' because it

i p172

Mark three answers

- **a** reduces noise pollution
- **b** uses diesel fuel
- **c** uses electricity
- **d** uses unleaded fuel
- **e** reduces parking spaces
- **f** reduces town traffic

68 Supertrams or Light Rapid Transit (LRT) systems are environmentally friendly because

Mark one answer   *i* p172

- **a** they use diesel power
- **b** they use quieter roads
- **c** they use electric power
- **d** they do not operate during rush hour

69 'Red routes' in major cities have been introduced to

Mark one answer   *i* p139

- **a** raise the speed limits
- **b** help the traffic flow
- **c** provide better parking
- **d** allow lorries to load more freely

70 Road humps, chicanes, and narrowings are

Mark one answer   *i* p125

- **a** always at major road works
- **b** used to increase traffic speed
- **c** at toll-bridge approaches only
- **d** traffic calming measures

71 The purpose of a catalytic converter is to reduce

Mark one answer

- **a** fuel consumption   *i* p209
- **b** the risk of fire
- **c** toxic exhaust gases
- **d** engine wear

72 Catalytic converters are fitted to make the

Mark one answer

- **a** engine produce more power   *i* p209
- **b** exhaust system easier to replace
- **c** engine run quietly
- **d** exhaust fumes cleaner

ANSWERS

54 b	60 a	66 c	72 d
55 a	61 a	67 a,c,f	
56 a	62 b,c,d,e	68 c	
57 a,c,d	63 a,d	69 b	
58 a,e	64 c,d	70 d	
59 c	65 a,b	71 c	

73 It is essential that tyre pressures are checked regularly. When should this be done?

Mark one answer **ℹ p203**

- **a** After any lengthy journey
- **b** After travelling at high speed
- **c** When tyres are hot
- **d** When tyres are cold

74 When should you NOT use your horn in a built-up area?

Mark one answer **ℹ p68**

- **a** Between 8 pm and 8 am
- **b** Between 9 pm and dawn
- **c** Between dusk and 8 am
- **d** Between 11.30 pm and 7 am

75 You will use more fuel if your tyres are

Mark one answer **ℹ 203**

- **a** under-inflated
- **b** of different makes
- **c** over-inflated
- **d** new and hardly used

76 How should you dispose of a used battery?

Mark two answers **ℹ p200**

- **a** Take it to a local authority site
- **b** Put it in the dustbin
- **c** Break it up into pieces
- **d** Leave it on waste land
- **e** Take it to a garage
- **f** Burn it on a fire

77 What is most likely to cause high fuel consumption?

Mark one answer **ℹ p209**

- **a** Poor steering control
- **b** Accelerating around bends
- **c** Staying in high gears
- **d** Harsh braking and accelerating

78 The fluid level in your battery is low. What should you top it up with?

Mark one answer **ℹ p200**

- **a** Battery acid
- **b** Distilled water
- **c** Engine oil
- **d** Engine coolant

79 You have too much oil in your engine. What could this cause?

Mark one answer **ℹ p202**

- **a** Low oil pressure
- **b** Engine overheating
- **c** Chain wear
- **d** Oil leaks

80 You are parked on the road at night. Where must you use parking lights?

Mark one answer **ℹ p139**

- **a** Where there are continuous white lines in the middle of the road
- **b** Where the speed limit exceeds 30 mph
- **c** Where you are facing oncoming traffic
- **d** Where you are near a bus stop

81 Which of these, if allowed to get low, could cause an accident?

Mark one answer **ℹ p200**

- **a** Anti-freeze level
- **b** Brake fluid level
- **c** Battery water level
- **d** Radiator coolant level

82 Motor vehicles can harm the environment. This has resulted in

Mark three answers **ℹ p209**

- **a** air pollution
- **b** damage to buildings
- **c** less risk to health
- **d** improved public transport
- **e** less use of electrical vehicles
- **f** using up of natural resources

83 Excessive or uneven tyre wear can be caused by faults in which THREE of the following?

Mark three answers   ℹ p203

- **a** The gearbox
- **b** The braking system
- **c** The accelerator
- **d** The exhaust system
- **e** Wheel alignment
- **f** The suspension

84 You need to top up your battery. What level should you fill to?

Mark one answer   ℹ p200

- **a** The top of the battery
- **b** Half-way up the battery
- **c** Just below the cell plates
- **d** Just above the cell plates

85 You are parking on a two-way road at night. The speed limit is 40mph. You should park on the

Mark one answer   ℹ p139

- **a** left with parking lights on
- **b** left with no lights on
- **c** right with parking lights on
- **d** right with dipped headlights on

86 Before starting a journey it is wise to plan your route. How can you do this?

Mark one answer   ℹ p75

- **a** Look at a map
- **b** Contact your local garage
- **c** Look in your vehicle handbook
- **d** Check your vehicle registration document

87 It can help to plan your route before starting a journey. You can do this by contacting

Mark one answer   ℹ p75

- **a** your local filling station
- **b** a motoring organisation
- **c** the Driver Vehicle Licensing Agency
- **d** your vehicle manufacturer

88 How can you plan your route before starting a long journey?

Mark one answer   ℹ p75

- **a** Check your vehicle's workshop manual
- **b** Ask your local garage
- **c** Use a route planner on the internet
- **d** Consult your travel agents

89 Planning your route before setting out can be helpful. How can you do this?

Mark one answer   ℹ p75

- **a** Look in a motoring magazine
- **b** Only visit places you know
- **c** Try to travel at busy times
- **d** Print or write down the route

90 Why is it a good idea to plan your journey to avoid busy times?

Mark one answer   ℹ p75

- **a** You will have an easier journey
- **b** You will have a more stressful journey
- **c** Your journey time will be longer
- **d** It will cause more traffic congestion

91 Planning your journey to avoid busy times has a number of advantages. One of these is

Mark one answer   ℹ p75

- **a** your journey will take longer
- **b** you will have a more pleasant journey
- **c** you will cause more pollution
- **d** your stress level will be greater

92 It is a good idea to plan your journey to avoid busy times. This is because

Mark one answer   ℹ p75

- **a** your vehicle will use more fuel
- **b** you will see less road works
- **c** it will help to ease congestion
- **d** you will travel a much shorter distance

ANSWERS

73 d	78 b	83 b,e,f	88 c
74 d	79 d	84 d	89 d
75 a	80 b	85 a	90 a
76 a,e	81 b	86 a	91 b
77 d	82 a,b,f	87 b	92 c

93 By avoiding busy times when travelling

Mark one answer **i** p75
- **a** you are more likely to be held up
- **b** your journey time will be longer
- **c** you will travel a much shorter distance
- **d** you are less likely to be delayed

94 It can help to plan your route before starting a journey. Why should you also plan an alternative route?

Mark one answer **i** p75
- **a** Your original route may be blocked
- **b** Your maps may have different scales
- **c** You may find you have to pay a congestion charge
- **d** Because you may get held up by a tractor

95 As well as planning your route before starting a journey, you should also plan an alternative route. Why is this?

Mark one answer **i** p75
- **a** To let another driver overtake
- **b** Your first route may be blocked
- **c** To avoid a railway level crossing
- **d** In case you have to avoid emergency vehicles

96 Who of these will not have to pay Congestion Charges in London?

Mark one answer **i** p125
- **a** A van driver making deliveries
- **b** A rider of a two-wheeled vehicle
- **c** A car driver whose vehicle is more than 1,000 cc
- **d** A driver who just wants to park in the area

97 You are making an appointment and will have to travel a long distance. You should

Mark one answer **i** p75
- **a** allow plenty of time for your journey
- **b** plan to go at busy times
- **c** avoid all national speed limit roads
- **d** prevent other drivers from overtaking

ANSWERS
93 d 96 b
94 a 97 a
95 b

SAFETY MARGINS

01 Your overall stopping distance will be longer when riding

Mark one answer ℹ️ p154
- **a** at night
- **b** in the fog
- **c** with a passenger
- **d** up a hill

02 On a wet road what is the safest way to stop?

Mark one answer ℹ️ p59
- **a** Change gear without braking
- **b** Use the back brake only
- **c** Use the front brake only
- **d** Use both brakes

03 You are riding in heavy rain when your rear wheel skids as you accelerate. To get control again you must

Mark one answer ℹ️ p189
- **a** change down to a lower gear
- **b** ease off the throttle
- **c** brake to reduce speed
- **d** put your feet down

04 It is snowing. Before starting your journey you should

Mark one answer ℹ️ p183
- **a** think if you need to ride at all
- **b** try to avoid taking a passenger
- **c** plan a route avoiding towns
- **d** take a hot drink before setting out

05 Why should you ride with a dipped headlight on in the daytime?

Mark one answer ℹ️ p37
- **a** It helps other road users to see you
- **b** It means that you can ride faster
- **c** Other vehicles will get out of the way
- **d** So that it is already on when it gets dark

06 Motorcyclists are only allowed to use high-intensity rear fog lights when

Mark one answer ℹ️ p186
- **a** a pillion passenger is being carried
- **b** they ride a large touring machine
- **c** visibility is 100 metres (328 feet) or less
- **d** they are riding on the road for the first time

07 When riding at night you should

Mark two answers ℹ️ p181
- **a** ride with your headlight on dipped beam
- **b** wear reflective clothing
- **c** wear a tinted visor
- **d** ride in the centre of the road
- **e** give arm signals

08 You MUST use your headlight

Mark three answers ℹ️ p181
- **a** when riding in a group
- **b** at night when street lighting is poor
- **c** when carrying a passenger
- **d** on motorways during darkness
- **e** at times of poor visibility
- **f** when parked on an unlit road

09 You are riding in town at night. The roads are wet after rain. The reflections from wet surfaces will

Mark one answer ℹ️ p184
- **a** affect your stopping distance
- **b** affect your road holding
- **c** make it easy to see unlit objects
- **d** make it hard to see unlit objects

ANSWERS

01 c	04 a	07 a,b
02 d	05 a	08 b,d,e
03 b	06 c	09 d

10 You are riding through a flood. Which TWO should you do?

Mark two answers **i** p185

- **a** Keep in a high gear and stand up on the footrests
- **b** Keep the engine running fast to keep water out of the exhaust
- **c** Ride slowly and test your brakes when you are out of the water
- **d** Turn your headlight off to avoid any electrical damage

11 You have just ridden through a flood. When clear of the water you should test your

Mark one answer **i** p185

- **a** starter motor
- **b** headlight
- **c** steering
- **d** brakes

12 When going through flood water you should ride

Mark one answer **i** p185

- **a** quickly in a high gear
- **b** slowly in a high gear
- **c** quickly in a low gear
- **d** slowly in a low gear

13 When riding at night you should NOT

Mark one answer **i** p181

- **a** switch on full beam headlights
- **b** overtake slower vehicles in front
- **c** use dipped beam headlights
- **d** use tinted glasses, lenses or visors

14 Which of the following should you do when riding in fog?

Mark two answers **i** p186

- **a** Keep close to the vehicle in front
- **b** Use your dipped headlight
- **c** Ride close to the centre of the road
- **d** Keep your visor or goggles clear
- **e** Keep the vehicle in front in view

15 You are riding in heavy rain. Why should you try to avoid this marked area?

i p119

Mark one answer

- **a** It is illegal to ride over bus stops
- **b** The painted lines may be slippery
- **c** Cyclists may be using the bus stop
- **d** Only emergency vehicles may drive over bus stops

16 When riding at night you should

Mark one answer **i** p24

- **a** wear reflective clothing
- **b** wear a tinted visor
- **c** ride in the middle of the road
- **d** always give arm signals

17 When riding in extremely cold conditions what can you do to keep warm?

Mark one answer **i** p26

- **a** Stay close to the vehicles in front
- **b** Wear suitable clothing
- **c** Lie flat on the tank
- **d** Put one hand on the exhaust pipe

18 You are riding at night. To be seen more easily you should

Mark two answers **i** p24

- **a** ride with your headlight on dipped beam
- **b** wear reflective clothing
- **c** keep the motorcycle clean
- **d** stay well out to the right
- **e** wear waterproof clothing

19 Your overall stopping distance will be much longer when riding

Mark one answer **i** p154

- **a** in the rain
- **b** in fog
- **c** at night
- **d** in strong winds

20 The road surface is very important to motorcyclists. Which FOUR of these are more likely to reduce the stability of your motorcycle?

Mark four answers *i* p119

- **a** Potholes
- **b** Drain covers
- **c** Concrete
- **d** Oil patches
- **e** Tarmac
- **f** Loose gravel

21 You are riding in very hot weather. What are TWO effects that melting tar has on the control of your motorcycle?

Mark two answers *i* p187

- **a** It can make the surface slippery
- **b** It can reduce tyre grip
- **c** It can reduce stopping distances
- **d** It can improve braking efficiency

22 You are riding past queuing traffic. Why should you be more cautious when approaching this road marking?

i p88

KEEP CLEAR

Mark one answer

- **a** Lorries will be unloading here
- **b** School children will be crossing here
- **c** Pedestrians will be standing in the road
- **d** Traffic could be emerging and may not see you

23 What can cause your tyres to skid and lose their grip on the road surface?

Mark one answer *i* p189

- **a** Giving hand signals
- **b** Riding one handed
- **c** Looking over your shoulder
- **d** Heavy braking

24 It has rained after a long dry spell. You should be very careful because the road surface will be unusually

Mark one answer *i* p187

- **a** loose
- **b** dry
- **c** sticky
- **d** slippery

25 When riding in heavy rain a film of water can build up between your tyres and the road surface. This may result in loss of control. What can you do to avoid this happening?

Mark one answer *i* p184

- **a** Keep your speed down
- **b** Increase your tyre pressures
- **c** Decrease your tyre pressures
- **d** Keep trying your brakes

26 When riding in heavy rain a film of water can build up between your tyres and the road. This is known as aquaplaning. What should you do to keep control?

Mark one answer *i* p184

- **a** Use your rear brakes gently
- **b** Steer to the crown of the road
- **c** Ease off the throttle smoothly
- **d** Change up into a higher gear

27 You are on a good, dry road surface and your motorcycle has good brakes and tyres. What is the typical overall stopping distance at 40mph?

Mark one answer *i* p154

- **a** 23 metres (75 feet)
- **b** 36 metres (120 feet)
- **c** 53 metres (175 feet)
- **d** 96 metres (315 feet)

ANSWERS

10 b,c	15 b	20 a,b,d,f	25 a
11 d	16 a	21 a,b	26 c
12 d	17 b	22 d	27 b
13 d	18 a,b	23 d	
14 b,d	19 a	24 d	

28 After riding through deep water you notice your scooter brakes do not work properly. What would be the best way to dry them out?

Mark one answer **i** p185

a Ride slowly, braking lightly
b Ride quickly, braking harshly
c Stop and dry them with a cloth
d Stop and wait for a few minutes

29 You have to ride in foggy weather. You should

Mark two answers **i** p186

a stay close to the centre of the road
b switch only your sidelights on
c switch on your dipped headlights
d be aware of others not using their headlights
e always ride in the gutter to see the kerb

30 Only a fool breaks the two-second rule refers to

Mark one answer **i** p154

a the time recommended when using the choke
b the separation distance when riding in good conditions
c restarting a stalled engine in busy traffic
d the time you should keep your foot down at a junction

31 At a mini roundabout it is important that a motorcyclist should avoid

Mark one answer **i** p115

a turning right
b using signals
c taking 'lifesavers'
d the painted area

32 You are riding on a motorway in a crosswind. You should take extra care when

Mark two answers **i** p187

a approaching service areas
b overtaking a large vehicle
c riding in slow-moving traffic
d approaching an exit
e riding in exposed places

33 Why should you try to avoid riding over this marked area?

i p119

Mark one answer

a It is illegal to ride over bus stops
b It will alter your machine's centre of gravity
c Pedestrians may be waiting at the bus stop
d A bus may have left patches of oil

34 Your overall stopping distance comprises thinking and braking distance. You are on a good, dry road surface with good brakes and tyres. What is the typical BRAKING distance at 50mph?

Mark one answer **i** p154

a 14 metres (46 feet)
b 24 metres (79 feet)
c 38 metres (125 feet)
d 55 metres (180 feet)

35 You are riding at speed through surface water. A thin film of water has built up between your tyres and the road surface. To keep control what should you do?

Mark one answer **i** p184

a Turn the steering quickly
b Use the rear brake gently
c Use both brakes gently
d Ease off the throttle

36 Braking distances on ice can be

Mark one answer **i** p154

a twice the normal distance
b five times the normal distance
c seven times the normal distance
d ten times the normal distance

37 Freezing conditions will affect the distance it takes you to come to a stop. You should expect stopping distances to increase by up to

Mark one answer **i** p154

a two times
b three times
c five times
d ten times

38 In windy conditions you need to take extra care when

Mark one answer **i** p187

- **a** using the brakes
- **b** making a hill start
- **c** turning into a narrow road
- **d** passing pedal cyclists

39 Your indicators may be difficult to see in bright sunlight. What should you do?

Mark one answer **i** p70

- **a** Put your indicator on earlier
- **b** Give an arm signal as well as using your indicator
- **c** Touch the brake several times to show the stop lights
- **d** Turn as quickly as you can

40 When approaching a right-hand bend you should keep well to the left. Why is this?

i p83

Mark one answer

- **a** To improve your view of the road
- **b** To overcome the effect of the road's slope
- **c** To let faster traffic from behind overtake
- **d** To be positioned safely if you skid

41 You should not overtake when

Mark three answers **i** p94

- **a** intending to turn left shortly afterwards
- **b** in a one-way street
- **c** approaching a junction
- **d** going up a long hill
- **e** the view ahead is blocked

42 You have just gone through deep water. To dry off the brakes you should

Mark one answer **i** p185

- **a** accelerate and keep to a high speed for a short time
- **b** go slowly while gently applying the brakes
- **c** avoid using the brakes at all for a few miles
- **d** stop for at least an hour to allow them time to dry

43 In very hot weather the road surface can become soft. Which TWO of the following will be most affected?

Mark two answers **i** p187

- **a** The suspension
- **b** The grip of the tyres
- **c** The braking
- **d** The exhaust

44 Where are you most likely to be affected by a side wind?

Mark one answer **i** p187

- **a** On a narrow country lane
- **b** On an open stretch of road
- **c** On a busy stretch of road
- **d** On a long, straight road

45 In good conditions, what is the typical stopping distance at 70mph?

Mark one answer **i** p154

- **a** 53 metres (175 feet)
- **b** 60 metres (197 feet)
- **c** 73 metres (240 feet)
- **d** 96 metres (315 feet)

46 What is the shortest overall stopping distance on a dry road at 60mph?

Mark one answer **i** p154

- **a** 53 metres (175 feet)
- **b** 58 metres (190 feet)
- **c** 73 metres (240 feet)
- **d** 96 metres (315 feet)

47 You are following a vehicle at a safe distance on a wet road. Another driver overtakes you and pulls into the gap you have left. What should you do?

Mark one answer **i** p88

- **a** Flash your headlights as a warning
- **b** Try to overtake safely as soon as you can
- **c** Drop back to regain a safe distance
- **d** Stay close to the other vehicle until it moves on

ANSWERS

28 a	33 d	38 d	43 b,c
29 c,d	34 c	39 b	44 b
30 b	35 d	40 a	45 d
31 d	36 d	41 a,c,e	46 c
32 b,e	37 d	42 b	47 c

THEORY QUESTIONS

HAZARD AWARENESS

01 You get cold and wet when riding. Which TWO are likely to happen?

Mark two answers   *i* p26

- **a** You may lose concentration
- **b** You may slide off the seat
- **c** Your visor may freeze up
- **d** Your reaction times may be slower
- **e** Your helmet may loosen

02 You are riding up to a zebra crossing. You intend to stop for waiting pedestrians. How could you let them know you are stopping?

Mark one answer   *i* p71

- **a** By signalling with your left arm
- **b** By waving them across
- **c** By flashing your headlight
- **d** By signalling with your right arm

03 You are about to ride home. You cannot find the glasses you need to wear. You should

Mark one answer   *i* p31

- **a** ride home slowly, keeping to quiet roads
- **b** borrow a friend's glasses and use those
- **c** ride home at night, so that the lights will help you
- **d** find a way of getting home without riding

04 Which THREE of these are likely effects of drinking alcohol?

Mark three answers   *i* p30

- **a** Reduced co-ordination
- **b** Increased confidence
- **c** Poor judgement
- **d** Increased concentration
- **e** Faster reactions
- **f** Colour blindness

05 You find that you need glasses to read vehicle number plates at the required distance. When MUST you wear them?

Mark one answer   *i* p31

- **a** Only in bad weather conditions
- **b** At all times when riding
- **c** Only when you think it necessary
- **d** Only in bad light or at night time

06 Drinking any amount of alcohol is likely to

Mark three answers   *i* p30

- **a** slow down your reactions to hazards
- **b** increase the speed of your reactions
- **c** worsen your judgement of speed
- **d** improve your awareness of danger
- **e** give a false sense of confidence

07 Which of the following types of glasses should NOT be worn when riding at night?

Mark one answer   *i* p181

- **a** Half-moon
- **b** Round
- **c** Bi-focal
- **d** Tinted

08 For which of these may you use hazard warning lights?

Mark one answer   *i* p69

- **a** When riding on a motorway to warn traffic behind of a hazard ahead
- **b** When you are double parked on a two way road
- **c** When your direction indicators are not working
- **d** When warning oncoming traffic that you intend to stop

09 When riding how can you help to reduce the risk of hearing damage?

Mark one answer   *i* p24

- **a** Wearing goggles
- **b** Using ear plugs
- **c** Wearing a scarf
- **d** Keeping the visor up

10 When riding long distances at speed, noise can cause fatigue. What can you do to help reduce this?

Mark one answer ***i*** p24
- **a** Vary your speed
- **b** Wear ear plugs
- **c** Use an open-face helmet
- **d** Ride in an upright position

11 Why should you wear ear plugs when riding a motorcycle?

Mark one answer ***i*** p24
- **a** To help to prevent ear damage
- **b** To make you less aware of traffic
- **c** To help to keep you warm
- **d** To make your helmet fit better

12 You are going out to a social event and alcohol will be available. You will be riding your motorcycle shortly afterwards. What is the safest thing to do?

Mark one answer ***i*** p30
- **a** Stay just below the legal limit
- **b** Have soft drinks and alcohol in turn
- **c** Don't go beyond the legal limit
- **d** Stick to non-alcoholic drinks

13 You are convicted of riding after drinking too much alcohol. How could this affect your insurance?

Mark one answer ***i*** p30
- **a** Your insurance may become invalid
- **b** The amount of excess you pay will be reduced
- **c** You will only be able to get third party cover
- **d** Cover will only be given for riding smaller motorcycles

14 Why should you check over your shoulder before turning right into a side road?

Mark one answer ***i*** p64
- **a** To make sure the side road is clear
- **b** To check for emerging traffic
- **c** To check for overtaking vehicles
- **d** To confirm your intention to turn

15 You are not sure if your cough medicine will affect you. What TWO things should you do?

Mark two answers ***i*** p29
- **a** Ask your doctor
- **b** Check the medicine label
- **c** Ride if you feel alright
- **d** Ask a friend or relative for advice

16 When should you use hazard warning lights?

Mark one answer ***i*** p69
- **a** When you are double-parked on a two-way road
- **b** When your direction indicators are not working
- **c** When warning oncoming traffic that you intend to stop
- **d** When your motorcycle has broken down and is causing an obstruction

17 It is a very hot day. What would you expect to find?

Mark one answer ***i*** p187
- **a** Mud on the road
- **b** A soft road surface
- **c** Roadworks ahead
- **d** Banks of fog

18 You see this road marking in between queuing traffic. What should you look out for?

Mark one answer ***i*** p88
- **a** Overhanging trees
- **b** Roadworks
- **c** Traffic wardens
- **d** Traffic emerging

19 Where would you expect to see these markers?

Mark two answers i p169

a On a motorway sign
b At the entrance to a narrow bridge
c On a large goods vehicle
d On a builder's skip placed on the road

20 What does this signal from a police officer, mean to oncoming traffic?

Mark one answer i p71

a Go ahead
b Stop
c Turn left
d Turn right

21 What is the main hazard shown in this picture?

Mark one answer i p144

a Vehicles turning right
b Vehicles doing U-turns
c The cyclist crossing the road
d Parked cars around the corner

22 Which road user has caused a hazard?

Mark one answer i p144

a The parked car (arrowed A)
b The pedestrian waiting to cross (arrowed B)
c The moving car (arrowed C)
d The car turning (arrowed D)

23 What should the driver of the car approaching the crossing do?

Mark one answer i p159

a Continue at the same speed
b Sound the horn
c Drive through quickly
d Slow down and get ready to stop

24 What THREE things should the driver of the grey car (arrowed) be especially aware of?

Mark three answers **i** p144
- **a** Pedestrians stepping out between cars
- **b** Other cars behind the grey car
- **c** Doors opening on parked cars
- **d** The bumpy road surface
- **e** Cars leaving parking spaces
- **f** Empty parking spaces

25 In heavy motorway traffic you are being followed closely by the vehicle behind. How can you lower the risk of an accident?

Mark one answer **i** p88
- **a** Increase your distance from the vehicle in front
- **b** Tap your foot on the brake pedal sharply
- **c** Switch on your hazard lights
- **d** Move onto the hard shoulder and stop

26 You see this sign ahead. You should expect the road to

Mark one answer **i** p120
- **a** go steeply uphill
- **b** go steeply downhill
- **c** bend sharply to the left
- **d** bend sharply to the right

27 You are approaching this cyclist. You should

Mark one answer **i** p167
- **a** overtake before the cyclist gets to the junction
- **b** flash your headlights at the cyclist
- **c** slow down and allow the cyclist to turn
- **d** overtake the cyclist on the left-hand side

28 Why must you take extra care when turning right at this junction?

Mark one answer **i** p104
- **a** Road surface is poor
- **b** Footpaths are narrow
- **c** Road markings are faint
- **d** There is reduced visibility

ANSWERS
19 c,d	22 a	25 a	28 d
20 b	23 d	26 c	
21 c	24 a,c,e	27 c	

29 When approaching this bridge you should give way to

Mark one answer   ℹ️ p169

- **a** bicycles
- **b** buses
- **c** motorcycles
- **d** cars

30 What type of vehicle could you expect to meet in the middle of the road?

Mark one answer   ℹ️ p169

- **a** Lorry
- **b** Bicycle
- **c** Car
- **d** Motorcycle

31 At this blind junction you must stop

Mark one answer   ℹ️ p104

- **a** behind the line, then edge forward to see clearly
- **b** beyond the line at a point where you can see clearly
- **c** only if there is traffic on the main road
- **d** only if you are turning to the right

32 A driver pulls out of a side road in front of you. You have to brake hard. You should

Mark one answer   ℹ️ p217

- **a** ignore the error and stay calm
- **b** flash your lights to show your annoyance
- **c** sound your horn to show your annoyance
- **d** overtake as soon as possible

33 You have just passed these warning lights. What hazard would you expect to see next?

Mark one answer   ℹ️ p145

- **a** A level crossing with no barrier
- **b** An ambulance station
- **c** A school crossing patrol
- **d** An opening bridge

34 An elderly person's driving ability could be affected because they may be unable to

Mark one answer ⓘ p217
- **a** obtain car insurance
- **b** understand road signs
- **c** react very quickly
- **d** give signals correctly

35 Why should you be especially cautious when going past this bus?

Mark two answers ⓘ p171
- **a** There is traffic approaching in the distance
- **b** The driver may open the door
- **c** It may suddenly move off
- **d** People may cross the road in front of it
- **e** There are bicycles parked on the pavement

36 You are planning a long journey. Do you need to plan rest stops?

Mark one answer ⓘ p151
- **a** Yes, you should plan to stop every half an hour
- **b** Yes, regular stops help concentration
- **c** No, you will be less tired if you get there as soon as possible
- **d** No, only fuel stops will be needed

37 A driver does something that upsets you. You should

Mark one answer ⓘ p217
- **a** try not to react
- **b** let them know how you feel
- **c** flash your headlights several times
- **d** sound your horn

38 The red lights are flashing. What should you do when approaching this level crossing?

Mark one answer ⓘ p175
- **a** Go through quickly
- **b** Go through carefully
- **c** Stop before the barrier
- **d** Switch on hazard warning lights

39 You are approaching crossroads. The traffic lights have failed. What should you do?

Mark one answer ⓘ p79
- **a** Brake and stop only for large vehicles
- **b** Brake sharply to a stop before looking
- **c** Be prepared to brake sharply to a stop
- **d** Be prepared to stop for any traffic

40 You are following a slower-moving vehicle on a narrow country road. There is a junction just ahead on the right. What should you do?

Mark one answer ⓘ p94
- **a** Overtake after checking your mirrors and signalling
- **b** Stay behind until you are past the junction
- **c** Accelerate quickly to pass before the junction
- **d** Slow down and prepare to overtake on the left

ANSWERS

29 b	32 a	35 c,d	38 c
30 a	33 c	36 b	39 d
31 a	34 c	37 a	40 b

41 What should the driver of the red car (arrowed) do?

Mark one answer **i** p159

- **a** Wave the pedestrians who are waiting to cross
- **b** Wait for the pedestrian in the road to cross
- **c** Quickly drive behind the pedestrian in the road
- **d** Tell the pedestrian in the road she should not have crossed

42 What should you do as you approach this overhead bridge?

Mark one answer **i** p169

- **a** Move out to the centre of the road before going through
- **b** Find another route, this is only for high vehicles
- **c** Be prepared to give way to large vehicles in the middle of the road
- **d** Move across to the right-hand side before going through

43 Why are mirrors often slightly curved (convex)?

Mark one answer **i** p63

- **a** They give a wider field of vision
- **b** They totally cover blind spots
- **c** They make it easier to judge the speed of following traffic
- **d** They make following traffic look bigger

44 You see this sign on the rear of a slow-moving lorry that you want to pass. It is travelling in the middle lane of a three-lane motorway. You should

Mark one answer **i** p137

- **a** cautiously approach the lorry then pass on either side
- **b** follow the lorry until you can leave the motorway
- **c** wait on the hard shoulder until the lorry has stopped
- **d** approach with care and keep to the left of the lorry

45 You think the driver of the vehicle in front has forgotten to cancel their right indicator. You should

Mark one answer **i** p69

- **a** flash your lights to alert the driver
- **b** sound your horn before overtaking
- **c** overtake on the left if there is room
- **d** stay behind and not overtake

46 What is the main hazard the driver of the red car (arrowed) should be aware of?

Mark one answer **i** p171

- **a** Glare from the sun may affect the driver's vision
- **b** The black car may stop suddenly
- **c** The bus may move out into the road
- **d** Oncoming vehicles will assume the driver is turning right

47 This yellow sign on a vehicle indicates this is

Mark one answer   *i* p171
- **a** a broken-down vehicle
- **b** a school bus
- **c** an ice cream van
- **d** a private ambulance

48 What TWO main hazards should you be aware of when going along this street?

Mark two answers   *i* p144
- **a** Glare from the sun
- **b** Car doors opening suddenly
- **c** Lack of road markings
- **d** The headlights on parked cars being switched on
- **e** Large goods vehicles
- **f** Children running out from between vehicles

49 A driver's behaviour has upset you. It may help if you

Mark one answer   *i* p217
- **a** stop and take a break
- **b** shout abusive language
- **c** gesture to them with your hand
- **d** follow their car, flashing your headlights

50 What is the main hazard you should be aware of when following this cyclist?

Mark one answer   *i* p167
- **a** The cyclist may move to the left and dismount
- **b** The cyclist may swerve out into the road
- **c** The contents of the cyclist's carrier may fall onto the road
- **d** The cyclist may wish to turn right at the end of the road

51 You are on a dual carriageway. Ahead you see a vehicle with an amber flashing light. What will this be?

Mark one answer   *i* p177
- **a** An ambulance
- **b** A fire engine
- **c** A doctor on call
- **d** A disabled person's vehicle

52 In areas where there are 'traffic calming' measures you should

Mark one answer   *i* p125
- **a** travel at a reduced speed
- **b** always travel at the speed limit
- **c** position in the centre of the road
- **d** only slow down if pedestrians are near

ANSWERS

41 b	44 d	47 b	50 b
42 c	45 d	48 b,f	51 d
43 a	46 c	49 a	52 a

53 When approaching this hazard why should you slow down?

Mark two answers   p145
- **a** Because of the bend
- **b** Because it's hard to see to the right
- **c** Because of approaching traffic
- **d** Because of animals crossing
- **e** Because of the level crossing

54 Why are place names painted on the road surface?

Mark one answer **i** p77
- **a** To restrict the flow of traffic
- **b** To warn you of oncoming traffic
- **c** To enable you to change lanes early
- **d** To prevent you changing lanes

55 Some two-way roads are divided into three lanes. Why are these particularly dangerous?

Mark one answer **i** p95
- **a** Traffic in both directions can use the middle lane to overtake
- **b** Traffic can travel faster in poor weather conditions
- **c** Traffic can overtake on the left
- **d** Traffic uses the middle lane for emergencies only

56 To avoid an accident when entering a contraflow system, you should

Mark three answers   p137
- **a** reduce speed in good time
- **b** switch lanes any time to make progress
- **c** choose an appropriate lane early
- **d** keep the correct separation distance
- **e** increase speed to pass through quickly
- **f** follow other motorists closely to avoid long queues

ANSWERS

53 a,e   54 c   55 a   56 a,c,d

272

VULNERABLE ROAD USERS

01 You should not ride too closely behind a lorry because

Mark one answer **i** p169

- **a** you will breathe in the lorry's exhaust fumes
- **b** wind from the lorry will slow you down
- **c** drivers behind you may not be able to see you
- **d** it will reduce your view ahead

02 You are riding along a main road with many side roads. Why should you be particularly careful?

Mark one answer **i** p145

- **a** Gusts of wind from the side roads may push you off course
- **b** Drivers coming out from side roads may not see you
- **c** The road will be more slippery where cars have been turning
- **d** Drivers will be travelling slowly when they approach a junction

03 You are riding on a country lane. You see cattle on the road. You should

Mark three answers **i** p165

- **a** slow down
- **b** stop if necessary
- **c** give plenty of room
- **d** rev your engine
- **e** sound your horn
- **f** ride up close behind them

04 A learner driver has begun to emerge into your path from a side road on the left. You should

Mark one answer **i** p217

- **a** be ready to slow down and stop
- **b** let them emerge then ride close behind
- **c** turn into the side road
- **d** brake hard, then wave them out

05 The vehicle ahead is being driven by a learner. You should

Mark one answer **i** p217

- **a** keep calm and be patient
- **b** ride up close behind
- **c** put your headlight on full beam
- **d** sound your horn and overtake

06 You are riding in fast-flowing traffic. The vehicle behind is following too closely. You should

Mark one answer **i** p88

- **a** slow down gradually to increase the gap in front of you
- **b** slow down as quickly as possible by braking
- **c** accelerate to get away from the vehicle behind you
- **d** apply the brakes sharply to warn the driver behind

07 You are riding towards a zebra crossing. Waiting to cross is a person in a wheelchair. You should

Mark one answer **i** p159

- **a** continue on your way
- **b** wave to the person to cross
- **c** wave to the person to wait
- **d** be prepared to stop

08 Why should you allow extra room when overtaking another motorcyclist on a windy day?

Mark one answer **i** p187

- **a** The rider may turn off suddenly to get out of the wind
- **b** The rider may be blown across in front of you
- **c** The rider may stop suddenly
- **d** The rider may be travelling faster than normal

ANSWERS

01 d	03 a,b,c	05 a	07 d
02 b	04 a	06 a	08 b

09 You have stopped at a pelican crossing. A disabled person is crossing slowly in front of you. The lights have now changed to green. You should

Mark two answers **i** p159

a allow the person to cross
b ride in front of the person
c ride behind the person
d sound your horn
e be patient
f edge forward slowly

10 Where should you take particular care to look out for other motorcyclists and cyclists?

Mark one answer **i** p99

a On dual carriageways
b At junctions
c At zebra crossings
d On one-way streets

11 What is a main cause of accidents among young and new motorcyclists?

Mark one answer **i** p213

a Using borrowed equipment
b Lack of experience and judgement
c Riding in bad weather conditions
d Riding on country roads

12 Young motorcyclists can often be the cause of accidents due to

Mark one answer **i** p213

a being too cautious at junctions
b riding in the middle of their lane
c showing off and being competitive
d riding when the weather is poor

13 Which of the following is applicable to young motorcyclists?

Mark one answer **i** p213

a They are normally better than experienced riders
b They are usually less likely to have accidents
c They are often over-confident of their own ability
d They are more likely to get cheaper insurance

14 Why is it vital for a rider to make a 'lifesaver' check before turning right?

Mark one answer **i** p64

a To check for any overtaking traffic
b To confirm that they are about to turn
c To make sure the side road is clear
d To check that the rear indicator is flashing

15 You are about to overtake horse riders. Which TWO of the following could scare the horses?

Mark two answers **i** p163

a Sounding your horn
b Giving arm signals
c Riding slowly
d Revving your engine

16 The road outside this school is marked with yellow zigzag lines. What do these lines mean?

Mark one answer **i** p125

a You may park on the lines when dropping off school children
b You may park on the lines when picking up school children
c You must not wait or park your motorcycle here
d You must stay with your motorcycle if you park here

17 Which sign means that there may be people walking along the road?

Mark one answer i p161

a

b

c

d

18 You are turning left at a junction. Pedestrians have started to cross the road. You should

Mark one answer i p99

a go on, giving them plenty of room
b stop and wave at them to cross
c blow your horn and proceed
d give way to them

19 You are turning left from a main road into a side road. People are already crossing the road into which you are turning. You should

Mark one answer i p99

a continue, as it is your right of way
b signal to them to continue crossing
c wait and allow them to cross
d sound your horn to warn them of your presence

20 You are at a road junction, turning into a minor road. There are pedestrians crossing the minor road. You should

Mark one answer i p99

a stop and wave the pedestrians across
b sound your horn to let the pedestrians know that you are there
c give way to the pedestrians who are already crossing
d carry on; the pedestrians should give way to you

ANSWERS

09 a,e	12 c	15 a,d	18 d
10 b	13 c	16 c	19 c
11 b	14 a	17 d	20 c

21 You are turning left into a side road. What hazards should you be especially aware of?

Mark one answer **i** p99

- **a** One way street
- **b** Pedestrians
- **c** Traffic congestion
- **d** Parked vehicles

22 You intend to turn right into a side road. Just before turning you should check for motorcyclists who might be

Mark one answer **i** p108

- **a** overtaking on your left
- **b** following you closely
- **c** emerging from the side road
- **d** overtaking on your right

23 A toucan crossing is different from other crossings because

Mark one answer **i** p161

- **a** moped riders can use it
- **b** it is controlled by a traffic warden
- **c** it is controlled by two flashing lights
- **d** cyclists can use it

24 At toucan crossings

Mark two answers **i** p161

- **a** there is no flashing amber light
- **b** cyclists are not permitted
- **c** there is a continuously flashing amber beacon
- **d** pedestrians and cyclists may cross
- **e** you only stop if someone is waiting to cross

25 What does this sign tell you?

Mark one answer **i** p167

- **a** No cycling
- **b** Cycle route ahead
- **c** Route for cycles only
- **d** End of cycle route

26 How will a school crossing patrol signal you to stop?

Mark one answer **i** p161

- **a** By pointing to children on the opposite pavement
- **b** By displaying a red light
- **c** By displaying a stop sign
- **d** By giving you an arm signal

27 Where would you see this sign?

i p171

Mark one answer

- **a** In the window of a car taking children to school
- **b** At the side of the road
- **c** At playground areas
- **d** On the rear of a school bus or coach

28 Which sign tells you that pedestrians may be walking in the road as there is no pavement?

Mark one answer **i** p161

a

b

c

d

29 What does this sign mean?

Mark one answer ℹ️ p167
- **a** No route for pedestrians and cyclists
- **b** A route for pedestrians only
- **c** A route for cyclists only
- **d** A route for pedestrians and cyclists

30 You see a pedestrian with a white stick and red band. This means that the person is

Mark one answer ℹ️ p159
- **a** physically disabled
- **b** deaf only
- **c** blind only
- **d** deaf and blind

31 What action would you take when elderly people are crossing the road?

Mark one answer ℹ️ p159
- **a** Wave them across so they know that you have seen them
- **b** Be patient and allow them to cross in their own time
- **c** Rev the engine to let them know that you are waiting
- **d** Tap the horn in case they are hard of hearing

32 You see two elderly pedestrians about to cross the road ahead. You should

Mark one answer ℹ️ p159
- **a** expect them to wait for you to pass
- **b** speed up to get past them quickly
- **c** stop and wave them across the road
- **d** be careful, they may misjudge your speed

33 You are coming up to a roundabout. A cyclist is signalling to turn right. What should you do?

Mark one answer ℹ️ p167
- **a** Overtake on the right
- **b** Give a horn warning
- **c** Signal the cyclist to move across
- **d** Give the cyclist plenty of room

34 You are approaching this roundabout and see the cyclist signal right. Why is the cyclist keeping to the left?

Mark one answer ℹ️ p167
- **a** It is a quicker route for the cyclist
- **b** The cyclist is going to turn left instead
- **c** The cyclist thinks The Highway Code does not apply to bicycles
- **d** The cyclist is slower and more vulnerable

35 When you are overtaking a cyclist you should leave as much room as you would give to a car. What is the main reason for this?

Mark one answer ℹ️ p167
- **a** The cyclist might change lanes
- **b** The cyclist might get off the bike
- **c** The cyclist might swerve
- **d** The cyclist might have to make a right turn

ANSWERS			
21 b	25 b	29 d	33 d
22 d	26 c	30 d	34 d
23 d	27 d	31 b	35 c
24 a,d	28 a	32 d	

36 Which TWO should you allow extra room when overtaking?

Mark two answers i p94

a Motorcycles
b Tractors
c Bicycles
d Road-sweeping vehicles

37 Why should you look particularly for motorcyclists and cyclists at junctions?

Mark one answer i p99

a They may want to turn into the side road
b They may slow down to let you turn
c They are harder to see
d They might not see you turn

38 You are waiting to come out of a side road. Why should you watch carefully for motorcycles?

Mark one answer i p99

a Motorcycles are usually faster than cars
b Police patrols often use motorcycles
c Motorcycles are small and hard to see
d Motorcycles have right of way

39 In daylight, an approaching motorcyclist is using a dipped headlight. Why?

Mark one answer i p37

a So that the rider can be seen more easily
b To stop the battery overcharging
c To improve the rider's vision
d The rider is inviting you to proceed

40 Motorcyclists should wear bright clothing mainly because

Mark one answer i p24

a they must do so by law
b it helps keep them cool in summer
c the colours are popular
d drivers often do not see them

41 There is a slow-moving motorcyclist ahead of you. You are unsure what the rider is going to do. You should

Mark one answer i p94

a pass on the left
b pass on the right
c stay behind
d move closer

42 Motorcyclists will often look round over their right shoulder just before turning right. This is because

Mark one answer i p63

a they need to listen for following traffic
b motorcycles do not have mirrors
c looking around helps them balance as they turn
d they need to check for traffic in their blind area

43 At road junctions which of the following are most vulnerable?

Mark three answers i p99

a Cyclists
b Motorcyclists
c Pedestrians
d Car drivers
e Lorry drivers

44 Motorcyclists are particularly vulnerable

Mark one answer i p99

a when moving off
b on dual carriageways
c when approaching junctions
d on motorways

45 An injured motorcyclist is lying unconscious in the road. You should

Mark one answer i p222

a remove the safety helmet
b seek medical assistance
c move the person off the road
d remove the leather jacket

46 You are approaching a roundabout. There are horses just ahead of you. You should

Mark two answers **i** p163

- **a** be prepared to stop
- **b** treat them like any other vehicle
- **c** give them plenty of room
- **d** accelerate past as quickly as possible
- **e** sound your horn as a warning

47 Which THREE should you do when passing sheep on a road?

Mark three answers **i** p165

- **a** Allow plenty of room
- **b** Go very slowly
- **c** Pass quickly but quietly
- **d** Be ready to stop
- **e** Briefly sound your horn

48 As you approach a pelican crossing the lights change to green. Elderly people are halfway across. You should

Mark one answer **i** p160

- **a** wave them to cross as quickly as they can
- **b** rev your engine to make them hurry
- **c** flash your lights in case they have not heard you
- **d** wait because they will take longer to cross

49 There are flashing amber lights under a school warning sign. What action should you take?

Mark one answer **i** p161

- **a** Reduce speed until you are clear of the area
- **b** Keep up your speed and sound the horn
- **c** Increase your speed to clear the area quickly
- **d** Wait at the lights until they change to green

50 You are approaching this crossing. You should

Mark one answer **i** p160

- **a** prepare to slow down and stop
- **b** stop and wave the pedestrians across
- **c** speed up and pass by quickly
- **d** drive on unless the pedestrians step out

51 You see a pedestrian with a dog. The dog has a bright orange lead and collar. This especially warns you that the pedestrian is

Mark one answer **i** p159

- **a** elderly
- **b** dog training
- **c** colour blind
- **d** deaf

52 These road markings must be kept clear to allow

Mark one answer **i** p125

- **a** school children to be dropped off
- **b** for teachers to park
- **c** school children to be picked up
- **d** a clear view of the crossing area

ANSWERS

36 a,c	41 c	46 a,c	51 d
37 c	42 d	47 a,b,d	52 d
38 c	43 a,b,c	48 d	
39 a	44 c	49 a	
40 d	45 b	50 a	

53 Where would you see this sign?

i p171

Mark one answer

a Near a school crossing
b At a playground entrance
c On a school bus
d At a 'pedestrians only' area

54 You are following two cyclists. They approach a roundabout in the left-hand lane. In which direction should you expect the cyclists to go?

Mark one answer   *i* p167

a Left
b Right
c Any direction
d Straight ahead

55 You are travelling behind a moped. You want to turn left just ahead. You should

Mark one answer   *i* p107

a overtake the moped before the junction
b pull alongside the moped and stay level until just before the junction
c sound your horn as a warning and pull in front of the moped
d stay behind until the moped has passed the junction

56 Which THREE of the following are hazards motorcyclists present in queues of traffic?

Mark three answers   *i* p88

a Cutting in just in front of you
b Riding in single file
c Passing very close to you
d Riding with their headlight on dipped beam
e Filtering between the lanes

57 You see a horse rider as you approach a roundabout. They are signalling right but keeping well to the left. You should

Mark one answer   *i* p163

a proceed as normal
b keep close to them
c cut in front of them
d stay well back

58 How would you react to drivers who appear to be inexperienced?

Mark one answer   *i* p217

a Sound your horn to warn them of your presence
b Be patient and prepare for them to react more slowly
c Flash your headlights to indicate that it is safe for them to proceed
d Overtake them as soon as possible

59 You are following a learner driver who stalls at a junction. You should

Mark one answer   *i* p217

a be patient as you expect them to make mistakes
b stay very close behind and flash your headlights
c start to rev your engine if they take too long to restart
d immediately steer around them and drive on

60 You are on a country road. What should you expect to see coming towards you on YOUR side of the road?

Mark one answer   *i* p127

a Motorcycles
b Bicycles
c Pedestrians
d Horse riders

61 You are turning left into a side road. Pedestrians are crossing the road near the junction. You must

Mark one answer **i** p99
- **a** wave them on
- **b** sound your horn
- **c** switch on your hazard lights
- **d** wait for them to cross

62 You are following a car driven by an elderly driver. You should

Mark one answer **i** p217
- **a** expect the driver to drive badly
- **b** flash your lights and overtake
- **c** be aware that the driver's reactions may not be as fast as yours
- **d** stay very close behind but be careful

63 You are following a cyclist. You wish to turn left just ahead. You should

Mark one answer **i** p107
- **a** overtake the cyclist before the junction
- **b** pull alongside the cyclist and stay level until after the junction
- **c** hold back until the cyclist has passed the junction
- **d** go around the cyclist on the junction

64 A horse rider is in the left-hand lane approaching a roundabout. You should expect the rider to

Mark one answer **i** p163
- **a** go in any direction
- **b** turn right
- **c** turn left
- **d** go ahead

65 Powered vehicles used by disabled people are small and hard to see. How do they give early warning when on a dual carriageway?

Mark one answer **i** p159
- **a** They will have a flashing red light
- **b** They will have a flashing green light
- **c** They will have a flashing blue light
- **d** They will have a flashing amber light

66 You should never attempt to overtake a cyclist

Mark one answer **i** p107
- **a** just before you turn left
- **b** on a left-hand bend
- **c** on a one-way street
- **d** on a dual carriageway

67 Ahead of you there is a moving vehicle with a flashing amber beacon. This means it is

Mark one answer **i** p177
- **a** slow moving
- **b** broken down
- **c** a doctor's car
- **d** a school crossing patrol

ANSWERS

53 c	57 d	61 d	65 d
54 c	58 b	62 c	66 a
55 d	59 a	63 c	67 a
56 a,c,e	60 c	64 a	

281

68 What does this sign mean?

Mark one answer   **i** p167

a Contraflow pedal cycle lane
b With-flow pedal cycle lane
c Pedal cycles and buses only
d No pedal cycles or buses

69 You notice horse riders in front. What should you do FIRST?

Mark one answer   **i** p163

a Pull out to the middle of the road
b Slow down and be ready to stop
c Accelerate around them
d Signal right

70 At night you see a pedestrian wearing reflective clothing and carrying a bright red light. What does this mean?

Mark one answer   **i** p159

a You are approaching roadworks
b You are approaching an organised walk
c You are approaching a slow-moving vehicle
d You are approaching an accident blackspot

71 You must not stop on these road markings because you may obstruct

Mark one answer   **i** p125

a children's view of the crossing area
b teachers' access to the school
c delivery vehicles' access to the school
d emergency vehicles' access to the school

72 The left-hand pavement is closed due to street repairs. What should you do?

Mark one answer   **i** p137

a Watch out for pedestrians walking in the road
b Use your right-hand mirror more often
c Speed up to get past the roadworks quicker
d Position close to the left-hand kerb

73 You are following a motorcyclist on an uneven road. You should

Mark one answer   **i** p119

a allow less room so you can be seen in their mirrors
b overtake immediately
c allow extra room in case they swerve to avoid potholes
d allow the same room as normal because road surfaces do not affect motorcyclists

74 You have just passed your test. How can you decrease your risk of accidents on the motorway?

Mark one answer   **i** p237

a By keeping up with the car in front
b By never going over 40 mph
c By staying only in the left-hand lane
d By taking further training

ANSWERS

68 b	70 b	72 a	74 d
69 b	71 a	73 c	

OTHER TYPES OF VEHICLE

01 You are riding behind a long vehicle. There is a mini-roundabout ahead. The vehicle is signalling left, but positioned to the right. You should

Mark one answer **i** p169

- **a** sound your horn
- **b** overtake on the left
- **c** keep well back
- **d** flash your headlights

02 Why should you be careful when riding on roads where electric trams operate?

Mark two answers **i** p173

- **a** They cannot steer to avoid you
- **b** They move quickly and quietly
- **c** They are noisy and slow
- **d** They can steer to avoid you
- **e** They give off harmful exhaust fumes

03 The road is wet. Why might a motorcyclist steer round drain covers on a bend?

Mark one answer **i** p119

- **a** To avoid puncturing the tyres on the edge of the drain covers
- **b** To prevent the motorcycle sliding on the metal drain covers
- **c** To help judge the bend using the drain covers as marker points
- **d** To avoid splashing pedestrians on the pavement

04 You are waiting to emerge left from a minor road. A large vehicle is approaching from the right. You have time to turn, but you should wait. Why?

Mark one answer **i** p105

- **a** The large vehicle can easily hide an overtaking vehicle
- **b** The large vehicle can turn suddenly
- **c** The large vehicle is difficult to steer in a straight line
- **d** The large vehicle can easily hide vehicles from the left

05 You are about to overtake a slow-moving motorcyclist. Which one of these signs would make you take special care?

Mark one answer **i** p95

- **a**
- **b**
- **c**
- **d**

06 You are following a long vehicle. It approaches a crossroads and signals left, but moves out to the right. You should

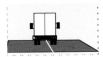

Mark one answer **i** p169

- **a** get closer in order to pass it quickly
- **b** stay well back and give it room
- **c** assume the signal is wrong and it is really turning right
- **d** overtake as it starts to slow down

ANSWERS

01 c	03 b	05 a
02 a,b	04 a	06 b

283

07 You are following a long vehicle approaching a crossroads. The driver signals right but moves close to the left-hand kerb. What should you do?

i p169

Mark one answer

a Warn the driver of the wrong signal
b Wait behind the long vehicle
c Report the driver to the police
d Overtake on the right-hand side

08 You are approaching a mini-roundabout. The long vehicle in front is signalling left but positioned over to the right. You should

i p169

Mark one answer

a sound your horn
b overtake on the left
c follow the same course as the lorry
d keep well back

09 Before overtaking a large vehicle you should keep well back. Why is this?

Mark one answer   *i* p169

a To give acceleration space to overtake quickly on blind bends
b To get the best view of the road ahead
c To leave a gap in case the vehicle stops and rolls back
d To offer other drivers a safe gap if they want to overtake you

10 Why is passing a lorry more risky than passing a car?

Mark one answer   *i* p169

a Lorries are longer than cars
b Lorries may suddenly pull up
c The brakes of lorries are not as good
d Lorries climb hills more slowly

11 You are travelling behind a bus that pulls up at a bus stop. What should you do?

Mark two answers   *i* p171

a Accelerate past the bus sounding your horn
b Watch carefully for pedestrians
c Be ready to give way to the bus
d Pull in closely behind the bus

12 You are following a large lorry on a wet road. Spray makes it difficult to see. You should

i p184

Mark one answer

a drop back until you can see better
b put your headlights on full beam
c keep close to the lorry, away from the spray
d speed up and overtake quickly

13 You are following a large articulated vehicle. It is going to turn left into a narrow road. What action should you take?

i p169

Mark one answer

a Move out and overtake on the right
b Pass on the left as the vehicle moves out
c Be prepared to stop behind
d Overtake quickly before the lorry moves out

14 You keep well back while waiting to overtake a large vehicle. A car fills the gap. You should

Mark one answer   *i* p88

a sound your horn
b drop back further
c flash your headlights
d start to overtake

15 You are following a long lorry. The driver signals to turn left into a narrow road. What should you do?

Mark one answer **i** p169

- **a** Overtake on the left before the lorry reaches the junction
- **b** Overtake on the right as soon as the lorry slows down
- **c** Do not overtake unless you can see there is no oncoming traffic
- **d** Do not overtake, stay well back and be prepared to stop

16 When you approach a bus signalling to move off from a bus stop you should

Mark one answer **i** p171

- **a** get past before it moves
- **b** allow it to pull away, if it is safe to do so
- **c** flash your headlights as you approach
- **d** signal left and wave the bus on

17 You wish to overtake a long, slow-moving vehicle on a busy road. You should

Mark one answer **i** p169

- **a** follow it closely and keep moving out to see the road ahead
- **b** flash your headlights for the oncoming traffic to give way
- **c** stay behind until the driver waves you past
- **d** keep well back until you can see that it is clear

18 Which of these is LEAST likely to be affected by crosswinds?

Mark one answer **i** p187

- **a** Cyclists
- **b** Motorcyclists
- **c** High-sided vehicles
- **d** Cars

19 What should you do as you approach this lorry?

Mark one answer **i** p169

- **a** Slow down and be prepared to wait
- **b** Make the lorry wait for you
- **c** Flash your lights at the lorry
- **d** Move to the right-hand side of the road

20 You are following a large vehicle approaching crossroads. The driver signals to turn left. What should you do?

Mark one answer **i** p169

- **a** Overtake if you can leave plenty of room
- **b** Overtake only if there are no oncoming vehicles
- **c** Do not overtake until the vehicle begins to turn.
- **d** Do not overtake when at or approaching a junction

ANSWERS

07 b	11 b,c	15 d	19 a
08 d	12 a	16 b	20 d
09 b	13 c	17 d	
10 a	14 b	18 d	

15

VEHICLE HANDLING

01 When you are seated on a stationary motorcycle, your position should allow you to

Mark one answer **i** p49

- **a** just touch the ground with your toes
- **b** place both feet on the ground
- **c** operate the centre stand
- **d** reach the switches by stretching

02 As a safety measure before starting your engine, you should

Mark two answers **i** p51

- **a** push the motorcycle forward to check the rear wheel turns freely
- **b** engage first gear and apply the rear brake
- **c** engage first gear and apply the front brake
- **d** glance at the neutral light on your instrument panel

03 When coming to a normal stop on a motorcycle, you should

Mark one answer **i** p53

- **a** only apply the front brake
- **b** rely just on the rear brake
- **c** apply both brakes smoothly
- **d** apply either of the brakes gently

04 You are approaching this junction. As the motorcyclist you should

Mark two answers **i** p144

- **a** prepare to slow down
- **b** sound your horn
- **c** keep near the left kerb
- **d** speed up to clear the junction
- **e** stop, as the car has right of way

05 What can you do to improve your safety on the road as a motorcyclist?

Mark one answer **i** p148

- **a** Anticipate the actions of others
- **b** Stay just above the speed limits
- **c** Keep positioned close to the kerbs
- **d** Remain well below speed limits

06 Which THREE of these can cause skidding?

Mark three answers **i** p189

- **a** Braking too gently
- **b** Leaning too far over when cornering
- **c** Staying upright when cornering
- **d** Braking too hard
- **e** Changing direction suddenly

07 It is very cold and the road looks wet. You cannot hear any road noise. You should

Mark two answers **i** p183

- **a** continue riding at the same speed
- **b** ride slower in as high a gear as possible
- **c** ride in as low a gear as possible
- **d** keep revving your engine
- **e** slow down as there may be black ice

08 When riding a motorcycle you should wear full protective clothing

Mark one answer **i** p24

- **a** at all times
- **b** only on faster, open roads
- **c** just on long journeys
- **d** only during bad weather

09 You have to make a journey in fog. What are the TWO most important things you should do before you set out?

Mark two answers **i** p186

- **a** Fill up with fuel
- **b** Make sure that you have a warm drink with you
- **c** Check that your lights are working
- **d** Check the battery
- **e** Make sure that your visor is clean

10 The best place to park your motorcycle is

Mark one answer   *i* p47
- **a** on soft tarmac
- **b** on bumpy ground
- **c** on grass
- **d** on firm, level ground

11 When riding in windy conditions, you should

Mark one answer   *i* p187
- **a** stay close to large vehicles
- **b** keep your speed up
- **c** keep your speed down
- **d** stay close to the gutter

12 In normal riding your position on the road should be

Mark one answer   *i* p83
- **a** about a foot from the kerb
- **b** about central in your lane
- **c** on the right of your lane
- **d** near the centre of the road

13 Your motorcycle is parked on a two-way road. You should get on from the

Mark one answer   *i* p49
- **a** right and apply the rear brake
- **b** left and leave the brakes alone
- **c** left and apply the front brake
- **d** right and leave the brakes alone

14 To gain basic skills in how to ride a motorcycle you should

Mark one answer   *i* p18
- **a** practise off-road with an approved training body
- **b** ride on the road on the first dry day
- **c** practise off-road in a public park or in a quiet cul-de-sac
- **d** ride on the road as soon as possible

15 You should not ride with your clutch lever pulled in for longer than necessary because it

Mark one answer   *i* p55
- **a** increases wear on the gearbox
- **b** increases petrol consumption
- **c** reduces your control of the motorcycle
- **d** reduces the grip of the tyres

16 You are approaching a road with a surface of loose chippings. What should you do?

Mark one answer   *i* p119
- **a** Ride normally
- **b** Speed up
- **c** Slow down
- **d** Stop suddenly

17 It rains after a long dry, hot spell. This may cause the road surface to

Mark one answer   *i* p187
- **a** be unusually slippery
- **b** give better grip
- **c** become covered in grit
- **d** melt and break up

18 The main causes of a motorcycle skidding are

Mark three answers   *i* p189
- **a** heavy and sharp braking
- **b** excessive acceleration
- **c** leaning too far when cornering
- **d** riding in wet weather
- **e** riding in the winter

ANSWERS

01	b	06	b,d,e	11	c	16	c
02	a,d	07	b,e	12	b	17	a
03	c	08	a	13	c	18	a,b,c
04	a,b	09	c,e	14	a		
05	a	10	d	15	c		

19 To stop your motorcycle quickly in an emergency you should apply

Mark one answer *i* p59

- **a** the rear brake only
- **b** the front brake only
- **c** the front brake just before the rear
- **d** the rear brake just before the front

20 Riding with the side stand down could cause an accident. This is most likely to happen when

Mark one answer *i* p47

- **a** going uphill
- **b** accelerating
- **c** braking
- **d** cornering

21 You leave the choke on for too long. This causes the engine to run too fast. When is this likely to make your motorcycle most difficult to control?

Mark one answer *i* p34

- **a** Accelerating
- **b** Going uphill
- **c** Slowing down
- **d** On motorways

22 You should NOT look down at the front wheel when riding because it can

Mark one answer *i* p52

- **a** make your steering lighter
- **b** improve your balance
- **c** use less fuel
- **d** upset your balance

23 You are entering a bend. Your side stand is not fully raised. This could

Mark one answer *i* p47

- **a** cause an accident
- **b** improve your balance
- **c** alter the motorcycle's centre of gravity
- **d** make the motorcycle more stable

24 In normal riding conditions you should brake

Mark one answer *i* p59

- **a** by using the rear brake first and then the front
- **b** when the motorcycle is being turned or ridden through a bend
- **c** by pulling in the clutch before using the front brake
- **d** when the motorcycle is upright and moving in a straight line

25 Which THREE of the following will affect your stopping distance?

Mark three answers *i* p154

- **a** How fast you are going
- **b** The tyres on your motorcycle
- **c** The time of day
- **d** The weather
- **e** The street lighting

26 You are on a motorway at night. You MUST have your headlights switched on unless

Mark one answer *i* p219

- **a** there are vehicles close in front of you
- **b** you are travelling below 50mph
- **c** the motorway is lit
- **d** your motorcycle is broken down on the hard shoulder

27 You have to park on the road in fog. You should

Mark one answer   **i** p187
- **a** leave parking lights on
- **b** leave no lights on
- **c** leave dipped headlights on
- **d** leave main beam headlights on

28 You ride over broken glass and get a sudden puncture. What should you do?

Mark one answer   **i** p219
- **a** Close the throttle and roll to a stop
- **b** Brake to a stop as quickly as possible
- **c** Release your grip on the handlebars
- **d** Steer from side to side to keep your balance

29 You are riding in wet weather. You see diesel fuel on the road. What should you do?

Mark one answer   **i** p119
- **a** Swerve to avoid the area
- **b** Accelerate through quickly
- **c** Brake sharply to a stop
- **d** Slow down in good time

30 Spilt fuel on the road can be very dangerous for you as a motorcyclist. How can this hazard be seen?

Mark one answer   **i** p119
- **a** By a rainbow pattern on the surface
- **b** By a series of skid marks
- **c** By a pitted road surface
- **d** By a highly polished surface

31 Which FOUR types of road surface increase the risk of skidding for motorcyclists?

Mark four answers   **i** p119
- **a** White lines
- **b** Dry tarmac
- **c** Tar banding
- **d** Yellow grid lines
- **e** Loose chippings

32 You leave the choke on for too long. This could make the engine run faster than normal. This will make your motorcycle

Mark one answer   **i** p34
- **a** handle much better
- **b** corner much safer
- **c** stop much more quickly
- **d** more difficult to control

33 You are riding on a wet road. When braking you should

Mark one answer   **i** p59
- **a** apply the rear brake well before the front
- **b** apply the front brake just before the rear
- **c** avoid using the front brake at all
- **d** avoid using the rear brake at all

34 The road is wet. You are passing a line of queuing traffic and riding on the painted road markings. You should take extra care, particularly when

Mark one answer   **i** p119
- **a** signalling
- **b** braking
- **c** carrying a passenger
- **d** checking your mirrors

ANSWERS

19 c	23 a	27 a	31 a,c,d,e
20 d	24 d	28 a	32 d
21 c	25 a,b,d	29 d	33 b
22 d	26 d	30 a	34 b

35 You are going ahead and will have to cross tram lines. Why should you be especially careful ?

Mark one answer **i** p173

- **a** Tram lines are always 'live'
- **b** Trams will be stopping here
- **c** Pedestrians will be crossing here
- **d** The steel rails can be slippery

36 You have to brake sharply and your motorcycle starts to skid. You should

Mark one answer **i** p189

- **a** continue braking and select a low gear
- **b** apply the brakes harder for better grip
- **c** select neutral and use the front brake only
- **d** release the brakes and reapply

37 You see a rainbow-coloured pattern across the road. What will this warn you of?

Mark one answer **i** p119

- **a** A soft uneven road surface
- **b** A polished road surface
- **c** Fuel spilt on the road
- **d** Water on the road

38 Traction Control Systems (TCS) are fitted to some motorcycles. What does this help to prevent?

Mark one answer **i** p189

- **a** Wheelspin when accelerating
- **b** Skidding when braking too hard
- **c** Uneven front tyre wear
- **d** Uneven rear tyre wear

39 Braking too hard has caused both wheels to skid. What should you do?

Mark one answer **i** p189

- **a** Release both brakes together
- **b** Release the front then the rear brake
- **c** Release the front brake only
- **d** Release the rear brake only

40 In which THREE of these situations may you overtake another vehicle on the left?

Mark three answers **i** p95

- **a** When you are in a one-way street
- **b** When approaching a motorway slip road where you will be turning off
- **c** When the vehicle in front is signalling to turn right
- **d** When a slower vehicle is travelling in the right-hand lane of a dual carriageway
- **e** In slow-moving traffic queues when traffic in the right-hand lane is moving more slowly

41 You are travelling in very heavy rain. Your overall stopping distance is likely to be

Mark one answer **i** p154

- **a** doubled
- **b** halved
- **c** up to ten times greater
- **d** no different

42 Which TWO of the following are correct? When overtaking at night you should

Mark two answers **i** p181

- **a** wait until a bend so that you can see the oncoming headlights
- **b** sound your horn twice before moving out
- **c** be careful because you can see less
- **d** beware of bends in the road ahead
- **e** put headlights on full beam

43 When may you wait in a box junction?

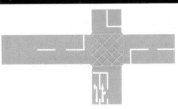

Mark one answer **i** p100

- **a** When you are stationary in a queue of traffic
- **b** When approaching a pelican crossing
- **c** When approaching a zebra crossing
- **d** When oncoming traffic prevents you turning right

44 Which of these plates normally appear with this road sign?

Mark one answer **i** p125

a Humps for ½ mile

b HumpBridge

c Low Bridge

d Soft Verge

45 Traffic calming measures are used to

Mark one answer **i** p125

a stop road rage
b help overtaking
c slow traffic down
d help parking

46 Why should you always reduce your speed when travelling in fog?

Mark one answer **i** p186

a Because the brakes do not work as well
b Because you could be dazzled by other people's fog lights
c Because the engine is colder
d Because it is more difficult to see events ahead

47 You are on a motorway in fog. The left-hand edge of the motorway can be identified by reflective studs. What colour are they?

Mark one answer **i** p186

a Green
b Amber
c Red
d White

48 A rumble device is designed to

Mark two answers **i** p77

a give directions
b prevent cattle escaping
c alert you to low tyre pressure
d alert you to a hazard
e encourage you to reduce speed

49 You are on a narrow road at night. A slower-moving vehicle ahead has been signalling right for some time. What should you do?

Mark one answer **i** p69

a Overtake on the left
b Flash your headlights before overtaking
c Signal right and sound your horn
d Wait for the signal to be cancelled before overtaking

50 Why should you test your brakes after this hazard?

Mark one answer **i** p185

a Because you will be on a slippery road
b Because your brakes will be soaking wet
c Because you will have gone down a long hill
d Because you will have just crossed a long bridge

ANSWERS

35 d	39 a	43 d	47 c
36 d	40 a,c,e	44 a	48 d,e
37 c	41 a	45 c	49 d
38 a	42 c,d	46 d	50 b

51 You have to make a journey in foggy conditions. You should

Mark one answer | *i* p186
- **a** follow other vehicles' tail lights closely
- **b** avoid using dipped headlights
- **c** leave plenty of time for your journey
- **d** keep two seconds behind other vehicles

52 You are overtaking a car at night. You must be sure that

Mark one answer | *i* p181
- **a** you flash your headlights before overtaking
- **b** you select a higher gear
- **c** you have switched your lights to full beam before overtaking
- **d** you do not dazzle other road users

53 You are on a road which has speed humps. A driver in front is travelling slower than you. You should

Mark one answer | *i* p125
- **a** sound your horn
- **b** overtake as soon as you can
- **c** flash your headlights
- **d** slow down and stay behind

54 You are following other vehicles in fog with your lights on. How else can you reduce the chances of being involved in an accident?

Mark one answer | *i* p186
- **a** Keep close to the vehicle in front
- **b** Use your main beam instead of dipped headlights
- **c** Keep together with the faster vehicles
- **d** Reduce your speed and increase the gap

55 You see these markings on the road. Why are they there?

Mark one answer | *i* p77
- **a** To show a safe distance between vehicles
- **b** To keep the area clear of traffic
- **c** To make you aware of your speed
- **d** To warn you to change direction

56 When MUST you use dipped headlights during the day?

Mark one answer | *i* p37
- **a** All the time
- **b** Along narrow streets
- **c** In poor visibility
- **d** When parking

57 Areas reserved for trams may have

Mark three answers | *i* p173
- **a** metal studs around them
- **b** white line markings
- **c** zigzag markings
- **d** a different coloured surface
- **e** yellow hatch markings
- **f** a different surface texture

58 You see a vehicle coming towards you on a single-track road. You should

Mark one answer | *i* p91
- **a** go back to the main road
- **b** do an emergency stop
- **c** stop at a passing place
- **d** put on your hazard warning lights

ANSWERS

51 c	53 d	55 c	57 b,d,f
52 d	54 d	56 c	58 c

01 Why is it particularly important to carry out a check on your motorcycle before making a long motorway journey?

Mark one answer | *i* p133

a You will have to do more harsh braking on motorways
b Motorway service stations do not deal with breakdowns
c The road surface will wear down the tyres faster
d Continuous high speeds may increase the risk of your motorcycle breaking down

02 On a motorway you may ONLY stop on the hard shoulder

Mark one answer | *i* p134

a in an emergency
b If you feel tired and need to rest
c if you go past the exit that you wanted to take
d to pick up a hitchhiker

03 The emergency telephones on a motorway are connected to the

Mark one answer | *i* p219

a ambulance service
b police control
c fire brigade
d breakdown service

04 You are intending to leave the motorway at the next exit. Before you reach the exit you should normally position your motorcycle

Mark one answer | *i* p134

a in the middle lane
b in the left-hand lane
c on the hard shoulder
d in any lane

05 For what reason may you use the right-hand lane of a motorway?

Mark one answer | *i* p133

a For keeping out of the way of lorries
b For riding at more than 70mph
c For turning right
d For overtaking other vehicles

06 You are joining a motorway from a slip road. You should

Mark one answer | *i* p134

a adjust your speed to the speed of the traffic on the motorway
b accelerate as quickly as you can and ride straight out
c ride onto the hard shoulder until a gap appears
d expect drivers on the motorway to give way to you

07 A motorcycle is not allowed on a motorway if it has an engine size smaller than

Mark one answer | *i* p133

a 50cc
b 125cc
c 150cc
d 250cc

08 To ride on a motorway your motorcycle must be

Mark one answer | *i* p133

a 50cc or more
b 100cc or more
c 125cc or more
d 250cc or more

09 On a three-lane motorway why should you normally ride in the left-hand lane?

Mark one answer | *i* p133

a The left-hand lane is only for lorries and motorcycles
b The left-hand lane should only be used by smaller vehicles
c The lanes on the right are for overtaking
d Motorcycles are not allowed in the far right-hand lane

ANSWERS

01 d	04 b	07 a
02 a	05 d	08 a
03 b	06 a	09 c

10 You are riding at 70mph on a three-lane motorway. There is no traffic ahead. Which lane should you use?

Mark one answer **i** p133
- **a** Any lane
- **b** Middle lane
- **c** Right-hand lane
- **d** Left-hand lane

11 You are riding on a motorway. Unless signs show otherwise you must NOT exceed

Mark one answer **i** p153
- **a** 50mph
- **b** 60mph
- **c** 70mph
- **d** 80mph

12 When joining a motorway you must always

Mark one answer **i** p134
- **a** use the hard shoulder
- **b** stop at the end of the acceleration lane
- **c** come to a stop before joining the motorway
- **d** give way to traffic already on the motorway

13 What is the national speed limit for cars and motorcycles in the centre lane of a three-lane motorway?

Mark one answer **i** p153
- **a** 40mph
- **b** 50mph
- **c** 60mph
- **d** 70mph

Mark one answer

14 What is the national speed limit on motorways for cars and motorcycles?

- **a** 30mph **i** p153
- **b** 50mph
- **c** 60mph
- **d** 70mph

15 The left-hand lane on a three-lane motorway is for use by

Mark one answer **i** p133
- **a** any vehicle
- **b** large vehicles only
- **c** emergency vehicles only
- **d** slow vehicles only

16 Which of these IS NOT allowed to travel in the right-hand lane of a three-lane motorway?

Mark one answer **i** p133
- **a** A small delivery van
- **b** A motorcycle
- **c** A vehicle towing a trailer
- **d** A motorcycle and side-car

17 You are travelling on a motorway. You decide you need a rest. You should

Mark two answers **i** p134
- **a** stop on the hard shoulder
- **b** go to a service area
- **c** park on the slip road
- **d** park on the central reservation
- **e** leave at the next exit

18 You break down on a motorway. You need to call for help. Why may it be better to use an emergency roadside telephone rather than a mobile phone?

Mark one answer **i** p219
- **a** It connects you to a local garage
- **b** Using a mobile phone will distract other drivers
- **c** It allows easy location by the emergency services
- **d** Mobile phones do not work on motorways

19 After a breakdown you need to rejoin the main carriageway of a motorway from the hard shoulder. You should

Mark one answer   **i** p219

a move out onto the carriageway then build up your speed

b move out onto the carriageway using your hazard lights

c gain speed on the hard shoulder before moving out onto the carriageway

d wait on the hard shoulder until someone flashes their headlights at you

20 A crawler lane on a motorway is found

Mark one answer   **i** p123

a on a steep gradient

b before a service area

c before a junction

d along the hard shoulder

21 You are driving on a motorway. There are red flashing lights above every lane. You must

Mark one answer   **i** p134

a pull onto the hard shoulder

b slow down and watch for further signals

c leave at the next exit

d stop and wait

22 What do these motorway signs show?

i p135

Mark one answer

a They are countdown markers to a bridge

b They are distance markers to the next telephone

c They are countdown markers to the next exit

d They warn of a police control ahead

23 On a motorway the amber reflective studs can be found between

Mark one answer   **i** p77

a the hard shoulder and the carriageway

b the acceleration lane and the carriageway

c the central reservation and the carriageway

d each pair of the lanes

24 What colour are the reflective studs between the lanes on a motorway?

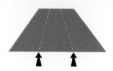

Mark one answer   **i** p77

a Green

b Amber

c White

d Red

25 What colour are the reflective studs between a motorway and its slip road?

Mark one answer   **i** p77

a Amber

b White

c Green

d Red

26 You have broken down on a motorway. To find the nearest emergency telephone you should always walk

Mark one answer   **i** p219

a with the traffic flow

b facing oncoming traffic

c in the direction shown on the marker posts

d in the direction of the nearest exit

ANSWERS

10 d	15 a	20 a	25 c
11 c	16 c	21 d	26 c
12 d	17 b,e	22 c	
13 d	18 c	23 c	
14 d	19 c	24 c	

27 You are joining a motorway. Why is it important to make full use of the slip road?

Mark one answer **ⓘ p134**

- **a** Because there is space available to turn round if you need to
- **b** To allow you direct access to the overtaking lanes
- **c** To build up a speed similar to traffic on the motorway
- **d** Because you can continue on the hard shoulder

28 How should you use the emergency telephone on a motorway?

Mark one answer **ⓘ p219**

- **a** Stay close to the carriageway
- **b** Face the oncoming traffic
- **c** Keep your back to the traffic
- **d** Stand on the hard shoulder

29 You are on a motorway. What colour are the reflective studs on the left of the carriageway?

Mark one answer **ⓘ p77**

- **a** Green
- **b** Red
- **c** White
- **d** Amber

30 On a three-lane motorway which lane should you normally use?

Mark one answer **ⓘ p133**

- **a** Left
- **b** Right
- **c** Centre
- **d** Either the right or centre

31 When going through a contraflow system on a motorway you should

ⓘ p137

Mark one answer

- **a** ensure that you do not exceed 30mph
- **b** keep a good distance from the vehicle ahead
- **c** switch lanes to keep the traffic flowing
- **d** stay close to the vehicle ahead to reduce queues

32 You are on a three-lane motorway. There are red reflective studs on your left and white ones to your right. Where are you?

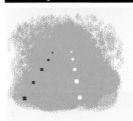

Mark one answer **ⓘ p186**

- **a** In the right-hand lane
- **b** In the middle lane
- **c** On the hard shoulder
- **d** In the left-hand lane

33 When may you stop on a motorway?

Mark three answers **ⓘ p134**

- **a** If you have to read a map
- **b** When you are tired and need a rest
- **c** If red lights show above every lane
- **d** When told to by the police
- **e** If your mobile phone rings
- **f** In an emergency or a breakdown

34 You are approaching roadworks on a motorway. What should you do?

Mark one answer **ⓘ p137**

- **a** Speed up to clear the area quickly
- **b** Always use the hard shoulder
- **c** Obey all speed limits
- **d** Stay very close to the vehicle in front

35 Which FOUR of these must NOT use motorways?

Mark four answers **ⓘ p133**

- **a** Learner car drivers
- **b** Motorcycles over 50cc
- **c** Double-deck buses
- **d** Farm tractors
- **e** Horse riders
- **f** Cyclists

36 Which FOUR of these must NOT use motorways?

Mark four answers   **i** p133

- **a** Learner car drivers
- **b** Motorcycles over 50cc
- **c** Double-deck buses
- **d** Farm tractors
- **e** Learner motorcyclists
- **f** Cyclists

37 Immediately after joining a motorway you should normally

Mark one answer   **i** p134

- **a** try to overtake
- **b** re-adjust your mirrors
- **c** position your vehicle in the centre lane
- **d** keep in the left-hand lane

38 What is the right-hand lane used for on a three-lane motorway?

Mark one answer   **i** p133

- **a** Emergency vehicles only
- **b** Overtaking
- **c** Vehicles towing trailers
- **d** Coaches only

39 What should you use the hard shoulder of a motorway for?

i p219

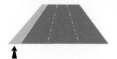

Mark one answer

- **a** Stopping in an emergency
- **b** Leaving the motorway
- **c** Stopping when you are tired
- **d** Joining the motorway

40 You are in the right-hand lane on a motorway. You see these overhead signs. This means

Mark one answer   **i** p135

- **a** move to the left and reduce your speed to 50mph
- **b** there are roadworks 50 metres (55 yards) ahead
- **c** use the hard shoulder until you have passed the hazard
- **d** leave the motorway at the next exit

41 You are allowed to stop on a motorway when you

Mark one answer   **i** p134

- **a** need to walk and get fresh air
- **b** wish to pick up hitchhikers
- **c** are told to do so by flashing red lights
- **d** need to use a mobile telephone

42 You are travelling along the left-hand lane of a three-lane motorway. Traffic is joining from a slip road. You should

Mark one answer   **i** p133

- **a** race the other vehicles
- **b** move to another lane
- **c** maintain a steady speed
- **d** switch on your hazard flashers

43 A basic rule when on motorways is

Mark one answer   **i** p133

- **a** use the lane that has least traffic
- **b** keep to the left-hand lane unless overtaking
- **c** overtake on the side that is clearest
- **d** try to keep above 50mph to prevent congestion

ANSWERS

27 c	32 d	37 d	42 b
28 b	33 c,d,f	38 b	43 b
29 b	34 c	39 a	
30 a	35 a,d,e,f	40 a	
31 b	36 a,d,e,f	41 c	

44 On motorways you should never overtake on the left unless

Mark one answer **i** p95

- **a** you can see well ahead that the hard shoulder is clear
- **b** the traffic in the right-hand lane is signalling right
- **c** you warn drivers behind by signalling left
- **d** there is a queue of slow-moving traffic to your right that is moving more slowly than you are

45 Motorway emergency telephones are usually linked to the police. In some areas they are now linked to

Mark one answer **i** p134

- **a** the Highways Agency Control Centre
- **b** the Driver Vehicle Licensing Agency
- **c** the Driving Standards Agency
- **d** the local Vehicle Registration Office

46 An Emergency Refuge Area is an area

Mark one answer **i** p134

- **a** on a motorway for use in cases of emergency or breakdown
- **b** for use if you think you will be involved in a road rage incident
- **c** on a motorway for a police patrol to park and watch traffic
- **d** for construction and road workers to store emergency equipment

47 What is an Emergency Refuge Area on a motorway for?

Mark one answer **i** p134

- **a** An area to park in when you want to use a mobile phone
- **b** To use in cases of emergency or breakdown
- **c** For an emergency recovery vehicle to park in a contra-flow system
- **d** To drive in when there is queuing traffic ahead

48 Highways Agency Traffic Officers

Mark one answer **i** p134

- **a** will not be able to assist at a breakdown or emergency
- **b** are not able to stop and direct anyone on a motorway
- **c** will tow a broken down vehicle and it's passengers home
- **d** are able to stop and direct anyone on a motorway

49 You are on a motorway. A red cross is displayed above the hard shoulder. What does this mean?

Mark one answer **i** p134

- **a** Pull up in this lane to answer your mobile phone
- **b** Use this lane as a running lane
- **c** This lane can be used if you need a rest
- **d** You should not travel in this lane

50 You are on a motorway in an Active Traffic Management (ATM) area. A mandatory speed limit is displayed above the hard shoulder. What does this mean?

Mark one answer **i** p134

- **a** You should not travel in this lane
- **b** The hard shoulder can be used as a running lane
- **c** You can park on the hard shoulder if you feel tired
- **d** You can pull up in this lane to answer a mobile phone

51 The aim of an Active Traffic Management scheme on a motorway is to

Mark one answer   **i** p134
- **a** prevent overtaking
- **b** reduce rest stops
- **c** prevent tailgating
- **d** reduce congestion

52 You are in an Active Traffic Management area on a motorway. When the Actively Managed mode is operating

Mark one answer   **i** p134
- **a** speed limits are only advisory
- **b** the national speed limit will apply
- **c** the speed limit is always 30mph
- **d** all speed limit signals are set

53 You are travelling on a motorway. A red cross is shown above the hard shoulder and mandatory speed limits above all other lanes. This means

Mark one answer   **i** p134
- **a** the hard shoulder can be used as a rest area if you feel tired
- **b** the hard shoulder is for emergency or breakdown use only
- **c** the hard shoulder can be used as a normal running lane
- **d** the hard shoulder has a speed limit of 50mph

54 Why can it be an advantage for traffic speed to stay constant over a longer distance?

Mark one answer   **i** p134
- **a** You will do more stop-start driving
- **b** You will use far more fuel
- **c** You will be able to use more direct routes
- **d** Your overall journey time will normally improve

55 You are travelling on a motorway. A red cross is shown above the hard shoulder. What does this mean?

Mark one answer   **i** p134
- **a** Use this lane as a rest area
- **b** Use this as a normal running lane
- **c** Do not use this lane to travel in
- **d** National speed limit applies in this lane

56 You see this sign on a motorway. It means you can use

Mark one answer   **i** p134
- **a** any lane except the hard shoulder
- **b** the hard shoulder only
- **c** the three right-hand lanes only
- **d** all the lanes including the hard shoulder

57 You should not normally travel on the hard shoulder of a motorway. When can you use it?

Mark one answer   **i** p134
- **a** When taking the next exit
- **b** When traffic is stopped
- **c** When signs direct you to
- **d** When traffic is slow moving

ANSWERS

44 d	48 d	52 d	56 d
45 a	49 d	53 b	57 c
46 a	50 b	54 d	
47 b	51 d	55 c	

01 You are riding slowly in a town centre. Before turning left you should glance over your left shoulder to

Mark one answer **i** p64

- **a** check for cyclists
- **b** help keep your balance
- **c** look for traffic signs
- **d** check for potholes

02 As a motorcycle rider which TWO lanes must you NOT use?

Mark two answers **i** p85

- **a** Crawler lane
- **b** Overtaking lane
- **c** Acceleration lane
- **d** Cycle lane
- **e** Tram lane

03 You are turning right at a large roundabout. Just before you leave the roundabout you should

Mark one answer **i** p114

- **a** take a 'lifesaver' glance over your left shoulder
- **b** take a 'lifesaver' glance over your right shoulder
- **c** put on your right indicator
- **d** cancel the left indicator

04 What does this sign mean?

Mark one answer **i** p141

- **a** No parking for solo motorcycles
- **b** Parking for solo motorcycles
- **c** Passing place for motorcycles
- **d** Police motorcycles only

05 You are riding on a busy dual carriageway. When changing lanes you should

Mark one answer **i** p64

- **a** rely totally on mirrors
- **b** always increase your speed
- **c** signal so others will give way
- **d** use mirrors and shoulder checks

06 You are looking for somewhere to park your motorcycle. The area is full EXCEPT for spaces marked 'disabled use'. You can

Mark one answer **i** p139

- **a** use these spaces when elsewhere is full
- **b** park if you stay with your motorcycle
- **c** use these spaces, disabled or not
- **d** not park there unless permitted

07 On which THREE occasions MUST you stop your motorcycle?

Mark three answers **i** p221 **i** p79 **i** p177

- **a** When involved in an accident
- **b** At a red traffic light
- **c** When signalled to do so by a police officer
- **d** At a junction with double broken white lines
- **e** At a pelican crossing when the amber light is flashing and no pedestrians are crossing

08 You are on a road with passing places. It is only wide enough for one vehicle. There is a car coming towards you. What should you do?

Mark one answer **i** p91

- **a** Pull into a passing place on your right
- **b** Force the other driver to reverse
- **c** Turn round and ride back to the main road
- **d** Pull into a passing place on your left

09 You are both turning right at this crossroads. It is safer to keep the car to your right so you can

Mark one answer **i** p111

a see approaching traffic
b keep close to the kerb
c keep clear of following traffic
d make oncoming vehicles stop

10 When filtering through slow-moving or stationary traffic you should

Mark three answers **i** p88

a watch for hidden vehicles emerging from side roads
b continually use your horn as a warning
c look for vehicles changing course suddenly
d always ride with your hazard lights on
e stand up on the footrests for a good view ahead
f look for pedestrians walking between vehicles

11 You are riding towards roadworks. The temporary traffic lights are at red. The road ahead is clear. What should you do?

Mark one answer **i** p137

a Ride on with extreme caution
b Ride on at normal speed
c Carry on if approaching cars have stopped
d Wait for the green light

12 You intend to go abroad and will be riding on the right-hand side of the road. What should you fit to your motorcycle?

Mark one answer **i** p195

a Twin headlights
b Headlight deflectors
c Tinted yellow brake lights
d Tinted red indicator lenses

13 You want to tow a trailer with your motorcycle. Your engine must be more than

Mark one answer **i** p207

a 50cc
b 125cc
c 525cc
d 1000cc

14 What is the national speed limit on a single carriageway?

Mark one answer **i** p153

a 40mph
b 50mph
c 60mph
d 70mph

15 What is the meaning of this sign?

Mark one answer **i** p155

a Local speed limit applies
b No waiting on the carriageway
c National speed limit applies
d No entry to vehicular traffic

16 What is the national speed limit on a single carriageway road for cars and motorcycles?

Mark one answer **i** p153

a 70mph
b 60mph
c 50mph
d 30mph

ANSWERS			
01 a	05 d	09 a	13 b
02 d,e	06 d	10 a,c,f	14 c
03 a	07 a,b,c	11 d	15 c
04 b	08 d	12 b	16 b

17 What is the national speed limit for cars and motorcycles on a dual carriageway?

Mark one answer **i** p153
- **a** 30mph
- **b** 50mph
- **c** 60mph
- **d** 70mph

18 There are no speed limit signs on the road. How is a 30 mph limit indicated?

Mark one answer **i** p153
- **a** By hazard warning lines
- **b** By street lighting
- **c** By pedestrian islands
- **d** By double or single yellow lines

19 Where you see street lights but no speed limit signs the limit is usually

Mark one answer **i** p153
- **a** 30mph
- **b** 40mph
- **c** 50mph
- **d** 60mph

20 What does this sign mean?

i p155

Mark one answer
- **a** Minimum speed 30mph
- **b** End of maximum speed
- **c** End of minimum speed
- **d** Maximum speed 30mph

21 There is a tractor ahead of you. You wish to overtake but you are NOT sure if it is safe to do so. You should

Mark one answer **i** p92
- **a** follow another overtaking vehicle through
- **b** sound your horn to the slow vehicle to pull over
- **c** speed through but flash your lights to oncoming traffic
- **d** not overtake if you are in doubt

22 Which three of the following are most likely to take an unusual course at roundabouts?

Mark three answers **i** p113
- **a** Horse riders
- **b** Milk floats
- **c** Delivery vans
- **d** Long vehicles
- **e** Estate cars
- **f** Cyclists

23 On a clearway you must not stop

Mark one answer **i** p139
- **a** at any time
- **b** when it is busy
- **c** in the rush hour
- **d** during daylight hours

24 What is the meaning of this sign?

Mark one answer **i** p141
- **a** No entry
- **b** Waiting restrictions
- **c** National speed limit
- **d** School crossing patrol

25 On a three-lane dual carriageway the right-hand lane can be used for

Mark one answer **i** p129
- **a** overtaking only, never turning right
- **b** overtaking or turning right
- **c** fast-moving traffic only
- **d** turning right only, never overtaking

26 You can park on the right-hand side of a road at night

Mark one answer   p139

- **a** in a one-way street
- **b** with your sidelights on
- **c** more than 10 metres (32 feet) from a junction
- **d** under a lamp-post

27 You are approaching a busy junction. There are several lanes with road markings. At the last moment you realise that you are in the wrong lane. You should

Mark one answer   p84

- **a** continue in that lane
- **b** force your way across
- **c** stop until the area has cleared
- **d** use clear arm signals to cut across

28 Where may you overtake on a one-way street?

Mark one answer *i* p85

- **a** Only on the left-hand side
- **b** Overtaking is not allowed
- **c** Only on the right-hand side
- **d** Either on the right or the left

29 When going straight ahead at a roundabout you should

Mark one answer *i* p114

- **a** indicate left before leaving the roundabout
- **b** not indicate at any time
- **c** indicate right when approaching the roundabout
- **d** indicate left when approaching the roundabout

30 Which vehicle might have to use a different course to normal at roundabouts?

Mark one answer *i* p113

- **a** Sports car
- **b** Van
- **c** Estate car
- **d** Long vehicle

31 You are going straight ahead at a roundabout. How should you signal?

Mark one answer *i* p114

- **a** Signal right on the approach and then left to leave the roundabout
- **b** Signal left as you leave the roundabout
- **c** Signal left on the approach to the roundabout and keep the signal on until you leave
- **d** Signal left just after you pass the exit before the one you will take

32 You may only enter a box junction when

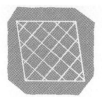

Mark one answer *i* p100

- **a** there are less than two vehicles in front of you
- **b** the traffic lights show green
- **c** your exit road is clear
- **d** you need to turn left

33 You may wait in a yellow box junction when

Mark one answer *i* p100

- **a** oncoming traffic is preventing you from turning right
- **b** you are in a queue of traffic turning left
- **c** you are in a queue of traffic to go ahead
- **d** you are on a roundabout

ANSWERS			
17 d	22 a,d,f	27 a	32 c
18 b	23 a	28 d	33 a
19 a	24 b	29 a	
20 c	25 b	30 d	
21 d	26 a	31 d	

34 You MUST stop when signalled to do so by which THREE of these?

Mark three answers   *i* p70

- **a** A police officer
- **b** A pedestrian
- **c** A school crossing patrol
- **d** A bus driver
- **e** A red traffic light

35 You will see these markers when approaching

Mark one answer   *i* p175

- **a** the end of a motorway
- **b** a concealed level crossing
- **c** a concealed speed limit sign
- **d** the end of a dual carriageway

36 Someone is waiting to cross at a zebra crossing. They are standing on the pavement. You should normally

Mark one answer   *i* p160

- **a** go on quickly before they step onto the crossing
- **b** stop before you reach the zigzag lines and let them cross
- **c** stop, let them cross, wait patiently
- **d** ignore them as they are still on the pavement

37 At toucan crossings, apart from pedestrians you should be aware of

Mark one answer   *i* p161

- **a** emergency vehicles emerging
- **b** buses pulling out
- **c** trams crossing in front
- **d** cyclists riding across

38 Who can use a toucan crossing?

Mark two answers   *i* p161

- **a** Trains
- **b** Cyclists
- **c** Buses
- **d** Pedestrians
- **e** Trams

39 At a pelican crossing, what does a flashing amber light mean?

Mark one answer   *i* p160

- **a** You must not move off until the lights stop flashing
- **b** You must give way to pedestrians still on the crossing
- **c** You can move off, even if pedestrians are still on the crossing
- **d** You must stop because the lights are about to change to red

40 You are waiting at a pelican crossing. The red light changes to flashing amber. This means you must

Mark one answer   *i* p160

- **a** wait for pedestrians on the crossing to clear
- **b** move off immediately without any hesitation
- **c** wait for the green light before moving off
- **d** get ready and go when the continuous amber light shows

41 When can you park on the left opposite these road markings?

Mark one answer   *i* p139

- **a** If the line nearest to you is broken
- **b** When there are no yellow lines
- **c** To pick up or set down passengers
- **d** During daylight hours only

42 You are intending to turn right at a crossroads. An oncoming driver is also turning right. It will normally be safer to

Mark one answer   *i* p111

- **a** keep the other vehicle to your RIGHT and turn behind it (offside to offside)
- **b** keep the other vehicle to your LEFT and turn in front of it (nearside to nearside)
- **c** carry on and turn at the next junction instead
- **d** hold back and wait for the other driver to turn first

43 You are on a road that has no traffic signs. There are street lights. What is the speed limit?

Mark one answer **i** p153
- **a** 20mph
- **b** 30mph
- **c** 40mph
- **d** 60mph

44 You are going along a street with parked vehicles on the left-hand side. For which THREE reasons should you keep your speed down?

Mark three answers **i** p84
- **a** So that oncoming traffic can see you more clearly
- **b** You may set off car alarms
- **c** Vehicles may be pulling out
- **d** Drivers' doors may open
- **e** Children may run out from between the vehicles

45 You meet an obstruction on your side of the road. You should

Mark one answer **i** p91
- **a** carry on, you have priority
- **b** give way to oncoming traffic
- **c** wave oncoming vehicles through
- **d** accelerate to get past first

46 You are on a two-lane dual carriageway. For which TWO of the following would you use the right-hand lane?

Mark two answers **i** p130
- **a** Turning right
- **b** Normal progress
- **c** Staying at the minimum allowed speed
- **d** Constant high speed
- **e** Overtaking slower traffic
- **f** Mending punctures

47 Who has priority at an unmarked crossroads?

Mark one answer **i** p100
- **a** The larger vehicle
- **b** No one has priority
- **c** The faster vehicle
- **d** The smaller vehicle

48 What is the nearest you may park to a junction?

Mark one answer **i** p53
- **a** 10 metres (32 feet)
- **b** 12 metres (39 feet)
- **c** 15 metres (49 feet)
- **d** 20 metres (66 feet)

49 In which THREE places must you NOT park?

Mark three answers **i** p53
- **a** Near the brow of a hill
- **b** At or near a bus stop
- **c** Where there is no pavement
- **d** Within 10 metres (32 feet) of a junction
- **e** On a 40mph road

50 You are waiting at a level crossing. A train has passed but the lights keep flashing. You must

Mark one answer **i** p175
- **a** carry on waiting
- **b** phone the signal operator
- **c** edge over the stop line and look for trains
- **d** park and investigate

51 You park overnight on a road with a 40mph speed limit. You should park

Mark one answer **i** p139
- **a** facing the traffic
- **b** with parking lights on
- **c** with dipped headlights on
- **d** near a street light

ANSWERS

34 a,c,e	39 b	44 c,d,e	49 a,b,d
35 b	40 a	45 b	50 a
36 c	41 c	46 a,e	51 b
37 d	42 a	47 b	
38 b,d	43 b	48 a	

52 At a crossroads there are no signs or road markings. Two vehicles approach. Which has priority?

Mark one answer *i* p100

- **a** Neither of the vehicles
- **b** The vehicle travelling the fastest
- **c** Oncoming vehicles turning right
- **d** Vehicles approaching from the right

53 What does this sign tell you?

Mark one answer *i* p141

- **a** That it is a no-through road
- **b** End of traffic calming zone
- **c** Free parking zone ends
- **d** No waiting zone ends

54 You are entering an area of roadworks. There is a temporary speed limit displayed. You should

Mark one answer *i* p137

- **a** not exceed the speed limit
- **b** obey the limit only during rush hour
- **c** ignore the displayed limit
- **d** obey the limit except at night

55 In which TWO places should you NOT park?

Mark two answers *i* p53

- **a** Near a school entrance
- **b** Near a police station
- **c** In a side road
- **d** At a bus stop
- **e** In a one-way street

56 You are travelling on a well-lit road at night in a built-up area. By using dipped headlights you will be able to

Mark one answer *i* p181

- **a** see further along the road
- **b** go at a much faster speed
- **c** switch to main beam quickly
- **d** be easily seen by others

57 The dual carriageway you are turning right onto has a very narrow central reservation. What should you do?

Mark one answer *i* p105

- **a** Proceed to the central reservation and wait
- **b** Wait until the road is clear in both directions
- **c** Stop in the first lane so that other vehicles give way
- **d** Emerge slightly to show your intentions

ANSWERS

52 a	54 a	56 d
53 d	55 a,d	57 b

01 How should you give an arm signal to turn left?

Mark one answer   p71

 a
 c

b
d

02 You are giving an arm signal ready to turn left. Why should you NOT continue with the arm signal while you turn?

 p71

Mark one answer

a Because you might hit a pedestrian on the corner
b Because you will have less steering control
c Because you will need to keep the clutch applied
d Because other motorists will think that you are stopping on the corner

03 This sign is of particular importance to motorcyclists. It means

 p95

Mark one answer

a side winds
b airport
c slippery road
d service area

04 Which one of these signs are you allowed to ride past on a solo motorcycle?

Mark one answer   p109

a
c

b
d

05 Which of these signals should you give when slowing or stopping your motorcycle

Mark one answer   p71

a
c

b
d

06 When drivers flash their headlights at you it means

Mark one answer   p68

a that there is a radar speed trap ahead
b that they are giving way to you
c that they are warning you of their presence
d that there is something wrong with your motorcycle

ANSWERS

01 c	03 a	05 a
02 b	04 d	06 c

307

07 Why should you make sure that you cancel your indicators after turning?

Mark one answer i p67

a To avoid flattening the battery
b To avoid misleading other road users
c To avoid dazzling other road users
d To avoid damage to the indicator relay

08 Your indicators are difficult to see due to bright sunshine. When using them you should

Mark one answer i p70

a also give an arm signal
b sound your horn
c flash your headlight
d keep both hands on the handlebars

09 You are riding on a motorway. There is a slow-moving vehicle ahead. On the back you see this sign. What should you do?

i p137

Mark one answer

a Pass on the right
b Pass on the left
c Leave at the next exit
d Drive no further

10 Traffic signs giving orders are generally which shape?

Mark one answer i p73

a

c

b

d

11 You MUST obey signs giving orders. These signs are mostly in

Mark one answer i p73

a green rectangles
b red triangles
c blue rectangles
d red circles

12 Which type of sign tells you NOT to do something?

Mark one answer i p73

a

c

b

d

13 What does this sign mean?

i p155

Mark one answer

a Maximum speed limit with traffic calming
b Minimum speed limit with traffic calming
c '20 cars only' parking zone
d Only 20 cars allowed at any one time

14 What does this sign mean?

i p109

Mark one answer

a No overtaking
b No motor vehicles
c Clearway (no stopping)
d Cars and motorcycles only

15 Which sign means no motor vehicles are allowed?

Mark one answer 🛈 p109

a

c

b

d

16 Which of these signs means no motor vehicles?

Mark one answer 🛈 p109

a

c

b

d

17 What does this sign mean?

Mark one answer 🛈 p155
- **a** New speed limit 20mph
- **b** No vehicles over 30 tonnes
- **c** Minimum speed limit 30mph
- **d** End of 20mph zone

18 What does this sign mean?

🛈 p109

Mark one answer
- **a** No parking
- **b** No road markings
- **c** No through road
- **d** No entry

19 What does this sign mean?

🛈 p109

Mark one answer
- **a** Bend to the right
- **b** Road on the right closed
- **c** No traffic from the right
- **d** No right turn

20 Which sign means 'no entry'?

Mark one answer 🛈 p109

a

c

b

d

ANSWERS			
07 b	11 d	15 b	19 d
08 a	12 a	16 a	20 d
09 b	13 a	17 d	
10 d	14 b	18 d	

21 What does this sign mean?

Mark one answer **i** p173
- **a** Route for trams only
- **b** Route for buses only
- **c** Parking for buses only
- **d** Parking for trams only

22 Which type of vehicle does this sign apply to?

Mark one answer **i** p169
- **a** Wide vehicles
- **b** Long vehicles
- **c** High vehicles
- **d** Heavy vehicles

23 Which sign means NO motor vehicles allowed?

Mark one answer **i** p109

a

c

b

d

24 What does this sign mean?

Mark one answer **i** p95
- **a** You have priority
- **b** No motor vehicles
- **c** Two-way traffic
- **d** No overtaking

25 What does this sign mean?

Mark one answer **i** p95
- **a** Keep in one lane
- **b** Give way to oncoming traffic
- **c** Do not overtake
- **d** Form two lanes

26 Which sign means no overtaking?

Mark one answer **i** p95

a

c

b

d

27 What does this sign mean?

Mark one answer   p141

- **a** Waiting restrictions apply
- **b** Waiting permitted
- **c** National speed limit applies
- **d** Clearway (no stopping)

28 What does this sign mean?

Mark one answer   p141

- **a** End of restricted speed area
- **b** End of restricted parking area
- **c** End of clearway
- **d** End of cycle route

29 Which sign means 'no stopping'?

Mark one answer   p141

a   **c**

b   **d**

30 What does this sign mean?

Mark one answer   p141

- **a** Roundabout
- **b** Crossroads
- **c** No stopping
- **d** No entry

31 You see this sign ahead. It means

Mark one answer   p141

- **a** national speed limit applies
- **b** waiting restrictions apply
- **c** no stopping
- **d** no entry

32 What does this sign mean?

Mark one answer   p141

- **a** Distance to parking place ahead
- **b** Distance to public telephone ahead
- **c** Distance to public house ahead
- **d** Distance to passing place ahead

311

33 What does this sign mean?

Mark one answer   **i** p141

a Vehicles may not park on the verge or footway
b Vehicles may park on the left-hand side of the road only
c Vehicles may park fully on the verge or footway
d Vehicles may park on the right-hand side of the road only

34 What does this traffic sign mean?

Mark one answer   **i** p90

a No overtaking allowed
b Give priority to oncoming traffic
c Two way traffic
d One-way traffic only

35 What is the meaning of this traffic sign?

Mark one answer   **i** p90

a End of two-way road
b Give priority to vehicles coming towards you
c You have priority over vehicles coming towards you
d Bus lane ahead

36 What does this sign mean?

Mark one answer   **i** p90

a No overtaking
b You are entering a one-way street
c Two-way traffic ahead
d You have priority over vehicles from the opposite direction

37 What shape is a STOP sign at a junction?

Mark one answer   **i** p73

a   c

b   d

38 At a junction you see this sign partly covered by snow. What does it mean?

Mark one answer   **i** p73

a Cross roads
b Give way
c Stop
d Turn right

ROAD & TRAFFIC SIGNS

39 What does this sign mean?

Mark one answer **ⓘ** p155

- **a** Service area 30 miles ahead
- **b** Maximum speed 30mph
- **c** Minimum speed 30mph
- **d** Lay-by 30 miles ahead

40 Which of these signs means turn left ahead?

Mark one answer **ⓘ** p85

a   **c**

b   **d**

41 What does this sign mean?

Mark one answer **ⓘ** p85

- **a** Give way to oncoming vehicles
- **b** Approaching traffic passes you on both sides
- **c** Turn off at the next available junction
- **d** Pass either side to get to the same destination

42 What does this sign mean?

Mark one answer **ⓘ** p173

- **a** Route for trams
- **b** Give way to trams
- **c** Route for buses
- **d** Give way to buses

43 What does a circular traffic sign with a blue background do?

Mark one answer **ⓘ** p73

- **a** Give warning of a motorway ahead
- **b** Give directions to a car park
- **c** Give motorway information
- **d** Give an instruction

44 Which of these signs means that you are entering a one-way street?

Mark one answer **ⓘ** p85

a   **c**

b   **d**

ANSWERS			
33 c	36 d	39 c	42 a
34 b	37 d	40 b	43 d
35 c	38 c	41 d	44 b

313

45 Where would you see a contraflow bus and cycle lane?

Mark one answer **i** p85
- **a** On a dual carriageway
- **b** On a roundabout
- **c** On an urban motorway
- **d** On a one-way street

46 What does this sign mean?

Mark one answer **i** p171
- **a** Bus station on the right
- **b** Contraflow bus lane
- **c** With-flow bus lane
- **d** Give way to buses

47 What does this sign mean?

Mark one answer **i** p171
- **a** With-flow bus and cycle lane
- **b** Contraflow bus and cycle lane
- **c** No buses and cycles allowed
- **d** No waiting for buses and cycles

48 What does a sign with a brown background show?

Mark one answer **i** p73
- **a** Tourist directions
- **b** Primary roads
- **c** Motorway routes
- **d** Minor routes

49 This sign means

Mark one answer **i** p73
- **a** tourist attraction
- **b** beware of trains
- **c** level crossing
- **d** beware of trams

50 What are triangular signs for?

Mark one answer **i** p73
- **a** To give warnings
- **b** To give information
- **c** To give orders
- **d** To give directions

51 What does this sign mean?

Mark one answer **i** p99
- **a** Turn left ahead
- **b** T-junction
- **c** No through road
- **d** Give way

52 What does this sign mean?

Mark one answer **i** p185
- **a** Multi-exit roundabout
- **b** Risk of ice
- **c** Six roads converge
- **d** Place of historical interest

53 What does this sign mean?

Mark one answer   *i* p99
- **a** Crossroads
- **b** Level crossing with gate
- **c** Level crossing without gate
- **d** Ahead only

54 What does this sign mean?

Mark one answer   *i* p99
- **a** Ring road
- **b** Mini-roundabout
- **c** No vehicles
- **d** Roundabout

55 Which FOUR of these would be indicated by a triangular road sign?

Mark four answers   *i* p73
- **a** Road narrows
- **b** Ahead only
- **c** Low bridge
- **d** Minimum speed
- **e** Children crossing
- **f** T-junction

56 What does this sign mean?

Mark one answer   *i* p167
- **a** Cyclists must dismount
- **b** Cycles are not allowed
- **c** Cycle route ahead
- **d** Cycle in single file

57 Which sign means that pedestrians may be walking along the road?

Mark one answer   *i* p161

a   **c**

b   **d**

58 Which of these signs warn you of a pedestrian crossing?

Mark one answer   *i* p161

a   **c**

b   **d**

ANSWERS			
45 d	49 a	53 a	57 a
46 b	50 a	54 d	58 a
47 a	51 b	55 a,c,e,f	
48 a	52 b	56 c	

59 What does this sign mean?

Mark one answer   **i** p161
- **a** No footpath ahead
- **b** Pedestrians only ahead
- **c** Pedestrian crossing ahead
- **d** School crossing ahead

60 What does this sign mean?

Mark one answer   **i** p161
- **a** School crossing patrol
- **b** No pedestrians allowed
- **c** Pedestrian zone – no vehicles
- **d** Pedestrian crossing ahead

61 Which of these signs means there is a double bend ahead?

Mark one answer   **i** p121

a

c

b

d

62 What does this sign mean?

Mark one answer   **i** p173
- **a** Wait at the barriers
- **b** Wait at the crossroads
- **c** Give way to trams
- **d** Give way to farm vehicles

63 What does this sign mean?

Mark one answer   **i** p124
- **a** Humpback bridge
- **b** Humps in the road
- **c** Entrance to tunnel
- **d** Soft verges

64 What does this sign mean?

Mark one answer   **i** p135
- **a** Low bridge ahead
- **b** Tunnel ahead
- **c** Ancient monument ahead
- **d** Accident black spot ahead

65 What does this sign mean?

Mark one answer   **i** p130
- **a** End of dual carriageway
- **b** Tall bridge
- **c** Road narrows
- **d** End of narrow bridge

66 Which sign means 'two-way traffic crosses a one-way road'?

Mark one answer **i** p85

a

c

b

d

67 Which of these signs means the end of a dual carriageway?

Mark one answer **i** p130

a

c

b

d

68 What does this sign mean?

Mark one answer **i** p95
- **a** Crosswinds
- **b** Road noise
- **c** Airport
- **d** Adverse camber

69 What does this traffic sign mean?

Mark one answer **i** p149
- **a** Slippery road ahead
- **b** Tyres liable to punctures ahead
- **c** Danger ahead
- **d** Service area ahead

70 You are about to overtake when you see this sign. You should

Hidden dip

Mark one answer **i** p95
- **a** overtake the other driver as quickly as possible
- **b** move to the right to get a better view
- **c** switch your headlights on before overtaking
- **d** hold back until you can see clearly ahead

71 What does this sign mean?

Mark one answer **i** p175
- **a** Level crossing with gate or barrier
- **b** Gated road ahead
- **c** Level crossing without gate or barrier
- **d** Cattle grid ahead

ANSWERS

59 c	63 b	67 d	71 a
60 d	64 b	68 a	
61 b	65 a	69 c	
62 c	66 b	70 d	

72 What does this sign mean?

Mark one answer **i** p173
- **a** No trams ahead
- **b** Oncoming trams
- **c** Trams crossing ahead
- **d** Trams only

73 What does this sign mean?

Mark one answer **i** p122
- **a** Adverse camber
- **b** Steep hill downwards
- **c** Uneven road
- **d** Steep hill upwards

74 What does this sign mean?

Mark one answer **i** p185
- **a** Uneven road surface
- **b** Bridge over the road
- **c** Road ahead ends
- **d** Water across the road

75 What does this sign mean?

Mark one answer **i** p109
- **a** Turn left for parking area
- **b** No through road on the left
- **c** No entry for traffic turning left
- **d** Turn left for ferry terminal

76 What does this sign mean?

Mark one answer **i** p109
- **a** T-junction
- **b** No through road
- **c** Telephone box ahead
- **d** Toilet ahead

77 Which sign means 'no through road'?

Mark one answer **i** p109

 a   c

b   d

78 You are driving through a tunnel and you see this sign. What does it mean?

Mark one answer **i** p135
- **a** Direction to emergency pedestrian exit
- **b** Beware of pedestrians, no footpath ahead
- **c** No access for pedestrians
- **d** Beware of pedestrians crossing ahead

79 Which is the sign for a ring road?

Mark one answer **i** p75

a

c

b

d

80 What does this sign mean?

Mark one answer **i** p137

a The right-hand lane ahead is narrow
b Right-hand lane for buses only
c Right-hand lane for turning right
d The right-hand lane is closed

81 What does this sign mean?

Mark one answer **i** p137

a Change to the left lane
b Leave at the next exit
c Contraflow system
d One-way street

82 What does this sign mean?

Mark one answer **i** p123

a Leave motorway at next exit
b Lane for heavy and slow vehicles
c All lorries use the hard shoulder
d Rest area for lorries

83 You are approaching a red traffic light. The signal will change from red to

Mark one answer **i** p79

a red and amber, then green
b green, then amber
c amber, then green
d green and amber, then green

84 A red traffic light means

Mark one answer **i** p79

a you should stop unless turning left
b stop, if you are able to brake safely
c you must stop and wait behind the stop line
d proceed with caution

85 At traffic lights, amber on its own means

Mark one answer **i** p79
- **a** prepare to go
- **b** go if the way is clear
- **c** go if no pedestrians are crossing
- **d** stop at the stop line

86 You are at a junction controlled by traffic lights. When should you NOT proceed at green?

Mark one answer **i** p79
- **a** When pedestrians are waiting to cross
- **b** When your exit from the junction is blocked
- **c** When you think the lights may be about to change
- **d** When you intend to turn right

87 You are in the left-hand lane at traffic lights. You are waiting to turn left. At which of these traffic lights must you NOT move on?

Mark one answer **i** p79

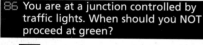

88 What does this sign mean?

Mark one answer **i** p79
- **a** Traffic lights out of order
- **b** Amber signal out of order
- **c** Temporary traffic lights ahead
- **d** New traffic lights ahead

89 When traffic lights are out of order, who has priority?

Mark one answer **i** p79
- **a** Traffic going straight on
- **b** Traffic turning right
- **c** Nobody
- **d** Traffic turning left

90 These flashing red lights mean STOP. In which THREE of the following places could you find them?

Mark three answers **i** p175
- **a** Pelican crossings
- **b** Lifting bridges
- **c** Zebra crossings
- **d** Level crossings
- **e** Motorway exits
- **f** Fire stations

91 What does this road marking mean?

Mark one answer **i** p83
- **a** Do not cross the line
- **b** No stopping allowed
- **c** You are approaching a hazard
- **d** No overtaking allowed

92 What do these zigzag lines at pedestrian crossings mean?

Mark one answer  *i* p159
- **a** No parking at any time
- **b** Parking allowed only for a short time
- **c** Slow down to 20mph
- **d** Sounding horns is not allowed

93 When may you cross a double solid white line in the middle of the road?

Mark one answer *i* p83
- **a** To pass traffic that is queuing back at a junction
- **b** To pass a car signalling to turn left ahead
- **c** To pass a road maintenance vehicle travelling at 10mph or less
- **d** To pass a vehicle that is towing a trailer

94 Where would you see this road marking?

Mark one answer *i* p125
- **a** At traffic lights
- **b** On road humps
- **c** Near a level crossing
- **d** At a box junction

95 Which is a hazard warning line?

Mark one answer *i* p83

 a   c

 b   d

96 At this junction there is a stop sign with a solid white line on the road surface. Why is there a stop sign here?

Mark one answer *i* p100
- **a** Speed on the major road is de-restricted
- **b** It is a busy junction
- **c** Visibility along the major road is restricted
- **d** There are hazard warning lines in the centre of the road

97 You see this line across the road at the entrance to a roundabout. What does it mean?

Mark one answer *i* p101
- **a** Give way to traffic from the right
- **b** Traffic from the left has right of way
- **c** You have right of way
- **d** Stop at the line

ANSWERS

85 d	89 c	93 c	97 a
86 b	90 b,d,f	94 b	
87 a	91 c	95 a	
88 a	92 a	96 c	

98 How will a police officer in a patrol vehicle normally get you to stop?

Mark one answer `i` p177

- **a** Flash the headlights, indicate left and point to the left
- **b** Wait until you stop, then approach you
- **c** Use the siren, overtake, cut in front and stop
- **d** Pull alongside you, use the siren and wave you to stop

99 You approach a junction. The traffic lights are not working. A police officer gives this signal. You should

Mark one answer `i` p71

- **a** turn left only
- **b** turn right only
- **c** stop level with the officer's arm
- **d** stop at the stop line

100 The driver of the car in front is giving this arm signal. What does it mean?

Mark one answer `i` p71

- **a** The driver is slowing down
- **b** The driver intends to turn right
- **c** The driver wishes to overtake
- **d** The driver intends to turn left

101 When may you NOT overtake on the left?

Mark one answer `i` p95

- **a** On a free-flowing motorway or dual carriageway
- **b** When the traffic is moving slowly in queues
- **c** On a one-way street
- **d** When the car in front is signalling to turn right

102 Where would you see these road markings?

Mark one answer `i` p133

- **a** At a level crossing
- **b** On a motorway slip road
- **c** At a pedestrian crossing
- **d** On a single-track road

103 What does this motorway sign mean?

Mark one answer `i` p135

- **a** Change to the lane on your left
- **b** Leave the motorway at the next exit
- **c** Change to the opposite carriageway
- **d** Pull up on the hard shoulder

104 What does this motorway sign mean?

Mark one answer `i` p135

- **a** Temporary minimum speed 50mph
- **b** No services for 50 miles
- **c** Obstruction 50 metres (164 feet) ahead
- **d** Temporary maximum speed 50mph

105 What does this sign mean?

Mark one answer `i` p135

- **a** Through traffic to use left lane
- **b** Right-hand lane T-junction only
- **c** Right-hand lane closed ahead
- **d** 11 tonne weight limit

106 On a motorway this sign means

Mark one answer **ℹ** p135
- **a** move over onto the hard shoulder
- **b** overtaking on the left only
- **c** leave the motorway at the next exit
- **d** move to the lane on your left

What does '25' mean on this motorway sign?

Mark one answer **ℹ** p75
- **a** The distance to the nearest town
- **b** The route number of the road
- **c** The number of the next junction
- **d** The speed limit on the slip road

108 The right-hand lane of a three-lane motorway is

Mark one answer **ℹ** p133
- **a** for lorries only
- **b** an overtaking lane
- **c** the right-turn lane
- **d** an acceleration lane

Where can you find reflective amber studs on a motorway?

Mark one answer **ℹ** p77
- **a** Separating the slip road from the motorway
- **b** On the left-hand edge of the road
- **c** On the right-hand edge of the road
- **d** Separating the lanes

110 Where on a motorway would you find green reflective studs?

Mark one answer **ℹ** p77
- **a** Separating driving lanes
- **b** Between the hard shoulder and the carriageway
- **c** At slip road entrances and exits
- **d** Between the carriageway and the central reservation

111 You are travelling along a motorway. You see this sign. You should

Mark one answer **ℹ** p135
- **a** leave the motorway at the next exit
- **b** turn left immediately
- **c** change lane
- **d** move onto the hard shoulder

112 What does this sign mean?

Mark one answer **ℹ** p135
- **a** No motor vehicles
- **b** End of motorway
- **c** No through road
- **d** End of bus lane

113 Which of these signs means that the national speed limit applies?

Mark one answer **ℹ** p155

a

c

b

d

ANSWERS			
98 a	102 b	106 d	110 c
99 d	103 a	107 c	111 a
100 d	104 d	108 b	112 b
101 a	105 c	109 c	113 d

114 What is the maximum speed on a single carriageway road?

Mark one answer *i* p153
- **a** 50mph
- **b** 60mph
- **c** 40mph
- **d** 70mph

115 What does this sign mean?

Mark one answer *i* p135
- **a** End of motorway
- **b** End of restriction
- **c** Lane ends ahead
- **d** Free recovery ends

116 This sign is advising you to

Mark one answer *i* p75
- **a** follow the route diversion
- **b** follow the signs to the picnic area
- **c** give way to pedestrians
- **d** give way to cyclists

117 Why would this temporary speed limit sign be shown?

Mark one answer *i* p137
- **a** To warn of the end of the motorway
- **b** To warn you of a low bridge
- **c** To warn you of a junction ahead
- **d** To warn of road works ahead

118 This traffic sign means there is

Mark one answer *i* p137
- **a** a compulsory maximum speed limit
- **b** an advisory maximum speed limit
- **c** a compulsory minimum speed limit
- **d** an advised separation distance

119 You see this sign at a crossroads. You should

Mark one answer *i* p79
- **a** maintain the same speed
- **b** carry on with great care
- **c** find another route
- **d** telephone the police

120 You are signalling to turn right in busy traffic. How would you confirm your intention safely?

Mark one answer *i* p70
- **a** Sound the horn
- **b** Give an arm signal
- **c** Flash your headlights
- **d** Position over the centre line

121 What does this sign mean?

Mark one answer *i* p109
- **a** Motorcycles only
- **b** No cars
- **c** Cars only
- **d** No motorcycles

122 You are on a motorway. You see this sign on a lorry that has stopped in the right-hand lane. You should

Mark one answer *i* p137
a move into the right-hand lane
b stop behind the flashing lights
c pass the lorry on the left
d leave the motorway at the next exit

123 You are on a motorway. Red flashing lights appear above your lane only. What should you do?

Mark one answer *i* p135
a Continue in that lane and look for further information
b Move into another lane in good time
c Pull onto the hard shoulder
d Stop and wait for an instruction to proceed

124 A red traffic light means

Mark one answer *i* p79
a you must stop behind the white stop line
b you may go straight on if there is no other traffic
c you may turn left if it is safe to do so
d you must slow down and prepare to stop if traffic has started to cross

125 The driver of this car is giving an arm signal. What are they about to do?

Mark one answer *i* p71
a Turn to the right
b Turn to the left
c Go straight ahead
d Let pedestrians cross

126 Which arm signal tells you that the car you are following is going to turn left?

Mark one answer *i* p71

a   **c**

b   **d**

127 When may you sound the horn?

Mark one answer *i* p68
a To give you right of way
b To attract a friend's attention
c To warn others of your presence
d To make slower drivers move over

128 You must not use your horn when you are stationary

Mark one answer *i* p68
a unless a moving vehicle may cause you danger
b at any time whatsoever
c unless it is used only briefly
d except for signalling that you have just arrived

129 What does this sign mean?

Mark one answer *i* p141
a You can park on the days and times shown
b No parking on the days and times shown
c No parking at all from Monday to Friday
d End of the urban clearway restrictions

ANSWERS

114 b	118 a	122 c	126 a
115 b	119 b	123 b	127 c
116 a	120 b	124 a	128 a
117 d	121 d	125 b	129 b

130 What does this sign mean?

Mark one answer   **i** p127

- **a** Quayside or river bank
- **b** Steep hill downwards
- **c** Uneven road surface
- **d** Road liable to flooding

131 Which sign means you have priority over oncoming vehicles?

Mark one answer   **i** p91

a

c

b

d

132 A white line like this along the centre of the road is a

Mark one answer   **i** p83

- **a** bus lane marking
- **b** hazard warning
- **c** give way marking
- **d** lane marking

133 What is the reason for the yellow criss-cross lines painted on the road here?

Mark one answer   **i** p100

- **a** To mark out an area for trams only
- **b** To prevent queuing traffic from blocking the junction on the left
- **c** To mark the entrance lane to a car park
- **d** To warn you of the tram lines crossing the road

134 What is the reason for the area marked in red and white along the centre of this road?

Mark one answer   **i** p83

- **a** It is to separate traffic flowing in opposite directions
- **b** It marks an area to be used by overtaking motorcyclists
- **c** It is a temporary marking to warn of the roadworks
- **d** It is separating the two sides of the dual carriageway

135 Other drivers may sometimes flash their headlights at you. In which situation are they allowed to do this?

Mark one answer   **i** p68

- **a** To warn of a radar speed trap ahead
- **b** To show that they are giving way to you
- **c** To warn you of their presence
- **d** To let you know there is a fault with your vehicle

136 There is a police car following you. The police officer flashes the headlights and points to the left. What should you do?

Mark one answer *i* p177

- **a** Turn left at the next junction
- **b** Pull up on the left
- **c** Stop immediately
- **d** Move over to the left

137 You see this amber traffic light ahead. Which light or lights, will come on next?

Mark one answer *i* p79

- **a** Red alone
- **b** Red and amber together
- **c** Green and amber together
- **d** Green alone

138 At roadworks which of the following can control traffic flow?

Mark three answers *i* p137

- **a** A STOP–GO board
- **b** Flashing amber lights
- **c** A police officer
- **d** Flashing red lights
- **e** Temporary traffic lights

139 In some narrow residential streets you may find a speed limit of

Mark one answer *i* p125

- **a** 20mph
- **b** 25mph
- **c** 35mph
- **d** 40mph

140 At a junction you see this signal. It means

Mark one answer *i* p173

- **a** cars must stop
- **b** trams must stop
- **c** both trams and cars must stop
- **d** both trams and cars can continue

141 Where would you find these road markings?

Mark one answer *i* p112

- **a** At a railway crossing
- **b** At a junction
- **c** On a motorway
- **d** On a pedestrian crossing

142 This broken white line painted in the centre of the road means

Mark one answer *i* p83

- **a** oncoming vehicles have priority over you
- **b** you should give priority to oncoming vehicles
- **c** there is a hazard ahead of you
- **d** the area is a national speed limit zone

143 You see this signal overhead on the motorway. What does it mean?

Mark one answer *i* p135

- **a** Leave the motorway at the next exit
- **b** All vehicles use the hard shoulder
- **c** Sharp bend to the left ahead
- **d** Stop, all lanes ahead closed

ANSWERS

130 a	134 a	138 a,c,e	142 c
131 c	135 c	139 a	143 a
132 b	136 b	140 b	
133 b	137 a	141 b	

144 What is the purpose of these yellow criss-cross lines on the road?

Mark one answer **i** p100

- **a** To make you more aware of the traffic lights
- **b** To guide you into position as you turn
- **c** To prevent the junction becoming blocked
- **d** To show you where to stop when the lights change

145 What MUST you do when you see this sign?

Mark one answer **i** p99

- **a** Stop, only if traffic is approaching
- **b** Stop, even if the road is clear
- **c** Stop, only if children are waiting to cross
- **d** Stop, only if a red light is showing

146 Which shape is used for a 'give way' sign?

Mark one answer **i** p73

147 What does this sign mean?

Mark one answer **i** p99

- **a** Buses turning
- **b** Ring road
- **c** Mini-roundabout
- **d** Keep right

148 What does this sign mean?

Mark one answer **i** p85

- **a** Two-way traffic straight ahead
- **b** Two-way traffic crosses a one-way road
- **c** Two-way traffic over a bridge
- **d** Two-way traffic crosses a two-way road

149 What does this sign mean?

Mark one answer **i** p85

- **a** Two-way traffic ahead across a one-way road
- **b** Traffic approaching you has priority
- **c** Two-way traffic straight ahead
- **d** Motorway contraflow system ahead

150 What does this sign mean?

Mark one answer **i** p126

- **a** Hump-back bridge
- **b** Traffic calming hump
- **c** Low bridge
- **d** Uneven road

151 Which of the following signs informs you that you are coming to a 'no through road'?

Mark one answer **i** p109

a

c

b

d

152 What does this sign mean?

Mark one answer **i** p141

- a Direction to park-and-ride car park
- b No parking for buses or coaches
- c Directions to bus and coach park
- d Parking area for cars and coaches

153 You are approaching traffic lights. Red and amber are showing. This means

Mark one answer **i** p79

- a pass the lights if the road is clear
- b there is a fault with the lights – take care
- c wait for the green light before you cross the stop line
- d the lights are about to change to red

154 This marking appears on the road just before a

Mark one answer **i** p101

- a 'no entry' sign
- b 'give way' sign
- c 'stop' sign
- d 'no through road' sign

155 At a railway level crossing the red light signal continues to flash after a train has gone by. What should you do?

Mark one answer **i** p175

- a Phone the signal operator
- b Alert drivers behind you
- c Wait
- d Proceed with caution

ANSWERS

144 c	147 c	150 a	153 c
145 b	148 b	151 c	154 b
146 d	149 c	152 a	155 c

DOCUMENTS

01 After passing your motorcycle test you must exchange the pass certificate for a full motorcycle licence within

Mark one answer **i** p237

- **a** six months
- **b** one year
- **c** two years
- **d** five years

02 For which TWO of these must you show your motorcycle insurance certificate?

Mark two answers **i** p194

- **a** When you are taking your motorcycle test
- **b** When buying or selling a machine
- **c** When a police officer asks you for it
- **d** When you are taxing your machine
- **e** When having an MoT inspection

03 Which of the following information is found on your motorcycle registration document?

Mark three answers **i** p193

- **a** Make and model
- **b** Service history record
- **c** Ignition key security number
- **d** Engine size and number
- **e** Purchase price
- **f** Year of first registration

04 A theory test pass certificate is valid for

Mark one answer **i** p14

- **a** two years
- **b** three years
- **c** four years
- **d** five years

05 Compulsory Basic Training (CBT) can only be carried out by

Mark one answer **i** p19

- **a** any ADI (Approved Driving Instructor)
- **b** any road safety officer
- **c** any DSA (Driving Standards Agency) approved training body
- **d** any motorcycle main dealer

06 Before riding anyone else's motorcycle you should make sure that

Mark one answer **i** p194

- **a** the owner has third party insurance cover
- **b** your own motorcycle has insurance cover
- **c** the motorcycle is insured for your use
- **d** the owner has the insurance documents with them

07 Vehicle excise duty is often called 'Road Tax' or 'The Tax Disc'. You must

Mark one answer **i** p195

- **a** keep it with your registration document
- **b** display it clearly on your motorcycle
- **c** keep it concealed safely in your motorcycle
- **d** carry it on you at all times

08 Motorcycles must FIRST have an MoT test certificate when they are

Mark one answer **i** p194

- **a** one year old
- **b** three years old
- **c** five years old
- **d** seven years old

09 Your motorcycle needs a current MoT certificate. You do not have one. Until you do have one you will not be able to renew your

Mark one answer **i** p194

- **a** driving licence
- **b** motorcycle insurance
- **c** road tax disc
- **d** motorcycle registration document

10 Which THREE of the following do you need before you can ride legally?

Mark three answers **i** p11

a A valid driving licence with signature
b A valid tax disc displayed on your motorcycle
c Proof of your identity
d Proper insurance cover
e Breakdown cover
f A vehicle handbook

11 Which THREE pieces of information are found on a registration document?

Mark three answers **i** p193

a Registered keeper
b Make of the motorcycle
c Service history details
d Date of the MoT
e Type of insurance cover
f Engine size

12 You have a duty to contact the licensing authority when

Mark three answers **i** p193

a you go abroad on holiday
b you change your motorcycle
c you change your name
d your job status is changed
e your permanent address changes
f your job involves travelling abroad

13 Your motorcycle is insured third party only. This covers

Mark two answers **i** p194

a damage to your motorcycle
b damage to other vehicles
c injury to yourself
d injury to others
e all damage and injury

14 Your motorcycle insurance policy has an excess of £100. What does this mean?

Mark one answer **i** p194

a The insurance company will pay the first £100 of any claim
b You will be paid £100 if you do not have an accident
c Your motorcycle is insured for a value of £100 if it is stolen
d You will have to pay the first £100 of any claim

15 When you apply to renew your motorcycle excise licence (tax disc) you must produce

Mark one answer **i** p195

a a valid insurance certificate
b the old tax disc
c the motorcycle handbook
d a valid driving licence

16 What is the legal minimum insurance cover you must have to ride on public roads?

Mark one answer **i** p194

a Third party, fire and theft
b Fully comprehensive
c Third party only
d Personal injury cover

17 Your motorcycle road tax is due to expire. As well as the renewal form and fee you will also need to produce an MoT (if required). What else will you need?

Mark one answer **i** p195

a Proof of purchase receipt
b Compulsory Basic Training certificate
c A valid certificate of insurance
d The Vehicle Registration Document

ANSWERS

01 c	06 c	11 a,b,f	16 c
02 c,d	07 b	12 b,c,e	17 c
03 a,d,f	08 b	13 b,d	
04 a	09 c	14 d	
05 c	10 a,b,d	15 a	

18 A Vehicle Registration Document will show

Mark one answer **i** p193
a the service history
b the year of first registration
c the purchase price
d the tyre sizes

19 What is the purpose of having a vehicle test certificate (MoT)?

Mark one answer **i** p194
a To make sure your motorcycle is roadworthy
b To certify how many miles per gallon it does
c To prove you own the motorcycle
d To allow you to park in restricted areas

20 Before taking a practical motorcycle test you need

Mark one answer **i** p14
a a full moped licence
b a full car licence
c a CBT (Compulsory Basic Training) certificate
d 12 months' riding experience

21 You must notify the licensing authority when

Mark three answers **i** p193 **i** p31
a your health affects your riding
b your eyesight does not meet a set standard
c you intend lending your motorcycle
d your motorcycle requires an MoT certificate
e you change your motorcycle

22 You have just passed your practical motorcycle test. This is your first full licence. Within two years you get six penalty points. You will have to

Mark two answers **i** p197
a retake only your theory test
b retake your theory and practical tests
c retake only your practical test
d reapply for your full licence immediately
e reapply for your provisional licence

23 You are a learner motorcyclist. The law states that you can carry a passenger when

Mark one answer **i** p206
a your motorcycle is no larger than 125cc
b your pillion passenger is a full licence-holder
c you have passed your test for a full licence
d you have had three years' experience of riding

24 You hold a provisional motorcycle licence. This means you must NOT

Mark three answers **i** p11
a exceed 30mph
b ride on a motorway
c ride after dark
d carry a pillion passenger
e ride without 'L' plates displayed

25 A full category A1 licence will allow you to ride a motorcycle up to

Mark one answer **i** p13
a 125cc
b 250cc
c 350cc
d 425cc

26 You have a CBT (Compulsory Basic Training) certificate issued from 1st February 2001. How long will this be valid for?

Mark one answer **i** p14
a one year
b two years
c three years
d four years

27 Which one of these details would you expect to see on an MoT?

Mark one answer **i** p194
a Your name, address and telephone number
b The vehicle registration and chassis number
c The previous owners' details
d The next due date for servicing

28 You want a licence to ride a large motorcycle via Direct Access. You will

Mark one answer ℹ p13

- **a** not require L-plates if you have passed a car test
- **b** require L-plates only when learning on your own machine
- **c** require L-plates while learning with a qualified instructor
- **d** not require L-plates if you have passed a moped test

29 A theory test pass certificate will not be valid after

Mark one answer ℹ p14

- **a** six months
- **b** one year
- **c** eighteen months
- **d** two years

30 A motorcyclist may only carry a pillion passenger when

Mark three answers ℹ p206

- **a** the rider has successfully completed CBT (Compulsory Basic Training)
- **b** the rider holds a full licence for the category of motorcycle
- **c** the motorcycle is fitted with rear footrests
- **d** the rider has a full car licence and is over 21
- **e** there is a proper passenger seat fitted
- **f** there is no sidecar fitted to the machine

31 An MoT certificate is normally valid for

Mark one answer ℹ p194

- **a** three years after the date it was issued
- **b** 10,000 miles
- **c** one year after the date it was issued
- **d** 30,000 miles

32 A cover note is a document issued before you receive your

Mark one answer ℹ p194

- **a** driving licence
- **b** insurance certificate
- **c** registration document
- **d** MoT certificate

33 You have just passed your practical test. You do not hold a full licence in another category. Within two years you get six penalty points on your licence. What will you have to do?

Mark two answers ℹ p197

- **a** Retake only your theory test
- **b** Retake your theory and practical tests
- **c** Retake only your practical test
- **d** Reapply for your full licence immediately
- **e** Reapply for your provisional licence

34 A police officer asks to see your documents. You do not have them with you. You may produce them at a police station within

Mark one answer ℹ p177

- **a** 5 days
- **b** 7 days
- **c** 14 days
- **d** 21 days

35 How long will a Statutory Off Road Notification (SORN) last for?

Mark one answer ℹ p195

- **a** 12 months
- **b** 24 months
- **c** 3 years
- **d** 10 years

ANSWERS

18 b	23 c	28 c	33 b,e
19 a	24 b,d,e	29 d	34 b
20 c	25 a	30 b,c,e	35 a
21 a,b,e	26 b	31 c	
22 b,e	27 b	32 b	

36 What is a Statutory Off Road Notification (SORN) declaration?

Mark one answer   **i** p195

- **a** A notification to tell VOSA that a vehicle does not have a current MoT
- **b** Information kept by the police about the owner of the vehicle
- **c** A notification to tell DVLA that a vehicle is not being used on the road
- **d** Information held by insurance companies to check the vehicle is insured

Statutory Off Road Notification (SORN) eclaration is

Mark one answer   **i** p195

- **a** to tell DVLA that your vehicle is being used on the road but the MoT has expired
- **b** to tell DVLA that you no longer own the vehicle
- **c** to tell DVLA that your vehicle is not being used on the road
- **d** to tell DVLA that you are buying a personal number plate

38 A Statutory Off Road Notification (SORN) is valid

Mark one answer   **i** p195

- **a** for as long as the vehicle has an MoT
- **b** for 12 months only
- **c** only if the vehicle is more than 3 years old
- **d** provided the vehicle is insured

tatutory Off Road Notification (SORN) l last

Mark one answer   **i** p195

- **a** for the life of the vehicle
- **b** for as long as you own the vehicle
- **c** for 12 months only
- **d** until the vehicle warranty expires

40 What is the maximum specified fine for driving without insurance?

Mark one answer   **i** p197

- **a** £50
- **b** £500
- **c** £1,000
- **d** £5,000

ANSWERS

36 c	38 b	40 d
37 c	39 c	

334

ACCIDENTS

01 Your motorcycle has broken down on a motorway. How will you know the direction of the nearest emergency telephone?

Mark one answer   *i* p219
- **a** By walking with the flow of traffic
- **b** By following an arrow on a marker post
- **c** By walking against the flow of traffic
- **d** By remembering where the last phone was

02 You are travelling on a motorway. A bag falls from your motorcycle. There are valuables in the bag. What should you do?

Mark one answer   *i* p219
- **a** Go back carefully and collect the bag as quickly as possible
- **b** Stop wherever you are and pick up the bag, but only when there is a safe gap
- **c** Stop on the hard shoulder and use the emergency telephone to inform the police
- **d** Stop on the hard shoulder and then retrieve the bag yourself

03 You are involved in an accident with another vehicle. Someone is injured. Your motorcycle is damaged. Which FOUR of the following should you find out?

Mark four answers   *i* p221
- **a** Whether the driver owns the other vehicle involved
- **b** The other driver's name, address and telephone number
- **c** The make and registration number of the other vehicle
- **d** The occupation of the other driver
- **e** The details of the other driver's vehicle insurance
- **f** Whether the other driver is licensed to drive

04 You should use the engine cut-out switch to

Mark one answer   *i* p221
- **a** stop the engine in an emergency
- **b** stop the engine on short journeys
- **c** save wear on the ignition switch
- **d** start the engine if you lose the key

05 You are riding on a motorway. The car in front switches on its hazard warning lights whilst moving. This means

Mark one answer   *i* p69
- **a** they are going to take the next exit
- **b** there is a danger ahead
- **c** there is a police car in the left lane
- **d** they are trying to change lanes

06 You are on the motorway. Luggage falls from your motorcycle. What should you do?

Mark one answer   *i* p219
- **a** Stop at the next emergency telephone and contact the police
- **b** Stop on the motorway and put on hazard lights whilst you pick it up
- **c** Walk back up the motorway to pick it up
- **d** Pull up on the hard shoulder and wave traffic down

07 You have broken down on a motorway. When you use the emergency telephone you will be asked

Mark three answers   *i* p219
- **a** for the number on the telephone that you are using
- **b** for your driving licence details
- **c** for the name of your vehicle insurance company
- **d** for details of yourself and your motorcycle
- **e** whether you belong to a motoring organisation

ANSWERS

01 b	03 a,b,c,e	05 b	07 a,d,e
02 c	04 a	06 a	

08 You are on a motorway. When can you use hazard warning lights?

Mark one answer   *i* p69

a When a vehicle is following too closely
b When you slow down quickly because of danger ahead
c When you are being towed by another vehicle
d When riding on the hard shoulder

Your motorcycle breaks down in a tunnel. What should you do?

Mark one answer   *i* p135

a Stay with your motorcycle and wait for the Police
b Stand in the lane behind your motorcycle to warn others
c Stand in front of your motorcycle to warn oncoming drivers
d Switch on hazard lights then go and call for help immediately

10 You are riding through a tunnel. Your motorcycle breaks down. What should you do?

Mark one answer   *i* p135

a Switch on hazard warning lights
b Remain on your motorcycle
c Wait for the police to find you
d Rely on CCTV cameras seeing you

11 You are involved in an accident. How can you reduce the risk of fire to your motorcycle?

Mark one answer   *i* p219

a Keep the engine running
b Open the choke
c Turn the fuel tap to reserve
d Use the engine cut-out switch

12 At the scene of an accident you should

Mark one answer   *i* p221

a not put yourself at risk
b go to those casualties who are screaming
c pull everybody out of their vehicles
d leave vehicle engines switched on

13 You are the first to arrive at the scene of an accident. Which FOUR of these should you do?

Mark four answers   *i* p221

a Leave as soon as another motorist arrives
b Switch off the vehicle engine(s)
c Move uninjured people away from the vehicle(s)
d Call the emergency services
e Warn other traffic

14 You are the first person to arrive at an accident where people are badly injured. Which THREE should you do?

Mark three answers   *i* p221

a Switch on your own hazard warning lights
b Make sure that someone telephones for an ambulance
c Try and get people who are injured to drink something
d Move the people who are injured clear of their vehicles
e Get people who are not injured clear of the scene

15 You arrive at the scene of a motorcycle accident. The rider is injured. When should the helmet be removed?

Mark one answer   *i* p222

a Only when it is essential
b Always straight away
c Only when the motorcyclist asks
d Always, unless they are in shock

16 You arrive at a serious motorcycle accident. The motorcyclist is unconscious and bleeding. Your main priorities should be to

Mark three answers   *i* p222

a try to stop the bleeding
b make a list of witnesses
c check the casualty's breathing
d take the numbers of the vehicles involved
e sweep up any loose debris
f check the casualty's airways

17 You arrive at an accident. A motorcyclist is unconscious. Your FIRST priority is the casualty's

Mark one answer **i** p222

a breathing
b bleeding
c broken bones
d bruising

18 At an accident a casualty is unconscious. Which THREE of the following should you check urgently?

Mark three answers **i** p222

a Circulation
b Airway
c Shock
d Breathing
e Broken bones

19 You arrive at the scene of an accident. It has just happened and someone is unconscious. Which of the following should be given urgent priority to help them?

Mark three answers **i** p222

a Clear the airway and keep it open
b Try to get them to drink water
c Check that they are breathing
d Look for any witnesses
e Stop any heavy bleeding
f Take the numbers of vehicles involved

20 At an accident someone is unconscious. Your main priorities should be to

Mark three answers **i** p222

a sweep up the broken glass
b take the names of witnesses
c count the number of vehicles involved
d check the airway is clear
e make sure they are breathing
f stop any heavy bleeding

21 You have stopped at the scene of an accident to give help. Which THREE things should you do?

Mark three answers **i** p222

a Keep injured people warm and comfortable
b Keep injured people calm by talking to them reassuringly
c Keep injured people on the move by walking them around
d Give injured people a warm drink
e Make sure that injured people are not left alone

22 You arrive at the scene of an accident. It has just happened and someone is injured. Which THREE of the following should be given urgent priority?

Mark three answers **i** p222

a Stop any severe bleeding
b Get them a warm drink
c Check that their breathing is OK
d Take numbers of vehicles involved
e Look for witnesses
f Clear their airway and keep it open

23 Which of the following should you NOT do at the scene of an accident?

Mark one answer **i** p221

a Warn other traffic by switching on your hazard warning lights
b Call the emergency services immediately
c Offer someone a cigarette to calm them down
d Ask drivers to switch off their engines

24 There has been an accident. The driver is suffering from shock. You should

Mark two answers **i** p222

a give them a drink
b reassure them
c not leave them alone
d offer them a cigarette
e ask who caused the accident

25 You have to treat someone for shock at the scene of an accident. You should

Mark one answer **i** p222

a reassure them constantly
b walk them around to calm them down
c give them something cold to drink
d cool them down as soon as possible

ANSWERS

08 b	13 b,c,d,e	18 a,b,d	23 c
09 d	14 a,b,e	19 a,c,e	24 b,c
10 a	15 a	20 d,e,f	25 a
11 d	16 a,c,f	21 a,b,e	
12 a	17 a	22 a,c,f	

26 You arrive at the scene of a motorcycle accident. No other vehicle is involved. The rider is unconscious, lying in the middle of the road. The first thing you should do is

Mark one answer **i** p222

a move the rider out of the road
b warn other traffic
c clear the road of debris
d give the rider reassurance

27 At an accident a small child is not breathing. When giving mouth to mouth you should breathe

Mark one answer **i** p222

a sharply
b gently
c heavily
d rapidly

28 When you are giving mouth to mouth you should only stop when

Mark one answer **i** p222

a you think the casualty is dead
b the casualty can breathe without help
c the casualty has turned blue
d you think the ambulance is coming

29 You arrive at the scene of an accident. There has been an engine fire and someone's hands and arms have been burnt. You should NOT

Mark one answer **i** p222

a douse the burn thoroughly with cool liquid
b lay the casualty down
c remove anything sticking to the burn
d reassure them constantly

30 You arrive at an accident where someone is suffering from severe burns. You should

Mark one answer **i** p222

a apply lotions to the injury
b burst any blisters
c remove anything stuck to the burns
d douse the burns with cool liquid

31 You arrive at the scene of an accident. A pedestrian has a severe bleeding wound on their leg, although it is not broken. What should you do?

Mark two answers **i** p222

a Dab the wound to stop bleeding
b Keep both legs flat on the ground
c Apply firm pressure to the wound
d Raise the leg to lessen bleeding
e Fetch them a warm drink

32 You arrive at the scene of an accident. A passenger is bleeding badly from an arm wound. What should you do?

Mark one answer **i** p222

a Apply pressure over the wound and keep the arm down
b Dab the wound
c Get them a drink
d Apply pressure over the wound and raise the arm

33 You arrive at the scene of an accident. A pedestrian is bleeding heavily from a leg wound but the leg is not broken. What should you do?

Mark one answer **i** p222

a Dab the wound to stop the bleeding
b Keep both legs flat on the ground
c Apply firm pressure to the wound
d Fetch them a warm drink

34 At an accident a casualty is unconscious but still breathing. You should only move them if

Mark one answer **i** p222

a an ambulance is on its way
b bystanders advise you to
c there is further danger
d bystanders will help you to

35 At an accident you suspect a casualty has back injuries. The area is safe. You should

Mark one answer **i** p222

a offer them a drink
b not move them
c raise their legs
d offer them a cigarette

36 At an accident it is important to look after the casualty. When the area is safe, you should

Mark one answer **i** p222

a get them out of the vehicle
b give them a drink
c give them something to eat
d keep them in the vehicle

37 A tanker is involved in an accident. Which sign would show that the tanker is carrying dangerous goods?

Mark one answer **i** p223

a
b
c
d

38 The police may ask you to produce which three of these documents following an accident?

Mark three answers **i** p192

a Vehicle registration document
b Driving licence
c Theory test certificate
d Insurance certificate
e MoT test certificate
f Road tax disc

39 You see a car on the hard shoulder of a motorway with a HELP pennant displayed. This means the driver is most likely to be

Mark one answer **i** p219

a a disabled person
b first aid trained
c a foreign visitor
d a rescue patrol person

40 For which TWO should you use hazard warning lights?

Mark two answers **i** p69

a When you slow down quickly on a motorway because of a hazard ahead
b When you have broken down
c When you wish to stop on double yellow lines
d When you need to park on the pavement

41 When are you allowed to use hazard warning lights?

Mark one answer **i** p69

a When stopped and temporarily obstructing traffic
b When travelling during darkness without headlights
c When parked for shopping on double yellow lines
d When travelling slowly because you are lost

42 You are on a motorway. A large box falls onto the road from a lorry. The lorry does not stop. You should

Mark one answer **i** p219

a go to the next emergency telephone and inform the police
b catch up with the lorry and try to get the driver's attention
c stop close to the box until the police arrive
d pull over to the hard shoulder, then remove the box

43 There has been an accident. A motorcyclist is lying injured and unconscious. Why should you usually not attempt to remove their helmet?

Mark one answer **i** p222

a Because they may not want you to
b This could result in more serious injury
c They will get too cold if you do this
d Because you could scratch the helmet

44 After an accident, someone is unconscious in their vehicle. When should you call the emergency services?

Mark one answer **i** p222

a Only as a last resort
b As soon as possible
c After you have woken them up
d After checking for broken bones

ANSWERS

26 b	31 c,d	36 d	41 a
27 b	32 d	37 b	42 a
28 b	33 c	38 b,d,e	43 b
29 c	34 c	39 a	44 b
30 d	35 b	40 a,b	

45 An accident casualty has an injured arm. They can move it freely, but it is bleeding. Why should you get them to keep it in a raised position?

Mark one answer **ℹ p222**
- **a** Because it will ease the pain
- **b** It will help them to be seen more easily
- **c** To stop them touching other people
- **d** It will help to reduce the bleeding

46 You are going through a congested tunnel and have to stop. What should you do?

Mark one answer **ℹ p135**
- **a** Pull up very close to the vehicle in front to save space
- **b** Ignore any message signs as they are never up to date
- **c** Keep a safe distance from the vehicle in front
- **d** Make a U-turn and find another route

47 You are going through a tunnel. What should you look out for that warns of accidents or congestion?

Mark one answer **ℹ p135**
- **a** Hazard warning lines
- **b** Other drivers flashing their lights
- **c** Variable message signs
- **d** Areas marked with hatch markings

48 You are going through a tunnel. What systems are provided to warn of any accidents or congestion?

Mark one answer **ℹ p135**
- **a** Double white centre lines
- **b** Variable message signs
- **c** Chevron 'distance markers'
- **d** Rumble strips

49 An accident has just happened. An injured person is lying in a busy road. What is the FIRST thing you should do to help?

Mark one answer **ℹ p222**
- **a** Treat the person for shock
- **b** Warn other traffic
- **c** Place them in the recovery position
- **d** Make sure the injured person is kept warm

50 At an accident a casualty has stopped breathing. You should

Mark two answers **ℹ p222**
- **a** remove anything that is blocking the mouth
- **b** keep the head tilted forwards as far as possible
- **c** raise the legs to help with circulation
- **d** try to give the casualty something to drink
- **e** tilt the head back gently to clear the airway

51 You are at the scene of an accident. Someone is suffering from shock. You should

Mark four answers **ℹ p222**
- **a** reassure them constantly
- **b** offer them a cigarette
- **c** keep them warm
- **d** avoid moving them if possible
- **e** avoid leaving them alone
- **f** give them a warm drink

52 To start mouth to mouth on a casualty you should

Mark three answers **ℹ p222**
- **a** tilt their head forward
- **b** clear the airway
- **c** turn them on their side
- **d** tilt their head back gently
- **e** pinch the nostrils together
- **f** put their arms across their chest

53 On the motorway, the hard shoulder should be used

Mark one answer **ℹ p134**
- **a** to answer a mobile phone
- **b** when an emergency arises
- **c** for a short rest when tired
- **d** to check a road atlas

ANSWERS

45 d	48 b	50 a,e	52 b,d,e
46 c	49 b	51 a,c,d,e	53 b
47 c			

VEHICLE LOADING

01 If a trailer swerves or snakes when you are towing it you should

Mark one answer **i** p207

- **a** ease off the throttle and reduce your speed
- **b** let go of the handlebars and let it correct itself
- **c** brake hard and hold the brake on
- **d** increase your speed as quickly as possible

02 When riding with a sidecar attached for the first time you should

Mark two answers **i** p207

- **a** keep your speed down
- **b** be able to stop more quickly
- **c** accelerate quickly round bends
- **d** approach corners more carefully

03 When may a learner motorcyclist carry a pillion passenger?

Mark one answer **i** p206

- **a** If the passenger holds a full licence
- **b** Not at any time
- **c** If the rider is undergoing training
- **d** If the passenger is over 21

04 When carrying extra weight on a motorcycle, you may need to make adjustments to the

Mark three answers **i** p205

- **a** headlight
- **b** gears
- **c** suspension
- **d** tyres
- **e** footrests

05 To obtain the full category 'A' licence through the accelerated or direct access scheme, your motorcycle must be

Mark one answer **i** p13

- **a** solo with maximum power 25kw (33bhp)
- **b** solo with maximum power of 11kw (14.6bhp)
- **c** fitted with a sidecar and have minimum power of 35kw (46.6bhp)
- **d** solo with minimum power of 35kw (46.6bhp)

06 Any load that is carried on a luggage rack MUST be

Mark one answer **i** p205

- **a** securely fastened when riding
- **b** carried only when strictly necessary
- **c** visible when you are riding
- **d** covered with plastic sheeting

07 Pillion passengers should

Mark one answer **i** p206

- **a** have a provisional motorcycle licence
- **b** be lighter than the rider
- **c** always wear a helmet
- **d** signal for the rider

08 Pillion passengers should

Mark one answer **i** p206

- **a** give the rider directions
- **b** lean with the rider when going round bends
- **c** check the road behind for the rider
- **d** give arm signals for the rider

09 When you are going around a corner your pillion passenger should

Mark one answer **i** p206

- **a** give arm signals for you
- **b** check behind for other vehicles
- **c** lean with you on bends
- **d** lean to one side to see ahead

10 Which of these may need to be adjusted when carrying a pillion passenger?

Mark one answer **i** p206

- **a** Indicators
- **b** Exhaust
- **c** Fairing
- **d** Headlight

ANSWERS

01	a	04	a,c,d	07	c	09	c
02	a,d	05	d	08	b	10	d
03	b	06	a				

11 You are towing a trailer with your motorcycle. You should remember that your

Mark one answer ⓘ p207
- **a** stopping distance may increase
- **b** fuel consumption will improve
- **c** tyre grip will increase
- **d** stability will improve

12 Heavy loads in a motorcycle top box may

Mark one answer ⓘ p205
- **a** improve stability
- **b** cause low-speed wobble
- **c** cause a puncture
- **d** improve braking

13 Overloading your motorcycle can seriously affect the

Mark two answers ⓘ p204
- **a** gearbox
- **b** steering
- **c** handling
- **d** battery life
- **e** journey time

14 Who is responsible for making sure that a motorcycle is not overloaded?

Mark one answer ⓘ p204
- **a** The rider of the motorcycle
- **b** The owner of the items being carried
- **c** The licensing authority
- **d** The owner of the motorcycle

15 Before fitting a sidecar to a motorcycle you should

Mark one answer ⓘ p207
- **a** have the wheels balanced
- **b** have the engine tuned
- **c** pass the extended bike test
- **d** check that the motorcycle is suitable

16 You are using throwover saddlebags. Why is it important to make sure they are evenly loaded?

Mark one answer ⓘ p205
- **a** They will be uncomfortable for you to sit on
- **b** They will slow your motorcycle down
- **c** They could make your motorcycle unstable
- **d** They will be uncomfortable for a pillion passenger to sit on

17 You are carrying a bulky tank bag. What could this affect?

Mark one answer ⓘ p205
- **a** Your ability to steer
- **b** Your ability to accelerate
- **c** Your view ahead
- **d** Your insurance premium

18 To carry a pillion passenger you must

Mark one answer ⓘ p206
- **a** hold a full car licence
- **b** hold a full motorcycle licence
- **c** be over the age of 21
- **d** be over the age of 25

19 When carrying a heavy load on your luggage rack, you may need to adjust your

Mark one answer ⓘ p205
- **a** carburettor
- **b** fuel tap
- **c** seating position
- **d** tyre pressures

20 You are carrying a pillion passenger. When following other traffic, which of he following should you do?

Mark one answer   **i** p206

a Keep to your normal following distance

b Get your passenger to keep checking behind

c Keep further back than you normally would

d Get your passenger to signal for you

21 You should only carry a child as a pillion passenger when

Mark one answer   **i** p206

a they are over 14 years old

b they are over 16 years old

c they can reach the floor from the seat

d they can reach the handholds and footrests

22 You have fitted a sidecar to your motorcycle. You should make sure that he sidecar

Mark one answer   **i** p207

a has a registration plate

b is correctly aligned

c has a waterproof cover

d has a solid cover

23 You are riding a motorcycle and sidecar. The extra weight

Mark one answer   **i** p207

a will allow you to corner more quickly

b will allow you to brake later for hazards

c may increase your stopping distance

d will improve your fuel consumption

24 You are carrying a pillion passenger. To allow for the extra weight which of the following is most likely to need adjustment?

Mark one answer   **i** p206

a Preload on the front forks

b Preload on the rear shock absorber(s)

c The balance of the rear wheel

d The front and rear wheel alignment

25 A trailer on a motorcycle must be no wider than

Mark one answer   **i** p207

a 0.5 metres (1 foot 8 inches)

b 1 metre (3 feet 3 inches)

c 1.5 metres (4 feet 11inches)

d 2 metres (6 feet 6 inches)

26 You want to tow a trailer with your motorcycle. Which one applies?

Mark one answer   **i** p207

a The motorcycle should be attached to a sidecar

b The trailer should weigh more than the motorcycle

c The trailer should be fitted with brakes

d The trailer should NOT be more than 1 metre (3 feet 3 inches) wide

27 You have a sidecar fitted to your motorcycle. What effect will it have?

Mark one answer   **i** p207

a Reduce stability

b Make steering lighter

c Increase stopping distance

d Increase fuel economy

28 Which THREE must a learner motorcyclist under 21 NOT do?

Mark three answers   **i** p11

a Ride a motorcycle with an engine capacity greater than 125cc

b Pull a trailer

c Carry a pillion passenger

d Ride faster than 30mph

e Use the right-hand lane on dual carriageways

ANSWERS

11 a	16 c	21 d	26 d
12 b	17 a	22 b	27 c
13 b,c	18 b	23 c	28 a,b,c
14 a	19 d	24 b	
15 d	20 c	25 b	

29 Carrying a heavy load in your top box may

Mark one answer **i** p205
- **a** cause high speed-weave
- **b** cause a puncture
- **c** use less fuel
- **d** improve stability

30 You want to tow a trailer behind your motorcycle. You should

Mark two answers **i** p205
- **a** display a 'long vehicle' sign
- **b** fit a larger battery
- **c** have a full motorcycle licence
- **d** ensure that your engine is more than 125cc
- **e** ensure that your motorcycle has shaft drive

31 To carry a pillion passenger your motorcycle should be fitted with

Mark two answers **i** p206
- **a** rear footrests
- **b** an engine of 250cc or over
- **c** a top box
- **d** a grab handle
- **e** a proper pillion seat

32 Your motorcycle is fitted with a top box. It is unwise to carry a heavy load in the top box because it may

Mark three answers **i** p205
- **a** reduce stability
- **b** improve stability
- **c** make turning easier
- **d** cause high-speed weave
- **e** cause low-speed wobble
- **f** increase fuel economy

33 You are towing a small trailer on a busy three-lane motorway. All the lanes are open. You must

Mark two answers **i** p207
- **a** not exceed 60mph
- **b** not overtake
- **c** have a stabiliser fitted
- **d** use only the left and centre lanes

ANSWERS

29 a	31 a,e	32 a,d,e	33 a,d
30 c,d			

INDEX

lights 36, 43, 199
lines on road
    double white 77, 83
    red 77
    yellow 77
loading 205
locks 140
loose chippings 119, 189
low-speed riding 52
luggage rack 205

M

maintenance 198-203
making progress 155
manhole covers 119, 189
medical transplant vehicles 177
medication 29
meeting 90-1
mines rescue vehicles 177
mirrors 63
MOT 195
motorcycle test
    booking 227, 231
    category A 15, 231
    category A1 15, 231
    failing 235
    fault assessment 235
    hazard perception test 228
    moped 11, 55, 231
    multiple-choice test 227
    passing 237
    practical 15, 230-35
    theory 14, 226-9
motorway
    breakdowns 133, 219
    joining 134
    junctions 133
    leaving 134
    service areas 134
    signals 134
    stopping on 134
mountain rescue vehicles 177
mounting 48
moving off 52
    at an angle 53, 234

N

New Driver Act 197
night
    noise at 181
    overtaking at 181
    parking at 139
no entry 109

O

observation 146-7
    rear 63-5
observation-signal-manoeuvre 65
odometer 40
offences 197
oil
    level 199
    light 43
one-way streets 84-5
organised walks 159
overtaking 92-5, 131, 181, 186, 187

P

panniers 205
parking 138-41
passing parked vehicles 84
passing places 127
pedestrian crossings 159-61
pedestrians 158-61
penalty points 197
pillion passengers 11, 181, 206, 235
police
    being stopped by 177
    directing traffic 70
pollution 209
positioning 82-5
position-speed-look 65
practice 21
puncture 202

R

rear observation 62-5
red routes 139
refuelling 199
registration document (V5) 193
rev counter 40
riding abroad 194
riding position 48
road
    markings 76-7, 119
    signs 72-3
    studs 77, 186
    surface 119
    tax (see Vehicle Excise Duty)
roads
    single track 127
    three-lane 95
roadworks 136-7
roundabouts 112-5
    mini- 115

LEARN TO RIDE

ACKNOWLEDGEMENTS

Author	Robert Davies
Project Manager	Louise McIntyre
Design and Page Build	Richard Parsons
Technical Advisors	Elliot Bloy
	of Dorsetbiker Ltd
Photographer	Jim Godden
Copy Editor	John Hardaker

Photo credits:

Freefoto.com	p176, 241
Tramlink Croydon Ltd	p172, 173
Watsonian-Squire	p15 (right) p207

The author and publishers would also like to thank the following companies:

Bransons of Yeovil
Quickstart Motorcycle Training